Early Praise for *Cucumber Recipes*

With *Cucumber Recipes* you feel like the authors are right there with you, offering you advice, showing you hidden gems, or gently chastising you for things you know you shouldn't be doing. From general advice about taming unruly test suites or scaling out across multiple servers, to craziness like testing embedded Arduino hardware projects, they manage to cover an enormous amount of ground in a small space. Prepare for a fun and informative ride.

➤ **Dan North**
Originator of BDD and author of the RSpec story runner (Cucumber's predecessor)

There are many cookbooks but very few "chef books." *Cucumber Recipes* is inspiring enough to qualify as a chef book. If there's a will and a desire to use Cucumber in the process, *Cucumber Recipes* will more than likely show you a way...or many ways! From the basic to the esoteric, there's something for everyone in *Cucumber Recipes*.

➤ **Michael Larsen**
Senior quality assurance engineer, SocialText

It is good to see that a free tool like Cucumber has been able to build up a community that treats BDD as its own child and carries it to nearly every possible platform and technology. This book provides a closer look at the details.

➤ **Gáspár Nagy**
Developer coach at TechTalk, creator of SpecFlow

If you're automating tests of any kind using Cucumber, in any language, against any type of software, you need this cookbook. Its recipes will help you write useful, easily maintained tests for even the most puzzling scenarios. Like all good cookbooks, it teaches good techniques and principles that will help you improve all your tests. Best of all, you can actually code the examples yourself, and learn by doing.

➤ **Lisa Crispin**
Co-author, *Agile Testing: A Practical Guide for Testers and Agile Teams*

Cucumber Recipes has testing solutions for a variety of platforms. It is a powerful book that gives us useful tips to use BDD in our chosen environment. To realize the power of BDD, *Cucumber Recipes* is a must on every software test engineer's table.

➤ **Kavitha Naveen**
Senior lead—quality engineering

Cucumber Recipes

Automate Anything with BDD Tools and Techniques

Ian Dees
Matt Wynne
Aslak Hellesøy

The Pragmatic Bookshelf
Dallas, Texas • Raleigh, North Carolina

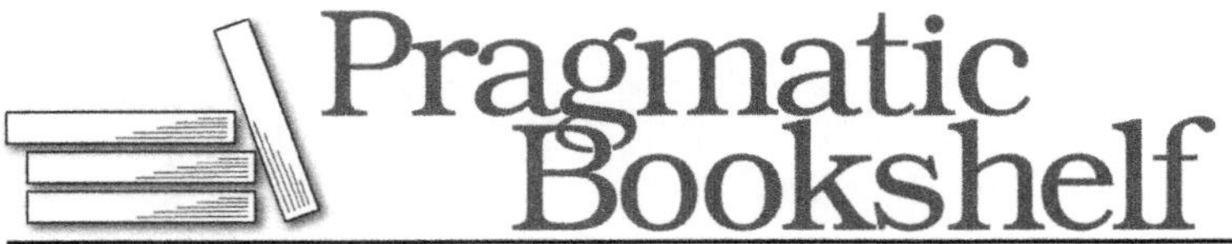

Our Pragmatic courses, workshops, and other products can help you and your team create better software and have more fun. For more information, as well as the latest Pragmatic titles, please visit us at *http://pragprog.com*.

The team that produced this book includes:

Jackie Carter (editor)
Potomac Indexing, LLC (indexer)
Kim Wimpsett (copyeditor)
David J Kelly (typesetter)
Janet Furlow (producer)
Juliet Benda (rights)
Ellie Callahan (support)

Printed in the United States of America.
ISBN-13: 978-1-937785-01-7
Printed on acid-free paper.
Book version: P2.0—November 2013

Contents

Foreword vii

Acknowledgments xi

Introduction xiii

1. Cucumber Techniques 1

Recipe 1. Compare and Transform Tables of Data 2
Recipe 2. Generate an RTF Report with a Custom Formatter 7
Recipe 3. Run Slow Setup/Teardown Code with Global Hooks 13
Recipe 4. Refactor to Extract Your Own Application Driver DSL 18
Recipe 5. Define Steps as Regular Ruby Methods 22
Recipe 6. Compare Images 27
Recipe 7. Test Across Multiple Cores 33
Recipe 8. Test Across Multiple Machines with SSH 36
Recipe 9. Run Your Features Automatically with Guard and Growl 41
Recipe 10. Add Cucumber to Your Continuous Integration Server 47
Recipe 11. Publish Your Documentation on Relish 55
Recipe 12. Test Through Multiple Interfaces Using Worlds 61
Recipe 13. Manipulate Time 67
Recipe 14. Drive Cucumber's Wire Protocol 72
Recipe 15. Implement a Wire Protocol Listener 75

2. Java 83

Recipe 16. Use Cucumber Directly with JRuby 84
Recipe 17. Use Cucumber with Java via Cucumber-JVM 87
Recipe 18. Drive a Spring + Hibernate Project 92
Recipe 19. Test a Grails App Using grails-cucumber 99

Recipe 20. Test Scala Code 104
Recipe 21. Test Clojure Code 109
Recipe 22. Drive a Swing Interface with FEST 111

3. .NET and Windows 117
Recipe 23. Get Good Text Output on Windows 118
Recipe 24. Test .NET Code with SpecFlow 124
Recipe 25. Drive a Windows App Using White 130
Recipe 26. Test Windows GUIs with AutoIt 135
Recipe 27. Test on Windows Phone 139

4. Mobile and Web 147
Recipe 28. Test on iOS Using Frank 148
Recipe 29. Test Android Apps with Calabash 153
Recipe 30. Parse HTML Tables 160
Recipe 31. Drive JavaScript/CoffeeScript Using Cucumber-JS 164
Recipe 32. Test a Web App Using Watir 168
Recipe 33. Test a PHP App with cuke4php 173
Recipe 34. Play Back Canned Network Data Using VCR 181
Recipe 35. Drive a Flash App Using Cuke4AS3 185
Recipe 36. Monitor a Web Service Using Nagios and Cucumber 195

5. Other Languages and Platforms 201
Recipe 37. Drive a Mac GUI Using AppleScript and System Events 202
Recipe 38. Drive a Mac GUI Using MacRuby and AXElements 209
Recipe 39. Test Python Code Using Lettuce 214
Recipe 40. Test Erlang Code 217
Recipe 41. Test Lua Code Using cucumber-lua 221
Recipe 42. Test a GUI on Linux, Mac, or Windows with Sikuli 225
Recipe 43. Test an Arduino Project Using Serial 230

A1. RSpec Expectations 237
A1.1 Basics 237
A1.2 Custom Matchers 238
A1.3 Alternatives 239

Bibliography 241

Index 243

Foreword

There was a time when one could analyze all that a program needed to do and then write the program that met that need. This stopped being a winning strategy when computers got big enough and fast enough to hold a description of the problem, not just the solution.

I embraced this change that went by the name of *object-oriented programming*. The advice was to divide large programs into parts that captured natural diversity. Then we were to program the parts to ask other parts for results without saying exactly how these results were to be achieved. This sounded simple. We no longer had to think everything through all of the time. Then, when we discovered one more case late in development, we were thankful we kept that complexity at a distance.

It was a good plan, but it turned out to be not quite that simple. Not only was there more than one way to chop up a program into parts, there was no easy way to tell which approach was going to prove to be leveraged when unforeseen needs surfaced, as they always do.

Agile

We forged ahead. We found dozens of techniques that helped keep track of what we had done, where we were going, and, especially, how to say "yes, we can" when asked to do something never once mentioned until our programs were used. When we say *Agile* today, we're distinguishing ourselves from the days when we would resist change even if it meant finishing a program that wouldn't be used.

We asked our pioneers to experiment. We asked that they try new things and share with each other how they worked out. We asked our best developers to think about these new problems: where have we been, where are we going, and how will we know when we get there?

This book carries that tradition forward. Let me explain how.

Patterns

A program is a mathematical object that follows precise rules. This stops being important when we can no longer fully analyze our problems as we might a proof. Our progress toward Agile accelerated when we started cataloging solutions rather than deriving new ones from scratch each time they occurred.

A recurring pattern became an object of interest. A recurring problem in a context and a solution known to work—this is something worth sharing. When we started naming and documenting these patterns, we created a literature that had not yet existed. Practical problem solving was respected. Well-worn solutions were judged valuable…more valuable even than the most innovative ideas.

Although Cucumber offers a new and innovative way of pushing Agile forward, there is no reason for every Cucumber user to rediscover the contents of this book. The solutions come from many, for sure. But the simple existence of this catalog will raise our collective competence as we come to know of solutions whether we need them right now or not.

This book covers lots of ground. Some of it you will use immediately; other parts you will later. However, you will be served well to know the range of problems already solved.

Platforms

We appreciate how computers become more powerful each year. We hardly think of them as computers anymore. But they still need to be programmed. When we say Agile means "yes, we can," we make a promise that becomes more difficult as capabilities proliferate. And each capability has its own constituents that want our attention.

Cucumber makes much of artifacts that can be shared across disciplines. A developer and a business analyst will bring different skills to a project. But if they are to coordinate their work, there must be some things they share. Cucumber meets that need.

This same distance from implementation allows Cucumber to straddle today's diverse implementation technologies. As our customers come to know many platforms, they expect us to know them too. As developers we begin to feel new pressure. Each platform has its quirks. That is where this book excels. As you are pressed into delivery on new platforms, you can bring Cucumber with you. But how do you hook it up? Read how here.

Progress

Remember that object-oriented programming promised that we would say what we want done, not how to do it. This works for objects because the *how* changes faster than the *what*. Our objects have some new longevity.

An only occasionally realized benefit of my own Framework for Integrated Test (FIT) was to create domain-based artifacts that could outlive the turnover of technology. Cucumber steps up to deliver broadly (based mostly on words) where my solution (based mostly on numbers) has been focused.

It's hard for any development team to think about the next technology when delivery on the current technology is so in demand. This book will help. Although you can jump to the solution you need today (and by all means do this!) and get today's work done, I ask that you familiarize yourself with all that is here so that you can understand the relentless pressure that innovation places on your work.

I've had the pleasure of following object technology out of the research laboratories and into the larger world. I've faced problems, many unanticipated, and found their solutions as interesting as they are useful. The recipes here are as interesting as they are useful. Enjoy.

Ward Cunningham
Inventor of FIT (inspiration to Cucumber)
Portland, Oregon, 2013

Acknowledgments

We are grateful to the many people who made this book possible. Thanks to our beta readers, who helped us catch bugs and steer the direction of the book. These include Chuck van der Linden, Massimo Manca, Bob Allen, gb, Dean Cornish, Pete Hodgson, Paul Harris, Wari Wahab, Ivan Ryan, Vijay Khurana, and Brett Giles. We would also like to thank our alert technical reviewers, including Gáspár Nagy, Luis Lavena, Josh Chisholm, Tom Coxen, Jeremy Crosen, Andrew Havens, Andy Lindeman, Kavitha Naveen, Perry Hunter, and Seth Craighead.

Special thanks to Ward Cunningham for his inspirational work in bringing software and people closer together and for the lovely foreword.

Thanks to our tireless editor, Jackie Carter, and to everyone else at the Pragmatic Programmers who helped shepherd this book from idea to release: Susannah Pfalzer, Janet Furlow, Dave Thomas, and Andy Hunt, to name a few.

Ian would like to thank his fellow authors, Matt and Aslak, for their guidance in the early days of the project and for the words and code they crafted for our readers. He'd also like to thank his wife, Lynn, and children, Avalon and Robin, for prying him away from the keyboard once in a while. Matt would like to thank Anna and Ian.

Introduction

You can use Cucumber to test anything. Websites, desktop programs, mobile applications, networked services, embedded devices—you name it.

Although it came to prominence in the Rails testing world, Cucumber is first and foremost a communication tool. It helps you express in clear terms what your software is supposed to do and why.

Cucumber is also a *polyglot* tool. It was designed from the beginning to be easily portable to different languages and platforms. The result is that you can enjoy the benefits of living documentation, no matter the software environment.

Who This Book Is For

This book isn't an introduction to Cucumber. If you're looking for a beginner's guide, you might want to start with *The Cucumber Book [WH11]* by Matt Wynne and Aslak Hellesøy (two of the contributors to the book you're reading now). There's also quite a bit of getting-started information on the official Cucumber site.[1]

Cucumber Recipes assumes you've grasped the basics of Cucumber and you understand the benefits of the outside-in development process.[2] Our book builds on the experience you've gained while using Cucumber on your team. We give you techniques to apply Cucumber in the various situations you'll encounter in the wild.

How to Use This Book

Each recipe in this book stands alone. In a few pages, we seek to show just enough information to get you started with each technique. We can't cover every nuance of the tool in this space, but we can get you over the most common hurdles and show you where to look next.

---

1. http://cukes.info
2. http://agilecoach.typepad.com/agile-coaching/2012/03/bdd-in-a-nutshell.html

You can read the recipes in any order. If you're a web developer, you may want to start with the block of recipes beginning with Recipe 30, *Parse HTML Tables*, on page 160. If Windows is your primary platform, see Chapter 3, *.NET and Windows*, on page 117. Java developers should start in Chapter 2, *Java*, on page 83.

To learn techniques for testing iOS and Android apps, visit Chapter 4, *Mobile and Web*, on page 147. For other languages and platforms such as Erlang, Python, Mac OS X, and Linux, see Chapter 5, *Other Languages and Platforms*, on page 201.

Throughout your exploration, you may want to refer to Chapter 1, *Cucumber Techniques*, on page 1 for general tips that will serve you well, no matter what platform you're on.

Getting the Tools You'll Need

This book contains recipes for Ruby, Java, C#, PHP, Scala, Clojure, Erlang, and more. Cucumber-Ruby is the original and most popular flavor of Cucumber, so several of our recipes use Ruby. Most of these will run across a variety of Ruby implementations, but we recommend version 1.9 unless otherwise noted in the ingredients.

On Mac and Linux systems, we recommend a managed Ruby environment such as RVM[3] or rbenv.[4] These tools make it easy to install Ruby and its dependencies. Both of these tools require a C compiler. Mac users will need to install the Xcode Command-Line Tools;[5] Ubuntu users should run sudo apt-get install build-essential.

For Windows, we suggest the RubyInstaller project[6] and its DevKit add-on,[7] paired with a Ruby switching tool such as Pik.[8]

Once you have Ruby, installing Cucumber is easy.

```
$ gem install cucumber
```

You'll also need an *assertion library* to mark whether each step is passing or failing. Cucumber doesn't care which one you use; for this book, we use the expectations system from RSpec.

3. http://rvm.beginrescueend.com
4. https://github.com/sstephenson/rbenv
5. https://developer.apple.com/xcode
6. http://rubyinstaller.org
7. http://rubyinstaller.org/add-ons/devkit
8. https://github.com/vertiginous/pik

```
$ gem install rspec-expectations
```

We like RSpec expectations for their ease of reading. If this is your first time writing this style of assertion, you might want to take a quick peek at our refresher course in Appendix 1, *RSpec Expectations*, on page 237.

Online Resources

This book has its own web page[9] where you can download the code for all the examples. In the electronic versions of this book, you can click the filename above any code example to download the source file directly. As we make changes to the code, we'll post them to the book's GitHub repository[10] as well.

The book's web page also has a discussion forum where you can connect to other readers and to us. If you find bugs, typos, or other annoyances, please let us and the world know about them on our errata page.

Last but not least, we're also running a blog[11] where we'll post bonus recipes on the topics we just didn't have room for in the book. We welcome guest recipe posts from anyone who'd like to fork the blog on GitHub.[12]

Now, let's jump into those recipes!

9. http://pragprog.com/titles/dhwcr
10. https://github.com/cucumber/cucumber-recipes-book-code
11. http://cukerecip.es
12. https://github.com/cucumber/cukerecip.es

CHAPTER 1

Cucumber Techniques

This chapter contains general Cucumber tips that aren't related to any particular platform. We'll look at ways to tame the complexity of a large test suite, produce custom-formatted reports, and test code that's running on a remote server or embedded device.

Recipe 1

Compare and Transform Tables of Data

Problem

Your tests are in English, but your data is in HTML. What you and your stakeholders call a last name, your app calls customer_name_last. What you call February 24, your app calls 2012-02-24T10:24:57-08:00. You need to translate between the two.

Ingredients

- Ast::Table,[1] Cucumber's table-crunching workhorse
- Ruby's built-in BigDecimal for representing currencies[2]

Solution

In this recipe, we'll assume we're getting data from our app using a GUI automation library or web scraping framework. The data will be in whatever format the behind-the-scenes API provides. This format may be grisly, so we don't want it in our human-readable Cucumber tests.

How do we address this mismatch between our top-level tests and the underlying API? We'll use Cucumber to transform the table in our .feature file to whatever the API needs. We can change columns, convert data inside cells, or perform tricky custom transformations.

This recipe comes in several flavors so that you can practice applying all these techniques.

Renaming Headers

Imagine you have the following test steps:

tables/tables.feature

```
Scenario: Renaming headers
  Given I am logged in as a buyer
  When I search for available cars
  Then I should see the following cars:
    | color | model   |
    | rust  | Camaro  |
    | blue  | Gremlin |
```

1. http://rdoc.info/github/cucumber/cucumber/Cucumber/Ast/Table
2. http://www.ruby-doc.org/stdlib-1.9.3/libdoc/bigdecimal/rdoc/index.html

Your team has standardized on the U.S. spelling of *color*, but the API you're calling to scrape the data from your app happens to use the U.K. spelling.

tables/step_definitions/table_steps.rb

```
When /^I search for available cars$/ do
  @cars = [{'colour' => 'rust', 'model' => 'Camaro'},
           {'colour' => 'blue', 'model' => 'Gremlin'}]
end
```

If you compare these tables directly in Cucumber, you'll get a test failure, because the color column name in your examples doesn't match the colour key returned by the API.

Cucumber's map_headers!() method lets you transform the table in your examples into the format expected by your underlying API.

tables/step_definitions/table_steps.rb

```
Then /^I should see the following cars:$/ do |table|
  table.map_headers! 'color' => 'colour'
  table.diff! @cars
end
```

If your team members have written several scenarios and have been alternating between spellings...well, you really should pick one and standardize. But in the meantime, you can pass a regular expression or a block to map_headers!() for more control over the column renaming.

```
table.map_headers! /colou?r/ => 'colour'
table.map_headers! { |name| name.sub('color', 'colour') }
```

What if you need to change the values inside the table, not just the headers?

Converting Data Inside Cells

Ast::Table can do more than just rename columns. It can manipulate the data inside cells too. Imagine you have the following scenario:

tables/tables.feature

```
Scenario: Converting cells
  Given I am logged in as a buyer
  When I view warranty options
  Then I should see the following options:
    | name     | price |
    | Platinum | $1000 |
    | Gold     | $500  |
    | Silver   | $200  |
```

Cucumber reads every table cell as a string. So, it will see the price of the platinum plan, for instance, as the string '$1000'.

Ian says:

Not a Moment Too Soon

One of our older projects used the RSpec Story Runner, Cucumber's predecessor. At the time, the Story Runner didn't support tables or tags. For one particularly repetitive test, we implemented our own ad hoc version.

```
# Modes: Regular, Analysis, Time
Scenario: Rounding
  When I enter 1.000001
  Then the value should be 1
```

We would preprocess the scenario in Ruby and generate three scenarios that would put the hardware into Regular, Analysis, or Time mode before running the test.

Thank goodness Cucumber came along!

But this hypothetical used-car API returns the prices as BigDecimal values like 1000.0. It also furnishes some extra information you're not using for this test: an administrative code for each plan.

tables/step_definitions/table_steps.rb

```
require 'bigdecimal'

When /^I view warranty options$/ do
  _1000 = BigDecimal.new '1000'
  _500  = BigDecimal.new '500'
  _200  = BigDecimal.new '200'

  @warranties = [{'name' => 'Platinum', 'price' => _1000, 'code' => 'P'},
                 {'name' => 'Gold',     'price' => _500,  'code' => 'G'},
                 {'name' => 'Silver',   'price' => _200,  'code' => 'S'}]
end
```

You need to convert the strings from your scenario into numbers to compare against your API. You can do this with Cucumber's map_column!() method. It takes a column name and a Ruby block to run on every cell in that column.

tables/step_definitions/table_steps.rb

```
Then /^I should see the following options:$/ do |table|
  table.map_column!(:price) { |cell| BigDecimal.new(cell.sub('$', '')) }
  table.diff! @warranties
end
```

Notice that Cucumber didn't complain that the API had an extra code column that's not used in the scenario. In the next section, we'll talk about these kinds of table structure differences.

Comparing Tables Flexibly

By default, Cucumber ignores *surplus columns*, that is, columns that are present in your internal data but not in your scenario. Any other difference in table structure—missing columns, surplus rows, or missing rows—will show up as a test failure.

You can change this default by passing an options hash to `diff!()` containing `:missing_col` or `:surplus_col` keys[3] with `true` or `false`. (`true` means "be strict.") For instance, if you want Cucumber to report the extra `code` column as a failure, you could use the following call:

```
table.diff! @warranties, :surplus_col => true
```

The three table operations you've seen so far—renaming headers, converting cells, and comparing structure—will get you through most of the situations where you need to map your Cucumber table to your underlying data. For those last few edge cases, you have one more trick up your sleeve.

Passing Cucumber Tables into Your Code

If your needs are really complex, you can always extract the data from where it's bottled up in the `Ast::Table` object and do whatever crunching you need on plain Ruby objects.

There are several ways to get the raw data out of a table. You can call `rows()` or `hashes()` to get the cells (minus the headers) as an array of arrays or an array of hashes. Here's what the output looks like with the table from the car scenario from the beginning of this recipe:

```
basic.rb(main):001:0> table.rows
=> [["rust", "Camaro"], ["blue", "Gremlin"]]
basic.rb(main):002:0> table.hashes
=> [{"color"=>"rust", "model"=>"Camaro"}, {"color"=>"blue", "model"=>"Gremlin"}]
basic.rb(main):003:0>
```

If you need the header row as well, you can call `raw()`.

```
raw.rb(main):001:0> table.raw
=> [["color", "model"], ["rust", "Camaro"], ["blue", "Gremlin"]]
raw.rb(main):002:0>
```

If your headers are in the first column (rather than the first row), you can `transpose()` the table or call `rows_hash()`.

3. Cucumber also allows you to ignore surplus or missing rows, but that use is rarer.

```
transpose.rb(main):001:0> table.transpose
=>
  |     color |     rust    |     blue    |
  |     model |     Camaro  |     Gremlin |

transpose.rb(main):002:0> table.rows_hash
=> {"color"=>"model", "rust"=>"Camaro", "blue"=>"Gremlin"}
transpose.rb(main):003:0>
```

Using the techniques in this recipe, you can keep your Cucumber features in the language of the problem domain. The mundane details of data formats and APIs will be confined to your Ruby step definitions, where they belong.

Further Exploration

This recipe assumes you're calling some underlying library, such as a GUI automation framework or a web scraping API, to get the values you're comparing against your scenarios. To see an example of how to parse HTML into a Cucumber-compatible table, see Recipe 30, *Parse HTML Tables*, on page 160.

Recipe 2

Generate an RTF Report with a Custom Formatter

Problem

You need the results of your tests to be in a specific format that's not one of the ones built into Cucumber. For instance, you might need everything typeset in a word processing document or sent to a network service.

Ingredients

- A Ruby 1.9–compatible update to an old RTF generation library, called clbustos-rtf[4]
- A word processor for viewing your report

Solution

In situations where you need a specific kind of output, you can write a *custom formatter*,[5] which is a simple Ruby class that generates the output format you need. All of Cucumber's built-in formatters—such as HTML and PDF—use the same technique.

This recipe will show you how to write a formatter to generate a minimal Rich Text Format (RTF) file, which can be read by most word processors.[6]

Our custom formatter will be just a plain Ruby class that follows a few simple conventions. Before we get into the specifics, let's talk about how formatters work.

Start with Callbacks

If you've ever parsed XML using a stream-based parser like `Nokogiri::SAX`, you've seen this flow before. You provide a Ruby class with a number of *callback* methods with names prescribed by the standard. The parser invokes one of your callbacks whenever it sees the start of an XML tag, the end of a document, and so on.

---

4. https://github.com/clbustos/rtf
5. https://github.com/cucumber/cucumber/wiki/Custom-Formatters
6. http://en.wikipedia.org/wiki/Rich_Text_Format

Cucumber provides a similar mechanism called *events*. While Cucumber runs, it will see various events: the beginning of a scenario, a passed or failed step, and others. For each event, it looks for a specific method in your formatter. The method names are self-descriptive: before_scenario(), after_step_result(), and so on.

You don't have to define a method for every possible event Cucumber might call; in fact, you don't have to define any of them. If your class is missing a particular event, Cucumber just moves on to the next one. So, you can actually start with an empty Ruby class and gradually add methods to it as you need.

Let's see that in action. Create a new project directory, and save the following text in humpty.feature:

formatters/humpty.feature

```
Feature: Humpty Dumpty

  Scenario: Fall
    Given I am on a wall
    When I lose my balance
    Then I should have a great fall

  Scenario: Reassembly
    Given all the king's horses
    And all the king's men
    When they attempt to put me back together again
    Then I should be in one piece
```

Make a support subdirectory; then add the following outline to support/rtf_formatter.rb:

formatters/support/rtf_formatter.rb

```
require 'rtf'

class RtfFormatter
end
```

Since this file is in the support directory, Cucumber will load it automatically. All you need to do to use your new formatter is pass the -f flag on the command line. Go ahead and try your new formatter.

```
$ cucumber -f RtfFormatter humpty.feature
```

Your formatter doesn't have any events yet, so the output isn't very interesting. It's time to change that.

Generate a Simple Document

When Cucumber starts a test run, it will create an instance of your RtfFormatter class. So, the initializer is a good place to create a new RTF document.

formatters/support/rtf_formatter.rb

```
Line 1 def initialize(step_mother, io, options)
2        @io   = io
3
4        font = RTF::Font.new(RTF::Font::SWISS, 'Verdana')
5        @rtf = RTF::Document.new font
6      end
```

Cucumber will always pass three arguments to your initializer, but you need to keep a reference only to the middle one, an IO object where you'll write the report.

On line 5, you create a new Document instance and hang onto it so your events can add text to it.

Now you're ready for your first event: after_step_result().

formatters/support/rtf_formatter.rb

```
def after_step_result(keyword, match, multiline, status,
                      exception, indent, background,
                      file_colon_line)
  @rtf.paragraph do |para|
    para << (status.to_s + ': ' + keyword + match.format_args)
  end
end
```

That's a lot of parameters! Fortunately, you need to worry only about three of them for now. keyword will be Given, When, or Then. match is a Ruby object containing information about the text and arguments of the step; you call its format_args() method to generate a simple string, such as " I am on a wall." status is a Symbol that indicates whether the step :passed, :failed, was :pending, and so on.

After all the features run, you'll generate the RTF output and send it to the IO object Cucumber handed to you. This behavior goes in the aptly named after_features() event.

formatters/support/rtf_formatter.rb

```
def after_features(features)
  @io.puts @rtf.to_rtf
end
```

Rerun your Cucumber script and direct output to a file.

```
$ cucumber -f RtfFormatter humpty.feature > report.rtf
```

When you open the report in a word processor, you should see something like Figure 1, *Basic RTF report*.

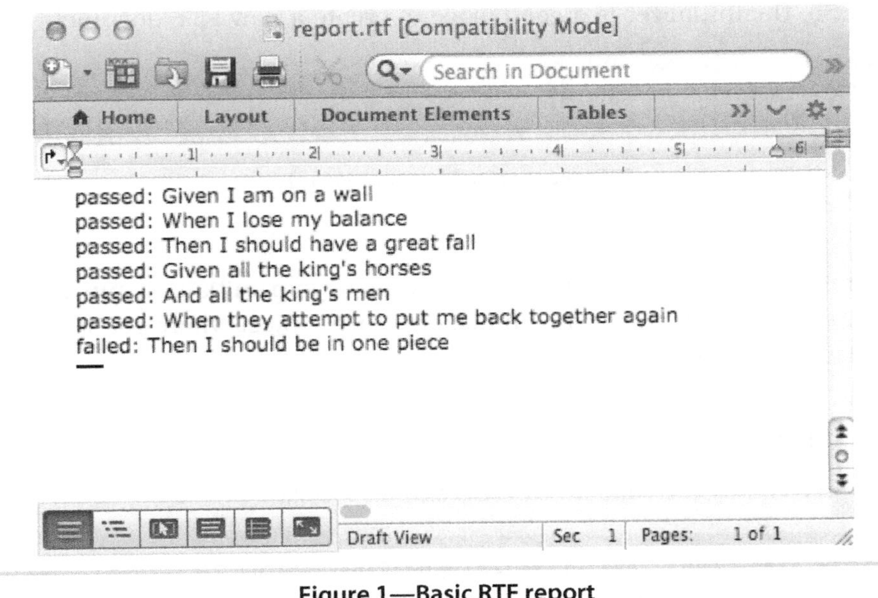

Figure 1—Basic RTF report

Add Formatting

So far, this RTF document looks like plain text. Let's add a little formatting. Since the goal here is to learn Cucumber rather than the full RTF standard, there's no need to get too crazy with the output. For now, a couple of changes of color and weight will be fine.

This RTF library uses the CharacterStyle class to represent properties such as color, bold, and italics. You'll store a few of these in a hash inside your RtfFormatter class so that you can look them up quickly when your event gets called with a status of :passed, :failed, and so on.

formatters/support/rtf_formatter.rb

```
Styles = {}
Styles.default = RTF::CharacterStyle.new

Styles[:passed] = RTF::CharacterStyle.new
Styles[:passed].foreground = RTF::Colour.new 0, 127, 0 # green

Styles[:failed] = RTF::CharacterStyle.new
Styles[:failed].foreground = RTF::Colour.new 127, 0, 0 # red
Styles[:failed].bold = true
```

Next, modify your after_step_result() method to apply a passing or failing style to each paragraph.

formatters/support/rtf_formatter.rb

```
def after_step_result(keyword, match, multiline, status,
                      exception, indent, background,
                      file_colon_line)
  @rtf.paragraph do |para|
    para.apply(Styles[status]) do |text|
      text << (status.to_s + ': ' + keyword + match.format_args)
    end
  end
end
```

To see what this looks like, write a couple of empty or failing step definitions for your Cucumber feature. Then, rerun Cucumber with your formatter. You should see something like Figure 2, *RTF report with formatting*.

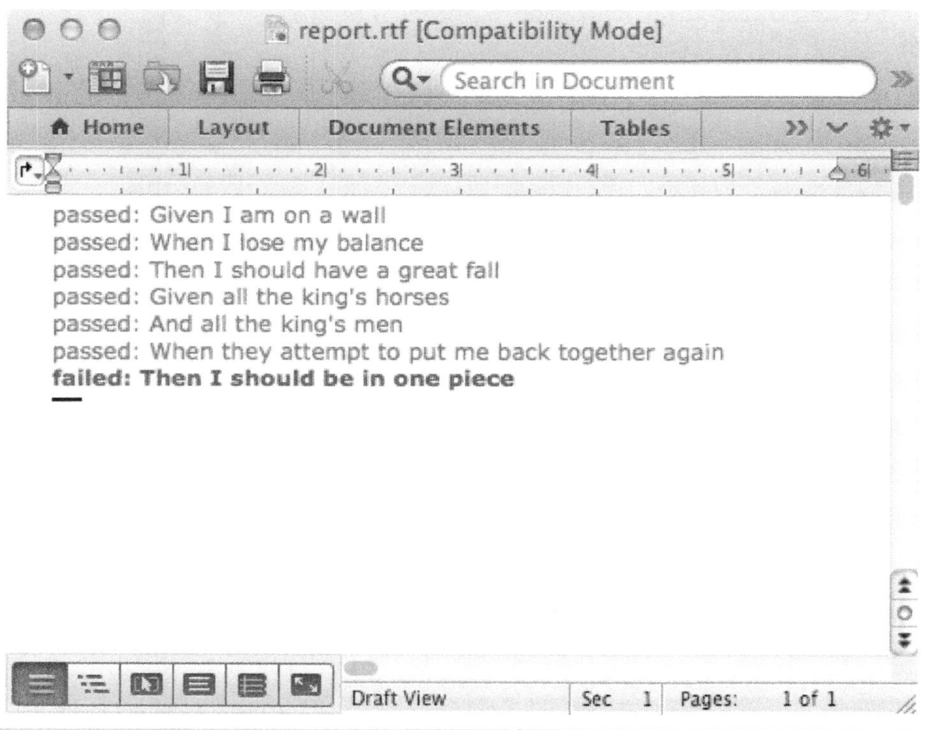

Figure 2—RTF report with formatting

Further Exploration

In this recipe, you've seen how to write a custom formatter and which methods are the most important ones for you to provide. Several other events are available to you, should you need to do something special with tags or tables. The formatter page on the Cucumber wiki has a complete list.[7] You can also pass the `-f debug` option when you run your tests to get a list of events as they occur.

Reading the source code for Cucumber's built-in formatters is a great way to learn events by example. In particular, the HTML formatter shows off a lot of the functionality available.[8] Third-party formatters like fuubar are another helpful learning resource.[9]

7. https://github.com/cucumber/cucumber/wiki/Custom-Formatters
8. https://github.com/cucumber/cucumber/tree/master/lib/cucumber/formatter/html.rb
9. https://github.com/jeffkreeftmeijer/fuubar

Recipe 3

Run Slow Setup/Teardown Code with Global Hooks

Problem

You need to do something that takes a while before your first test, such as launching a browser or waiting for a desktop application to load. You're familiar with Cucumber's Before hook, which runs once per scenario. But you want something that runs just once overall so that your setup code doesn't slow down your test too much.

Ingredients

- Cucumber's built-in env.rb file for setup code
- Ruby's built-in at_exit() hook for teardown code[10]
- The Selenium WebDriver browser automation library[11]
- The Firefox web browser[12]

Solution

This recipe starts with a simple web testing project. Before we make our improvements, the code to start and stop the web browser executes inside regular Cucumber scenario hooks—and so the tests run more slowly than they should. We're going to see how to migrate that slow code to global hooks so it runs only once.

You don't have to use any special hooks to run setup code when Cucumber starts. Just put your one-time start-up code in env.rb, and Cucumber will run it before the first test.

That just leaves one question. With the Before hook, there was a corresponding After hook where you could shut down whatever application or browser you were using. Where do you put global teardown code that needs to run only once?

The answer is to use Ruby's built-in at_exit() method, which allows you to register a hook that runs just as Cucumber is exiting.

---

10. http://www.ruby-doc.org/core-1.9.2/Kernel.html#method-i-at_exit
11. http://seleniumhq.org/docs/03_webdriver.html#ruby
12. http://www.firefox.com

Let's look at a test that suffers from repeated setup code and how you might convert it to use global hooks.

Setup

First, install Selenium WebDriver.

```
$ gem install selenium-webdriver
```

Now, create a simple test that has multiple scenarios.

global_hooks/bank.feature

```
Feature: Banking

  Scenario: Deposit
    Given I have $0 in my account
    # ...

  Scenario: Withdrawal
    Given I have $100 in my account
    # ...
```

Fill in a step definition that requires a web browser.

global_hooks/step_definitions/bank_steps.rb

```
Given /^I have \$(\d+) in my account$/ do |balance|
  @browser.navigate.to 'http://example.com/banking'
end
```

This code presumes you've launched a browser and stored a reference to it in the @browser variable. The traditional approach to managing that variable is to use Before and After hooks. Let's look at that technique first and then migrate to global hooks.

Scenario Hooks

Here's how you might have added per-scenario setup and teardown code without this recipe:

global_hooks/support/hooks.rb

```
require 'selenium-webdriver'

Before do
  @browser = Selenium::WebDriver.for :firefox
end

After do
  @browser.quit
end
```

Go ahead and run your feature, taking care to time the results. On Mac and Linux, you'd type the following:

```
$ time cucumber bank.feature
```

On Windows with PowerShell installed, you'd type this instead:[13]

```
C:\Hooks> Measure-Command {cucumber bank.feature}
```

You should see Firefox launch and exit before and after every step, and the total execution time will show it. It's time to migrate your start-up code to global hooks.

Global Hooks

You're going to move your browser-launching code out of the Before hook. But where to? You may recall that Cucumber is guaranteed to run code in env.rb before any of your other support code. That makes this file a good place for one-time setup.

The simplest approach is to run the setup code at file scope and store any state you need in a global.

global_hooks/support/env.rb

```ruby
require 'selenium-webdriver'

$browser = Selenium::WebDriver.for :firefox
at_exit { $browser.quit }
```

Notice the symmetry between the creation of the $browser object and the registering of an at_exit() hook to tear it down when Ruby exits.

Before you run off and change your step definition to use the $browser global variable, it's worth considering the maintenance problems that globals can cause down the road. Take a moment to package up this code into a module and change the global variable to a class-level attribute instead.

global_hooks/support/env.rb

```ruby
require 'selenium-webdriver'

module HasBrowser
  @@browser = Selenium::WebDriver.for :firefox
  at_exit { @@browser.quit }
end
```

13. PowerShell comes with Windows 7 and can also be downloaded from http://www.microsoft.com/powershell.

Ian says:

To Restart or Not to Restart?

Keeping a long-running program alive works really well for web testing. Since the app you're testing is running on a server you control, it's easy to get it into a known state before each scenario.

If you're testing a desktop GUI app, you'll have to consider the trade-offs. You'll save time by launching the app only once. But if it gets into a bizarre state during one scenario, all the subsequent tests could fail.

One approach is to add a "reset" command to your app so that you can quickly get it back to a default mode at the beginning of each scenario, without suffering the overhead of quitting and relaunching it.

Notice that you're now storing the browser in a class-level attribute @@browser so that its value will be available across scenarios. In a minute, we'll add an accessor function for your step definitions to call.

First, though, take a look at the at_exit() hook. You're probably used to seeing these at file scope, so it may seem a little weird to use it inside a module definition. It will work just fine here.

Now, about that accessor function. Add the following code inside your module definition:

```
def browser
  @@browser
end
```

One last thing: how do you make the browser() method available to your step definitions? You add it to the *world*,[14] a container provided by Cucumber to store state between steps. You can do this by calling World() at file scope and passing it the name of your module.

```
World(HasBrowser)
```

Don't forget to change your step definition to use the new browser() method.

global_hooks/step_definitions/bank_steps.rb

```
Given /^I have \$(\d+) in my account$/ do |balance|
  browser.navigate.to 'http://example.com/banking'
end
```

14. https://github.com/cucumber/cucumber/wiki/A-Whole-New-World

Now if you rerun your test, you should see that Firefox starts only once at the beginning of the run and exits only once at the end. The total execution time will be cut almost in half.

Further Exploration

This recipe covered attaching hooks to the World object, which the Cucumber runtime creates for each scenario. For more on how you can customize this object's behavior, see Chapter 7 of *The Cucumber Book [WH11]*.

Most of the time, env.rb is the best place for global setup code. But if your hook must run specifically after configuration is complete, while still finishing before the first scenario runs, you can use the AfterConfiguration hook instead.[15]

15. https://github.com/cucumber/cucumber/wiki/Hooks

Recipe 4

Refactor to Extract Your Own Application Driver DSL

Problem

Your step definition code is growing out of control. When you jump down the stack from your nice, readable Cucumber scenarios into the step definitions behind them, you're suddenly besieged by masses of Ruby code. You have a nagging feeling that there are little bits of duplication all over the place, but you just can't see it. You need to clean things up.

Ingredients

- Ruby's built-in module[16] mixins
- Cucumber's built-in `World()` method[17] for registering extension modules
- The capybara gem[18] for automating browsers
- The Firefox web browser[19]

Solution

In this recipe, we'll start with an existing Cucumber scenario for testing a website. The step definitions are difficult to read and maintain, because they're full of irrelevant details about which buttons to click.

You'll soon fix these problems. Through a series of refactorings—small transformations that improve the maintainability of the code without changing its behavior—you'll move the low-level details into their own Ruby module. The new step definitions will drive the application through easy-to-read method names like `log_in_as()`. This technique of wrapping your application's user interface in an easy-to-use API is called an application driver *domain-specific language* (DSL).

Let's consider a simple scenario that tests the behavior of Squeaker,[20] an up-and-coming micro-blogging platform.

---

16. http://ruby-doc.org/core-1.9.2/Module.html
17. http://rdoc.info/github/cucumber/cucumber/Cucumber/RbSupport/RbDsl:World
18. http://rubygems.org/gems/capybara
19. http://www.firefox.com
20. http://squeaker.heroku.com

Matt says: Swap in Drivers to Connect to Your Application at Different Levels

One interesting possibility once you've introduced this extra layer into your test suite is that you can swap in a different driver module without the step definitions knowing anything about it. I've used this on projects that use a hexagonal architecture[a] to run a set of very fast Cucumber tests using a driver that connected directly to my domain model. I use an environment variable to choose which driver to plug in.

```
if ENV['SLOW']
  World(EndToEndDriver)
else
  World(FastDriver)
end
```

The cost of this is that I have to maintain two driver DSL modules: one that connects to my domain model and another that hits the user interface and database. The payback is that this allows me to still have the confidence of running a full (but slow) suite of end-to-end tests when I want. The rest of the time I can run the same features and step definitions against my domain model instead and get lightning-quick feedback.

a. http://alistair.cockburn.us/Hexagonal+architecture

dsl/before/features/greet_user.feature

```
Feature: Greet user

  Scenario: Greet users who are logged in
    Given I am logged in as "matt"
    When I visit the homepage
    Then I should see "Hello matt"
```

To drive the Squeaker web interface, we'll install Capybara into our Cucumber suite.

dsl/before/features/support/env.rb

```
require 'capybara/cucumber'

Capybara.default_driver = :selenium
Capybara.app_host = 'http://squeaker.heroku.com'
```

Right now the step definitions to drive this scenario look like this:

dsl/before/features/step_definitions/steps.rb

```
Before { visit '/reset' }
When /^I visit the homepage$/ do
  visit '/'
end
```

```
Given /^I am logged in as "(.*?)"$/ do |username|
  # create account
  visit '/'
  click_link 'create an account'
  fill_in 'Username', with: username
  click_button 'Create My Account'
  click_button 'Log Out'
  # log in
  click_link 'log in'
  fill_in 'Username', with: username
  click_button 'Log in'
end
Then /^I should see "(.*?)"$/ do |expected_text|
  page.should have_content(expected_text)
end
```

The problem here is in the step that logs you in. It's really long and contains a lot of detail that makes it hard to follow. Let's refactor it to extract a couple of helper methods.

dsl/after/features/step_definitions/steps.rb

```
Before { visit '/reset' }

When /^I visit the homepage$/ do
  visit '/'
end

Given /^I am logged in as "(.*?)"$/ do |username|
  create_user_named username
  log_in_as username
end

Then /^I should see "(.*?)"$/ do |expected_text|
  page.should have_content(expected_text)
end
```

This step definition is much easier to read. Now, when you move from the Gherkin feature into this file, the jump in abstraction is much gentler and less jarring. We're also starting to build up our own DSL for driving our application. As we go on, we can add more helper methods to carry out common tasks such as posting messages and following users.

You might be wondering where we define these methods. We're going to define them on a module and use Cucumber's World() method to register them with Cucumber as an extension. Create features/support/squeaker_driver.rb with the following content:

dsl/after/features/support/squeaker_driver.rb

```
module SqueakerDriver
  def create_user_named(username)
    visit '/'
    click_link 'create an account'
    fill_in 'Username', with: username
    click_button 'Create My Account'
    click_button 'Log Out'
  end
  def log_in_as(username)
    visit '/'
    click_link 'log in'
    fill_in 'Username', with: username
    click_button 'Log in'
  end
end
World(SqueakerDriver)
```

Cucumber will automatically load this file (it loads everything in features/support automatically) on start-up, which registers the methods defined in SqueakerDriver as being available to your step definitions.

Further Exploration

For a deep dive into the different types of DSLs and how they're implemented, see Martin Fowler's *Domain-Specific Languages [Fow10].*

Recipe 5

Define Steps as Regular Ruby Methods

Problem

You'd like your step definitions to be plain Ruby methods so that they're easier to edit, test, and maintain.

Ingredients

- Cucumber's built-in support for invoking Ruby methods directly[21]
- (Optional) Mechanize[22] to run the examples with live data

Solution

Cucumber step definitions are pretty easy to put together. You just tie together a regular expression with a block of code. Ideally, these blocks of code should be really short—perhaps a method invocation or two and some data massaging.

Over time, it can be tempting to let more and more code creep into your step definitions. They can become harder to read and maintain.

Regular Ruby methods don't have this problem. They're easy to refactor when they get complex. They're easy to test with any one of the great frameworks written for Ruby.

With *step methods*, you can bring the maintainability benefits of plain Ruby into your step definition code. In this recipe, we're going to start with a traditional Cucumber test and then move the step definitions into an easy-to-test Ruby module.

The techniques we show here will work for any kind of Cucumber test: desktop, mobile, web, and so on. We'll show a web app for the purposes of the example.

Traditional Test

Consider the following Cucumber test to look for a book's related titles on the Pragmatic Programmers website:

---

21. https://github.com/cucumber/cucumber/blob/master/features/step_definitions.feature#L21
22. http://mechanize.rubyforge.org

methods/before/features/book.feature

```
Feature: Book landing page
  Scenario: Related titles
    Given I am on the page for "Cucumber Recipes"
    When I look for related titles
    Then I should see "The Cucumber Book"
```

A quick-and-dirty implementation of the Given step might look something like this:

methods/before/features/step_definitions/book_steps.rb

```
Given /^I am on the page for "(.*?)"$/ do |title|
  urls    = {'Cucumber Recipes' => 'http://pragprog.com/titles/dhwcr'}
  url     = urls[title] || raise("Unknown title #{title}")
  browser = Mechanize.new
  @page   = browser.get url
end
```

Here, we're using Mechanize to fetch and scrape the page. To run this example with a live page, you'll need to install the mechanize gem.

```
$ gem install mechanize
```

Then load the library in features/support/env.rb.

methods/before/features/support/env.rb

```
require 'mechanize'
```

Now, you can define the Then step.

methods/before/features/step_definitions/book_steps.rb

```
When /^I look for related titles$/ do
  css = 'table#related-books td.description a'
  @related = @page.search(css).map &:content
end
```

Mechanize uses Nokogiri[23] for HTML parsing, so we can just locate the Related Titles section by CSS descriptors and then extract the text. Once we have that, the Then step is simple.

methods/before/features/step_definitions/book_steps.rb

```
Then /^I should see "(.*?)"$/ do |title|
  @related.should include(title)
end
```

Go ahead and run the test now; you should get a passing result. Then, look back at the step definitions. We have low-level CSS selectors tangled up with high-level concepts like book titles. How can we tease these apart?

23. http://nokogiri.org

Method Steps

The first thing you might do is apply the concepts of Recipe 4, *Refactor to Extract Your Own Application Driver DSL*, on page 18 and extract that low-level HTML scraping code into a Ruby module.

methods/dsl/lib/knows_book_page.rb

```
module KnowsBookPage
  def visit_book_page(title)
    urls    = {'Cucumber Recipes' => 'http://pragprog.com/titles/dhwcr'}
    url     = urls[title] || raise("Unknown title #{title}")
    browser = Mechanize.new
    @page   = browser.get url
  end

  def find_related_titles
    css = 'table#related-books td.description a'
    @related = @page.search(css).map &:content
  end

  def verify_related_title(title)
    @related.should include(title)
  end
end
```

You can then include this module in the World, as in Recipe 12, *Test Through Multiple Interfaces Using Worlds*, on page 61.

methods/dsl/features/support/env.rb

```
require 'mechanize'
require './lib/knows_book_page'

World(KnowsBookPage)
```

Now, the step definitions become simple wrappers around the methods in KnowsBookPage.

methods/dsl/features/step_definitions/book_steps.rb

```
Given /^I am on the page for "(.*?)"$/ do |title|
  visit_book_page title
end

When /^I look for related titles$/ do
  find_related_titles
end

Then /^I should see "(.*?)"$/ do |title|
  verify_related_title title
end
```

Once that's done, you may wonder why we need even this thin layer. That's where step methods come in. If the entire contents of your step definition would be a method call on World, you can replace the step definition body with the method name.

methods/steps/features/step_definitions/book_steps.rb

```
Given /^I am on the page for "(.*?)"$/, :visit_book_page
When /^I look for related titles$/,     :find_related_titles
Then /^I should see "(.*?)"$/,          :verify_related_title
```

Notice that this technique even works with step definitions that take parameters, like our Given and Then steps. Any capture groups in the regular expression—in this case, the book titles—get passed into the method as parameters.

Plain Ol' Ruby Objects

Implementing step definitions in a module has a couple of advantages. It forces us to keep our step definition code in a conventional Ruby module, where we can more easily "test the tests." It also makes it easier to apply typical Ruby refactorings when our code starts to get complex.

You'll notice that we used a Ruby module to group our step definition methods and make them callable from the Cucumber World. Often, a class is a better way to organize code. For these cases, you can specify what object Cucumber should call your step definition methods on.

If we have a BookPage class in lib/book_page.rb,

methods/object/lib/book_page.rb

```
class BookPage
  include RSpec::Matchers
  def visit_book_page(title)
    urls    = {'Cucumber Recipes' => 'http://pragprog.com/titles/dhwcr'}
    url     = urls[title] || raise("Unknown title #{title}")
    browser = Mechanize.new
    @page   = browser.get url
  end

  def find_related_titles
    css = 'table#related-books td.description a'
    @related = @page.search(css).map &:content
  end
  def verify_related_title(title)
    @related.should include(title)
  end
end
```

then we can create a single instance and use it from our World.

methods/object/features/support/env.rb

```
require 'mechanize'
require './lib/book_page'
module KnowsBookPage
  def page
    @page ||= BookPage.new
  end
end
World(KnowsBookPage)
```

Now, all we need to do is tell our step definitions to call methods on the page object instead of the World.

methods/object/features/step_definitions/book_steps.rb

```
Given /^I am on the page for "(.*?)"$/, :visit_book_page, :on => lambda { page }
When /^I look for related titles$/, :find_related_titles, :on => lambda { page }
Then /^I should see "(.*?)"$/,     :verify_related_title, :on => lambda { page }
```

With these techniques, you can lavish the same attention on your Cucumber step definitions that you do on the rest of your Ruby code.

Recipe 6

Compare Images

Problem

You're using Cucumber to test an app that generates or manipulates images. You want to compare the result to a reference picture—with a little wiggle room for minor differences.

Ingredients

- pdiff (short for "perceptual diff"),[24] a command-line image comparison tool that accounts for the way people perceive images
- chunky_png[25] for generating PNG files in the example code

Solution

It sounds so simple, doesn't it? "Compare these two pictures and tell me whether they match." But the devil is in the details. What does it mean for two images to match?

Do they need to be pixel-for-pixel identical? If not, what percentage difference is acceptable? What about images that are slightly rotated or scaled? Or discolored by a tiny amount? Your answers to these questions will determine how you compare the images. Here are a few approaches you might take:

- Compare the pixels one by one and count how many are different.
- For each pixel, compute the delta between the reference image and your app's image. For example, a pixel that is only a slightly different shade of red would result in a smaller difference than one that's a completely different color or brightness.
- Reduce, or *downsample*, the number of colors or pixels in the images before comparing them. This will build in a little tolerance for differences.
- Compute a hash of the image's contents, giving it a fingerprint you can use for comparison.

---

24. http://pdiff.sf.net
25. https://github.com/wvanbergen/chunky_png/wiki

- Use a heavyweight algorithm like SURF[26] to look for common features between the two pictures, accounting for rotation and scale.

For this recipe, we're going to use a tool called pdiff, or "perceptual diff." It compares pixels directly but gives more weight to differences that are likely to stand out to the human eye. This kind of comparison is suitable when you want to build in a little tolerance for differences but don't care about matching rotated or scaled images.

The app we're writing will draw a simple image, which we will compare to a reference image using pdiff.

Setup

First, let's get the software installed. pdiff is pretty easy to build from source, but the project also posts binaries for Windows, Mac, and Linux.[27] Grab the perceptualdiff executable for your platform and save it somewhere on your PATH.

To generate the image from our app, we're going to use chunky_png, a pure-Ruby library for generating PNG files. Go ahead and install the gem.

```
$ gem install chunky_png
```

We'll need a little setup code as well. Create a file called support/env.rb, where we can bring in the libraries we'll be using. This is also where we'll add a Cucumber hook to remove the generated image before each test.

compare_images/support/env.rb

```
require 'fileutils'
require 'chunky_png'

include ChunkyPNG

Before do
  FileUtils.rm_f 'generated.png'
end
```

Now that setup is complete, we can move on to the feature.

Feature

Let's write a feature defining the behavior for a simple automated drawing program.

26. http://www.vision.ee.ethz.ch/~surf
27. http://sourceforge.net/projects/pdiff/files/pdiff/

compare_images/drawing.feature

```
Feature: Drawing

  Scenario: Green circle
    Given a white background
    When I draw a green circle
    Then the result should resemble "circle.png"
```

The chunky_png API is pretty simple. We create a new Canvas object and then call the circle() method to draw into it.

compare_images/step_definitions/drawing_steps.rb

```
Given /^a white background$/ do
  @canvas = Canvas.new 300, 200, Color::WHITE
end

When /^I draw a green circle$/ do
  green = Color.rgb 0, 255, 0
  @canvas.circle 150, 100, 50, green, green
end
```

In the final step definition, we'll save the file and see how closely it resembles the picture we expect. Before we do that, we need to talk a little about the mechanics of comparing images.

Comparing Images

Our expected image is 300x200 pixels, with a lime green circle in the middle that has a radius of 50. You can create this image manually in a graphics editor, or you can download the one we drew for this book.[28] Either way, save the file as reference.png.

Before we add pdiff to our Cucumber feature, let's try using it from the command line. Run your feature once to create generated.png. Then, execute perceptualdiff with the -verbose option.

```
$ perceptualdiff -verbose reference.png generated.png
Field of view is 45.000000 degrees
Threshold pixels is 100 pixels
The Gamma is 2.200000
The Display's luminance is 100.000000 candela per meter squared
Converting RGB to XYZ
Constructing Laplacian Pyramids
Performing test
FAIL: Images are visibly different
229 pixels are different
```

---

28. http://media.pragprog.com/titles/dhwcr/code/compare_images/reference.png

Even though 229 pixels sounds like it's a lot, in a 60,000-pixel image it's not that big a difference. See for yourself: the following image contains both the reference image and the generated image.

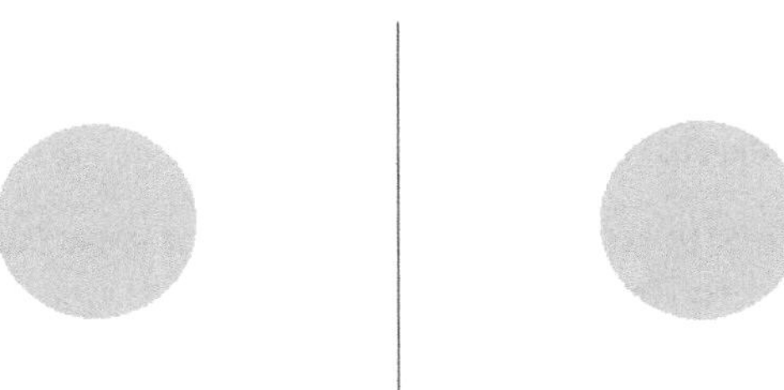

pdiff can actually show you exactly which pixels are different; just pass the -output flag.

```
$ perceptualdiff -output diff.png reference.png generated.png
```

This will produce a file showing the difference between the two images. As you can see in the close-up below, the only difference is around the border of the circle. This is likely because of a slight difference in the way my graphics editor and chunky_png render circles.

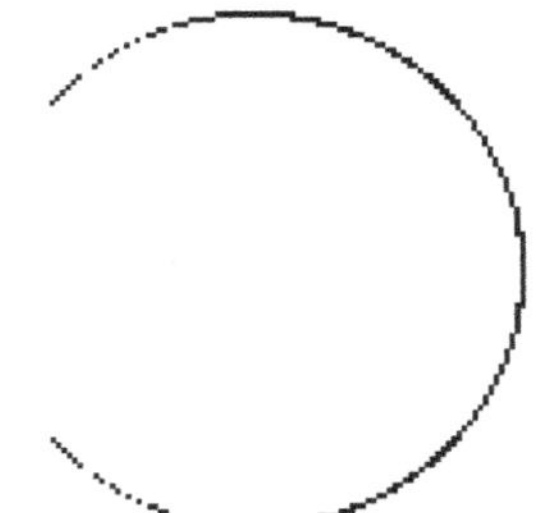

Either way, our end user is unlikely to care about the difference. For this project, we're assuming pixel-exact matching is not required.

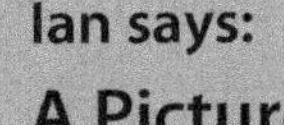

Ian says:

A Picture Is Worth...

Think image comparison sounds like a big hack? Sometimes it's all you have. A friend of mine tests on an OS where there are no developer hooks into the GUI. The only testing activity it supports is taking a full screenshot.

He's able to test with the same sophistication as the rest of us, thanks to his suite of computer vision algorithms. He can even detect subtle differences in readouts that human testers missed.

There are a couple of ways to relax our criteria a bit so that pdiff will consider our images as being similar enough. We could pass the -tolerance option to increase the number of pixels that pdiff allows to be different. Or we could reduce the size of the image before comparing, by passing the -downsample option. We have a slight preference for the latter because it relies less on discovering a magic threshold number that's neither too strict nor too forgiving.

Here's how to downsample the image by a factor of two:

```
$ perceptualdiff -downsample 2 -verbose reference.png generated.png
Downsampling by 2
Downsampling by 4
Field of view is 45.000000 degrees
Threshold pixels is 100 pixels
The Gamma is 2.200000
The Display's luminance is 100.000000 candela per meter squared
Converting RGB to XYZ
Constructing Laplacian Pyramids
Performing test
PASS: Images are perceptually indistinguishable
68 pixels are different
```

Now that we have a handle on using pdiff manually, let's call it from our Cucumber feature.

Results

In the previous section, we saw how to run pdiff from the command line. How do we incorporate the tool into our step definition?

Like any good command-line tool, pdiff uses an exit code to signal whether the comparison succeeded. We can use Ruby's $? variable to retrieve the exit code; this object has a success?() method we can call from our Then step.

compare_images/step_definitions/drawing_steps.rb

```
Then /^the result should resemble "([^"]*)"$/ do |filename|
  @canvas.save 'generated.png'
  `perceptualdiff -downsample 2 #{filename} generated.png`
  $?.should be_success
end
```

Now, if you run your feature again, you should see a passing result.

Further Exploration

As we've said, there are a lot of different ways to compare images, depending on what your needs are. Jeff Kreeftmeijer has written a tutorial on simple color differences using chunky_png.[29] Mike Perham's phashion library[30] calculates a single fingerprint for each image and then compares the fingerprints.

For really heavy-duty stuff such as detecting scaling and rotation, you may need to bring out the power tools like OpenCV,[31] the open source computer vision library. This software is not for the faint of heart, but sometimes a powerful algorithm like SURF is what fits your application best.

29. http://jeffkreeftmeijer.com/2011/comparing-images-and-creating-image-diffs
30. http://www.mikeperham.com/2010/05/21/detecting-duplicate-images-with-phashion/
31. http://opencv.willowgarage.com/wiki

Recipe 7

Test Across Multiple Cores

Problem

You want to give your tests a quick speed boost by distributing them across all the cores on your development machine.

Ingredients

- The parallel gem[32] for distributing tasks within a single test
- The parallel_tests gem[33] for distributing entire features across multiple cores

Solution

Unless you tell it otherwise, Cucumber typically runs your features in a single process containing a single thread. Modern desktop machines often have multiple cores; even my little travel computer has two. By breaking work into pieces and farming them out to all the cores on your machine, you can run your tests faster.

Parallel Tasks

Imagine you have the following scenario in features/shipping.feature:

multiple_cores/parallel/features/shipping.feature

```
Feature: Shipping

  Scenario: Packing the containers
    Given an order for 20 tons of material
    When I pack 4 shipping containers
    Then the order should be complete
```

Here's the definition of the When step (you can leave the other two definitions empty):

multiple_cores/parallel/features/step_definitions/shipping_steps.rb

```
When /^I pack (\d+) shipping containers$/ do |count|
  last = count.to_i
```

32. https://github.com/grosser/parallel
33. https://github.com/grosser/parallel_tests

```
  (1..last).each do |i|
    Shipping.pack_container i
  end
end
```

The definition of the Shipping class goes in features/support/env.rb.

multiple_cores/parallel/features/support/env.rb

```
class Shipping
  @@logger = Logger.new 'shipping.log'
  def self.pack_container(container)
    @@logger.info "Container ##{container} - START"
    sleep 2
    @@logger.info "Container ##{container} - DONE"
  end
end
```

We've added a call to sleep() to simulate the lengthy calculation of how best to fill the shipping container (a problem known to be computationally difficult).

When you run this feature, you should see something like this at the end of Cucumber's output:

```
0m8.007s
```

Each of the four containers took two seconds to fill; the overall test time was about eight seconds.

Calculating properties of shipping containers is pure math. It doesn't hit a database, the file system, or any other global state. It's safe to run the calculation in parallel across all your cores. To do so, we're going to install the parallel gem.

```
$ gem install parallel
```

Then, replace the call to each() in your step definition with Parallel.each().

multiple_cores/parallel/features/step_definitions/shipping_steps.rb

```
When /^I pack (\d+) shipping containers$/ do |count|
  last = count.to_i

➤ Parallel.each(1..last) do |i|
    Shipping.pack_container i
  end
end
```

Notice that we didn't need to make any changes to our code under test—just the Cucumber step definition. Now, if you run your test again, the overall time should drop based on the number of cores you have. On my two-core laptop, the time dropped almost in half, to 4.102 seconds.

Parallel Features

Parallel.each is fine for breaking a single task into pieces you can run on all your machine's cores. But what about spreading your entire Cucumber suite across cores?

The parallel_tests gem, built on the parallel gem we've just discussed, will spawn one Cucumber process per core on your machine and then run a different subset of your features on each core.

Let's see what that looks like. Remove the call to Parallel.each() from your previous step definition, and just go back to Ruby's regular each() method. Add a new Cucumber file called receiving.feature with the following contents:

multiple_cores/parallel_tests/features/receiving.feature

```
Feature: Receiving

  Scenario: Filling the warehouse
    Given I have received 20 tons of raw material
    When I unload the order into the warehouse
    Then I should have 15% space remaining
```

Fill in empty definitions for these steps, and throw a fixed sleep() inside the When step. I used four seconds on mine. So, the eight-second shipping test plus the four-second receiving test take a total of twelve seconds on a single core.

Go ahead and install parallel_tests so that you can run your features in parallel.

```
$ gem install parallel_tests
```

The only thing you have to do differently to run your Cucumber tests on multiple cores is to run the parallel_cucumber command instead of just plain cucumber.

```
$ parallel_cucumber features
```

Now, the total test time should be close to the length of the longest test, around eight seconds.

Further Exploration

This recipe deals with speeding up tests on your own development machine by using all your cores. The next logical step is to farm your tests out to multiple machines; Recipe 8, *Test Across Multiple Machines with SSH*, on page 36 will show you how to do that.

Recipe 8

Test Across Multiple Machines with SSH

Problem

You're testing a complex application, and your tests take a while to complete. You'd like to run your tests in parallel across multiple machines to save overall execution time.

Ingredients

- Cucumber tags[34] for sorting your features into groups that can be run across multiple machines
- An SSH client[35] for connecting to the remote machines
- rsync[36] for copying your Cucumber features to each computer

Solution

We strive to make our Cucumber tests run as fast as possible. But let's say you've optimized everything you can, and your tests still take an hour to run. What can you do?

One approach is to run only a subset of the tests, at least while you're actively developing a specific feature. Another is to break your tests into groups and run each group on its own dedicated machine.

There are libraries that can help with this process, but they tend to stay tied to a particular workflow or Cucumber version. For this recipe, we're going to use something much simpler and future-proof: good ol' SSH. We'll use a single development computer and two remote test machines.

We'll start with some long-running features, manually assign them to groups, copy the code to each remote machine, and use SSH to run the tests there.

Long-Running Features

Imagine you're writing some acceptance tests for a flight reservation system. These take quite a while, because at this level you're exercising the entire stack.

34. https://github.com/cucumber/cucumber/wiki/tags
35. https://en.wikipedia.org/wiki/Secure_Shell
36. http://rsync.samba.org

Here are a couple of scenarios for flight.feature:

multiple_machines/flight.feature

```
Feature: Flights
  @group1
  Scenario: Route exists
    Given a nonstop flight exists
    When I plan my trip
    Then I should see the nonstop options first

  @group2
  Scenario: No route exists
    Given no nonstop flight exists
    When I plan my trip
    Then I should be shown connecting flights
```

You'll notice we've added @group1 and @group2 tags to the scenarios. This will make it easy to split this scenario across multiple machines later.

Create a new file called step_definitions/flight_steps.rb and add empty step definitions to it. Then, add a delay to the middle step to simulate this long-running action.

multiple_machines/step_definitions/flight_steps.rb

```
When /^I plan my trip$/ do
  sleep 10
end
```

If you run these scenarios, you'll see that they take a while to complete. Once we get SSH set up, we'll be able to reduce overall test time by distributing the workload.

Remote Machine Setup

Let's say you have two Linux machines, remote1 and remote2. At the simplest level, you could run a test script on remote1 by passing the appropriate command directly to ssh.

```
$ ssh user@remote1 'cd /path/to/tests && run_some_tests'
```

This would work, but you'd have to enter your password every time. Instead, let's use *public key authentication*, the standard SSH replacement for passwords. This typically involves the following steps:

1. Generate a public/private *key pair* on your development machine.
2. Paste the newly generated public key into the authorized_keys file in the $HOME/.ssh directory on each remote machine.

First, run the following command on your development computer:

```
$ ssh-keygen
```

Now, copy ~/.ssh/id_rsa.pub to your home directory on remote1. Log into remote1 and run the following commands:

```
$ echo ~/id_rsa.pub >> ~/.ssh/authorized_keys
$ rm ~/id_rsa.pub
```

As an alternative to manual copying, you can use a tool like ssh-copy-id[37] or ssh-forever.[38]

Copy the same key to remote2 and add it to the authorized_keys file the way you did for remote1. This will enable you to log in to either machine without a password.

```
$ ssh remote1
```

Now that you can connect easily to both remote machines from your development machine, it's time to transfer your Cucumber tests to them.

Copying Your Tests

There are a myriad of ways to copy your Cucumber features to your remote machines. You could use FTP, the scp command, your revision control system, or even sneakernet (physically carrying a USB thumb drive to each machine).

One of the most low-maintenance methods is rsync. This tool can synchronize a local directory with a remote one in an efficient way—and it doesn't require you to commit your tests to revision control before trying them remotely.

rsync comes with a baffling array of options. The only flags you need for this exercise are -a (a set of common options for archiving), -v (to show all the file names being transferred), and --delete (to delete remote files that you've removed locally). Run the following commands on your development machine:

```
$ rsync -av --delete . remote1:flight
$ rsync -av --delete . remote2:flight
```

Log into your remote machines and look in the flight directory on each. All your tests should be there.

Running Your Tests

Now that your tests are copied to the remote machines, make sure to install Cucumber and any dependencies. The easiest way to do this is to use Bundler. Create a Gemfile in your project directory on your development machine with the following contents:

37. http://linux.die.net/man/1/ssh-copy-id
38. https://github.com/mattwynne/ssh-forever

multiple_machines/Gemfile

```
source :rubygems

gem 'cucumber'
```

Re-rsync your project so that both remote machines have the new file. Then, ssh from your development box into each remote to run the bundle command and install your dependencies.

```
$ ssh remote1 'cd flight && bundle'
$ ssh remote2 'cd flight && bundle'
```

When you're ready to run your tests, just pass the -t option to cucumber to specify that the scenarios tagged @group1 should run on remote1 and those tagged @group2 should run on remote2. From your development computer, run these commands:

```
$ ssh remote1 'cd flight && cucumber -t@group1 flight.feature' &
$ ssh remote2 'cd flight && cucumber -t@group2 flight.feature' &
```

The two machines will run these steps in parallel, reporting their results on the local console. This approach takes a bit of manual work but scales easily and isn't dependent on any specific Cucumber version (or even on Cucumber itself).

Further Exploration

In this recipe, we kept both the scenarios in a single .feature file and used tags to separate them into groups. On a real project, you're likely to have multiple .feature files, perhaps spread across several different directories. You may be able to use the file system instead of Cucumber tags to split your scenarios across multiple machines, like so:

```
$ ssh remote1 'cd proj && cucumber login/*.feature' &
$ ssh remote2 'cd proj && cucumber admin/*.feature' &
```

If all your machines are on the same network, you might try a tool like Specjour,[39] which coordinates the machines using the Bonjour network configuration technology.[40]

In Recipe 10, *Add Cucumber to Your Continuous Integration Server*, on page 47, we show how to run Cucumber tests from the Jenkins continuous integration server. Jenkins has its own distributed build tool[41] that you can use with the remote testing techniques we've discussed here.

39. https://github.com/sandro/specjour
40. http://www.apple.com/support/bonjour
41. https://wiki.jenkins-ci.org/display/JENKINS/Distributed+builds

One last note: there's nothing special about the number of test machines we used for this recipe. You can get some of the advantages of remote testing—such as testing on a fast server that closely resembles your production environment—with just one remote machine.

Recipe 9

Run Your Features Automatically with Guard and Growl

Problem

You're in the zone, jumping back and forth between adding new scenarios and filling in step definitions. Every time you have to switch to the command line and rerun Cucumber, it disrupts your train of thought. You want Cucumber to run your tests automatically whenever you save a change to one of your project files.

Ingredients

- Guard,[42] a Ruby library for watching project files
- Guard::Cucumber,[43] a Cucumber-aware plug-in for Guard
- A desktop notification system such as Growl for Mac,[44] Growl for Windows,[45] or Snarl for Linux[46] to tell you when the tests are done
- ruby_gntp,[47] a Ruby library for sending desktop notifications

Solution

Guard is an open source library that watches your project files and performs tasks automatically for you. What sort of tasks? Generating documentation, running tests, reporting results, whatever you want! (We're using it to regenerate this chapter's PDF every time we save changes to the document.) Each type of task is supported by a specific Guard plug-in. In this recipe, we'll use the Cucumber::Guard plug-in to run Cucumber tests whenever the source code or tests change.

We'll start with a Cucumber project that has a couple of features and scenarios but no automation yet. We'll see how to connect Guard::Cucumber to an existing project and verify that it's running the features at the right time. Finally, we'll add desktop notifications to the mix so that you don't have to keep checking your console logs to find out whether the tests passed.

42. https://github.com/guard/guard
43. https://github.com/guard/guard-cucumber
44. http://growl.info
45. http://www.growlforwindows.com
46. https://sites.google.com/site/snarlapp/home
47. http://snaka.info/ruby_gntp

Setup

Let's imagine you're using Cucumber to test an event logging library. Presumably, the individual classes have unit tests, and you're using Cucumber for something a little higher-level. You have one .feature file for writing to the log…

guard/features/appending.feature

```
Feature: Appending to a log
  Scenario: Initially empty log
    Given a log containing:
      """
      """
    When I append the warning "Disk space low"
    Then the log should read:
      """
      W Disk space low
      """
```

and one for reading from it.

guard/features/parsing.feature

```
Feature: Parsing a log
  Scenario: Multiple lines
    Given a log containing:
      """
      W Disk space low
      I Backup complete
      """
    When I parse the log
    Then the entries should be:
      | priority    | message         |
      | warning     | Disk space low  |
      | information | Backup complete |
```

Go ahead and run Cucumber on what you have so far, and verify that you get a bunch of pending steps.

Now, install Guard::Cucumber.

```
$ gem install guard-cucumber
```

You may see a few warnings about Guard being used outside the Bundler packaging tool. That's just Guard kvetching and can be safely ignored for this recipe.

Guard needs a list of files it should watch, plus instructions on what commands to run when those files change. Just as the Rake build tool uses a Rakefile, Guard uses a Guardfile. You can create this file by hand, but it's easier to have Guard::Cucumber do it.

```
$ guard init cucumber
```

Take a look at your initial Guardfile (we've made a couple alignment tweaks here but no major changes).

guard/Guardfile

```
1 # A sample Guardfile
2 # More info at https://github.com/guard/guard#readme
3 guard 'cucumber' do
4   watch(%r{^features/.+\.feature$})
5   watch(%r{^features/support/.+$}) { 'features' }
6   watch(%r{^features/step_definitions/(.+)_steps\.rb$}) { |m|
7     Dir[File.join("**/#{m[1]}.feature")][0] || 'features'
8   }
9 end
```

Each line inside the block contains a regular expression describing which files to watch. Note that these are not the same as the filename wildcards you'd use at the command line. For instance, to pick up C source files, you'd use \.c$ rather than *.c.

Line 4 tells Watchr to run just a single .feature file if that's all that changes. Line 5 runs all the features if anything in the support directory changes.

Line 6 watches the step definitions. If a file named *xyz*_steps.rb changes, Cucumber::Guard will rerun just *xyz*.feature. If it can't find a match, it reruns everything.

Matt says:

A Better Guard Rule

The third rule in the default Guardfile assumes you'll have one step definition file per feature, which is an antipattern. Instead, you should have one step file per domain model, as we've done in this recipe.

The default behavior isn't hurting us here. But in your own projects, you might want to replace the third rule with the following line:

```
watch(%r{^features/step_definitions/.+_steps\.rb$}) { 'features' }
```

That will just rerun all the features when you update any step definition; it's much safer.

If you had any files outside the usual Cucumber layout, such as a lib directory, you'd add them here. But this default configuration is all you'll need for this project.

Now that Guard is installed and configured, it's time to run it.

Using Guard

From your project directory, launch Guard on the command line and leave it running.

```
$ guard
```

Guard will report your pending steps and will then appear to freeze. It's watching your project for changes; let's give it something to see. First, here are the steps for appending to the log:

guard/features/step_definitions/log_steps.rb

```
When /^I append the ([a-z]+) "([^"]*)"$/ do
  | priority, message |

  @log.append priority, message
end
Then /^the log should read:$/ do |expected|
  @log.contents.should == expected
end
```

As soon as you save this file, Guard will rerun the steps. Take a peek at your command prompt and verify that you now have a step failure (because the @log variable is still undefined).

Now, add the step definitions for reading the log.

guard/features/step_definitions/log_steps.rb

```
When /^I parse the log$/ do
  @entries = @log.parse
end
Then /^the entries should be:$/ do |table|
  table.diff! @entries
end
```

The step for creating a new log is shared by both your features.

guard/features/step_definitions/log_steps.rb

```
Given /^a log containing:$/ do |contents|
  @log = Log.new contents
end
```

Now, it's time to add the implementation of the Log class. Add the following code to features/support/log.rb:

guard/features/support/log.rb

```
class Log
  attr_reader :contents
  def initialize(contents)
    @contents = contents
  end
```

```
  def append(priority, message)
    @contents << priority[0].upcase << ' ' << message
  end

  def parse
    @contents.split("\n").map do |line|
      initial, message = line.split(" ", 2)
      priorities = { 'I' => 'information', 'W' => 'warning' }
      { 'priority' => priorities[initial], 'message' => message }
    end
  end
end
```

Guard has been rerunning your features with each change you've made. With this one last change, all your steps should be green now.

It's definitely saved a few keystrokes not having to keep tabbing over to your shell to type Up Enter and rerun the tests every time you make a change. But it's still inconvenient to have to leave your text editor and watch the tests to see whether they passed or failed. Wouldn't it be nice to be able to see what happened with your steps without leaving your text editor?

Displaying Notifications

How do you find out what happened with your tests without having to babysit the output constantly? You find out the same way as with any other background operation such as a backup or file download: by using notifications.

The granddaddy of desktop notification systems on the Mac is Growl. Rather than your web browser and your backup software having to ship their own custom notification systems (each with its own jarringly different look and feel), both can just plug into Growl.

Developers have written systems similar to Growl on other platforms. Windows users have the aptly named Growl for Windows, while Linux users have Snarl.

Guard has the ability to detect several different desktop notification systems. If you're using one of the ones it knows about, there's no configuration needed.

First, download and install the appropriate notification framework for your platform. For a list of links, see *Ingredients*, on page 41.

All three of these tools speak the same protocol, Growl Network Transport Protocol (GNTP). That means they're all supported by a single library, ruby_gntp. Go ahead and install that now.

```
$ gem install ruby_gntp
```

Now make a change to one of your step definitions and save the file. A few seconds later, you should see a temporary pop-up window like Figure 3, *Guard notifications in Growl*.

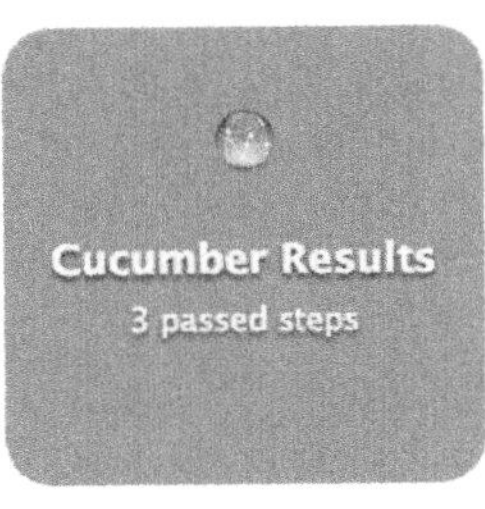

Figure 3—Guard notifications in Growl

Further Exploration

Why use Guard over some of the other Ruby libraries that start tests automatically, like autotest[48] or Watchr?[49] These will also work fine with Cucumber; we chose Guard for this recipe for its seamless Cucumber and Growl integration.

Since Guard does not exit immediately but instead continues to run and monitor your tests, you may wonder whether it is compatible with global teardown code you might put in an at_exit() hook, as in Recipe 3, *Run Slow Setup/Teardown Code with Global Hooks*, on page 13. Indeed, this still works; Guard spins up a separate Ruby instance to run your features.

Unlike most of the recipes in this book, this recipe uses Cucumber to test a library, rather than an application. For more on using Cucumber in this capacity, see Dr Nic Williams' presentation *Integration Testing with Cucumber: How to Test Anything*.[50]

48. https://github.com/seattlerb/zentest
49. https://github.com/mynyml/watchr
50. http://www.slideshare.net/drnic/integration-testing-with-cucumber-how-to-test-anything-j-a-o-o-2009

Recipe 10

Add Cucumber to Your Continuous Integration Server

Problem

You want to run your Cucumber tests automatically on a shared machine every time someone on your team checks in a change.

Ingredients

- Jenkins, the open source continuous integration server[51]
- The Git version control system[52]
- Jenkins plug-ins for Git and Rake (installed using the admin tools)
- A post-commit hook[53] for notifying Jenkins that your source code has changed
- cURL[54] for interacting with Jenkins from command-line scripts

Solution

In Recipe 9, *Run Your Features Automatically with Guard and Growl*, on page 41, we saw how the Guard library can watch the files on an individual developer's machine and rerun Cucumber tests whenever the source code changes. A *continuous integration* (CI) server performs a similar service for your entire team, watching the common code base and triggering a build/test cycle when anyone pushes new code to the server.

In this recipe, we're going to connect Cucumber to Jenkins, an open source CI server that enjoys a broad base of community support. We'll start by checking a simple Cucumber project into revision control using Git. We'll use a local installation of Jenkins just to get a feel for it (rather than the more typical use with a dedicated server). We'll see a couple of different ways for Jenkins to run your tests.

- Polling the source code at regular intervals, which is easier to set up
- Installing a *post-commit hook* into Git so that you notify Jenkins immediately when you make a change

Ready to get started?

---

51. http://jenkins-ci.org
52. http://git-scm.com
53. http://progit.org/book/ch7-3.html
54. http://curl.haxx.se

Project Setup

If you don't already have Git on your machine, go ahead and install it.[55] Create a repository called cone_of_silence.

```
$ git init cone_of_silence
```

Add the following to cone_of_silence/cone.feature:

continuous_integration/cone.feature

```
Feature: Cone of silence

  Scenario: Activation
    Given I am writing a book
    When I activate the cone of silence
    Then I should not hear my children for the next hour
```

Jenkins understands Rake, so give your project a Rakefile to kick off the tests.

continuous_integration/Rakefile

```
require 'cucumber/rake/task'

Cucumber::Rake::Task.new :features do |t|
  t.cucumber_opts = '*.feature'
end
```

Make sure your Rakefile is correctly set up by triggering a test run.

```
$ rake features
```

Go ahead and copy the boilerplate step definitions Cucumber gives you into step_definitions/cone_steps.rb, and remove the calls to pending().

Once your tests are passing, check everything into Git.

```
$ git add .
$ git commit -m "Initial commit"
```

Now that you have a Git repository, you can install Jenkins and point it at your code.

Install Jenkins

You can try Jenkins right from your web browser without installing anything.[56] Or you can download the .war file[57] and run it from the command line.

```
$ java -jar jenkins.war
```

---

55. http://git-scm.com/download
56. https://wiki.jenkins-ci.org/display/JENKINS/Meet+Jenkins
57. http://mirrors.jenkins-ci.org/war/latest/jenkins.war

Once Jenkins is running, you should be able to point your browser at http://localhost:8080 and see something like Figure 4, *The main Jenkins screen*.

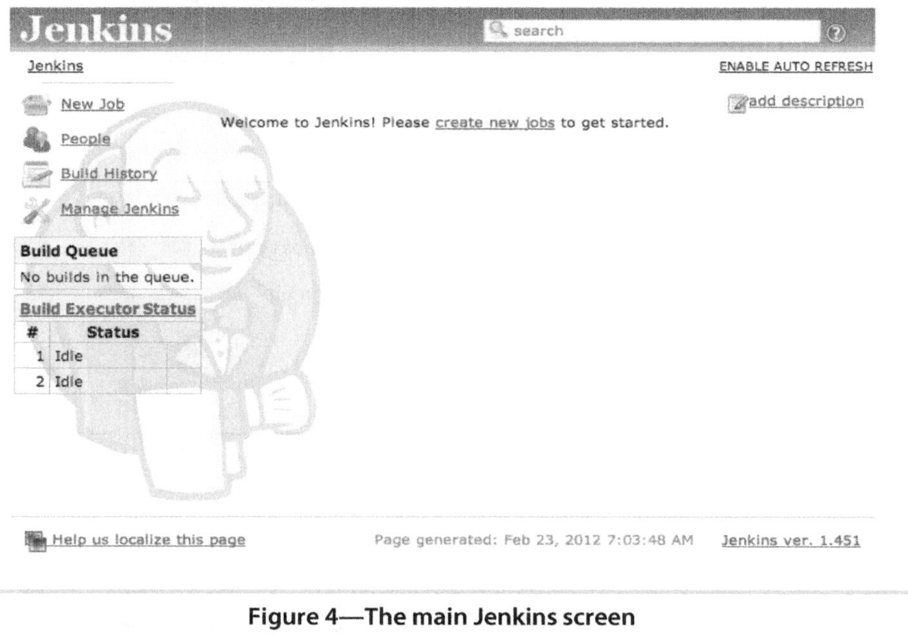

Figure 4—The main Jenkins screen

Some features of Jenkins (such as triggering a build automatically) require you to turn on password protection. Click Manage Jenkins in the list of links on the left. Then click Configure System. Select the "Enable security" checkbox.

Under Access Control / Security Realm, choose Jenkins' own user database, and select the "Allow users to sign up" checkbox. In the Authorization section just below it, choose "Logged-in users can do anything."

When you're done, your security settings should look like Figure 5, *Jenkins security settings*.[58] Click Save to go back to the main screen. Follow the sign-up link in the upper-right corner and create an account for yourself.

There's one last configuration step: installing the two plug-ins you need for this recipe. Follow the Manage Jenkins link again, but this time, choose Manage Plugins. On the Available tab, fill in the checkboxes next to the Git plug-in (under Source Code Management) and the Rake plug-in (under Build Tools). Click "Download now and install after restart," and follow the instructions to restart Jenkins.

58. You'd want to do considerably more than this to lock down a production server, of course.

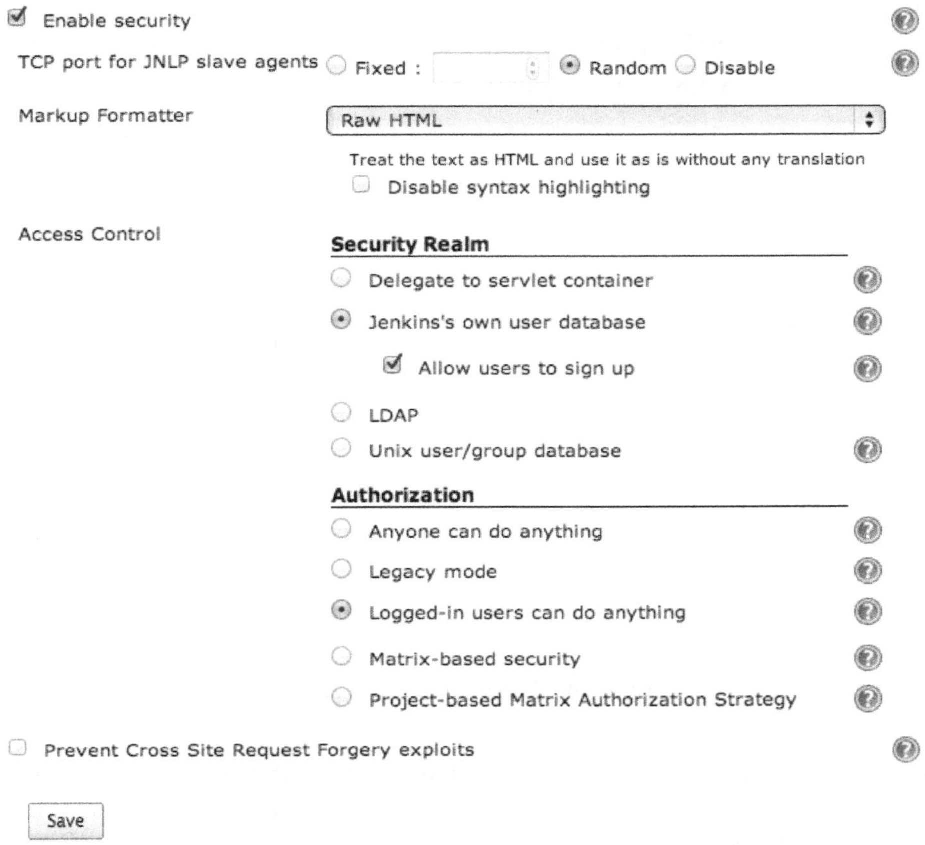

Enable security

TCP port for JNLP slave agents ○ Fixed : ◉ Random ○ Disable

Markup Formatter: Raw HTML

Treat the text as HTML and use it as is without any translation

Disable syntax highlighting

Access Control

Security Realm

○ Delegate to servlet container
◉ Jenkins's own user database
Allow users to sign up
○ LDAP
○ Unix user/group database

Authorization

○ Anyone can do anything
○ Legacy mode
◉ Logged-in users can do anything
○ Matrix-based security
○ Project-based Matrix Authorization Strategy

Prevent Cross Site Request Forgery exploits

Save

Figure 5—Jenkins security settings

Timed Builds

On the left side of the page, click New Job. Give Cone of Silence for the job name, and choose "Build a free-style software project." Click OK.

Under Source Code Management, choose Git. For the repository URL, type file:///path/to/cone_of_silence, substituting the full path of the directory you created at the beginning of this recipe.

In the Build Triggers section, choose Poll SCM. In the "Schedule text" field, enter five asterisks separated by spaces: * * * * * . This will poll every minute of every hour of every day. The syntax is similar to that used by the cron command on UNIX systems.[59]

59. http://pubs.opengroup.org/onlinepubs/9699919799/utilities/crontab.html

Under Build, click "Add build step," and choose Invoke Rake from the drop-down. In the Tasks text field, type features, the name you gave the Cucumber tests in your Rakefile.

When your project is correctly configured, the screen will look like Figure 6, *Jenkins project settings*, on page 52. Click Save, and then follow the Back to Dashboard link. You should see something like Figure 7, *The project dashboard*, on page 53.

If you wait a minute or so and then reload the page, Jenkins will change the project status to Success. Click build #1 in the Last Success column, and follow the Console Output link on the left to verify that your Cucumber steps ran. Then head back to the dashboard.

Let's see whether Jenkins is really checking the result of each test. Introduce a deliberate test failure in your step definitions.

continuous_integration/step_definitions/cone_steps.rb

```
Then /^I should not hear my children for the next hour$/ do
  raise 'a ruckus'
end
```

Wait another minute, and verify that Jenkins has marked the build as failed; it should look like Figure 8, *A failing project*, on page 53.

Now you have a fully functional continuous integration server. But wouldn't it be nice not to have to wait after every change for the build to kick in?

Triggered Build

The finishing touch for this recipe will be to trigger a build immediately when your source code changes. Click the Cone of Silence project in Jenkins, and follow the Configure link on the left. Deselect the Build Periodically checkbox, and instead choose "Trigger builds remotely." (If you don't see this option, it's because Jenkins's security settings are too lax; go back to *Install Jenkins*, on page 48, and make sure you have security enabled.)

You need to come up with some kind of unique, secret key to protect your build server from accidental or malicious triggers. You can use the command-line uuidgen utility[60] or just make up something.

From the command line, verify that you can trigger a build (substitute your token at the end of the URL).

```
$ curl http://localhost:8080/job/Cone%20of%20Silence/build?token=BackToBrooklyn
```

60. http://linux.about.com/library/cmd/blcmdl1_uuidgen.htm

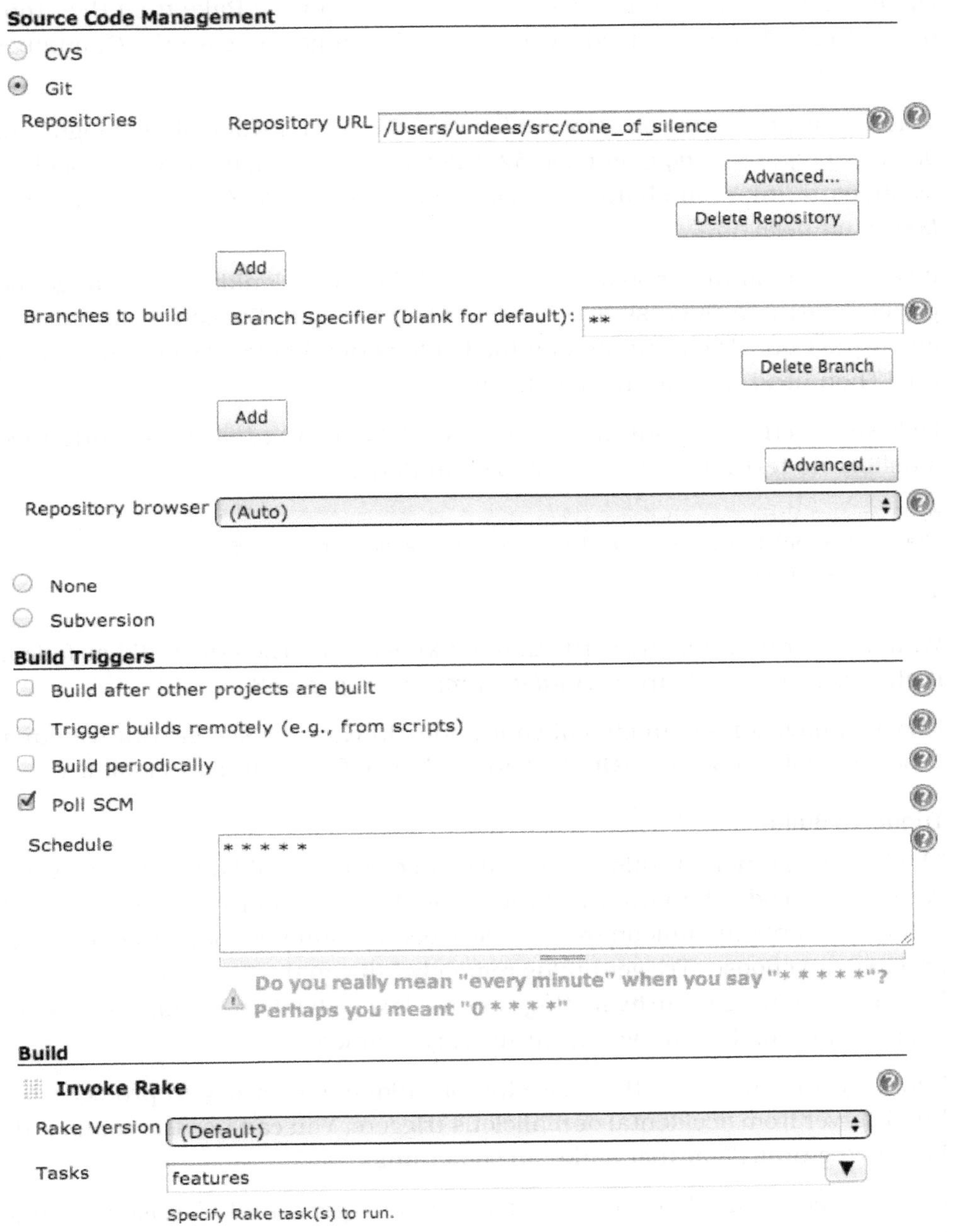

Source Code Management

CVS

Git

Repositories | Repository URL /Users/undees/src/cone_of_silence

Advanced...

Delete Repository

Add

Branches to build | Branch Specifier (blank for default): **

Delete Branch

Add

Advanced...

Repository browser (Auto)

None

Subversion

Build Triggers

Build after other projects are built

Trigger builds remotely (e.g., from scripts)

Build periodically

Poll SCM

Schedule * * * * *

Do you really mean "every minute" when you say "* * * * *"? Perhaps you meant "0 * * * *"

Build

Invoke Rake

Rake Version (Default)

Tasks features

Specify Rake task(s) to run.

Figure 6—Jenkins project settings

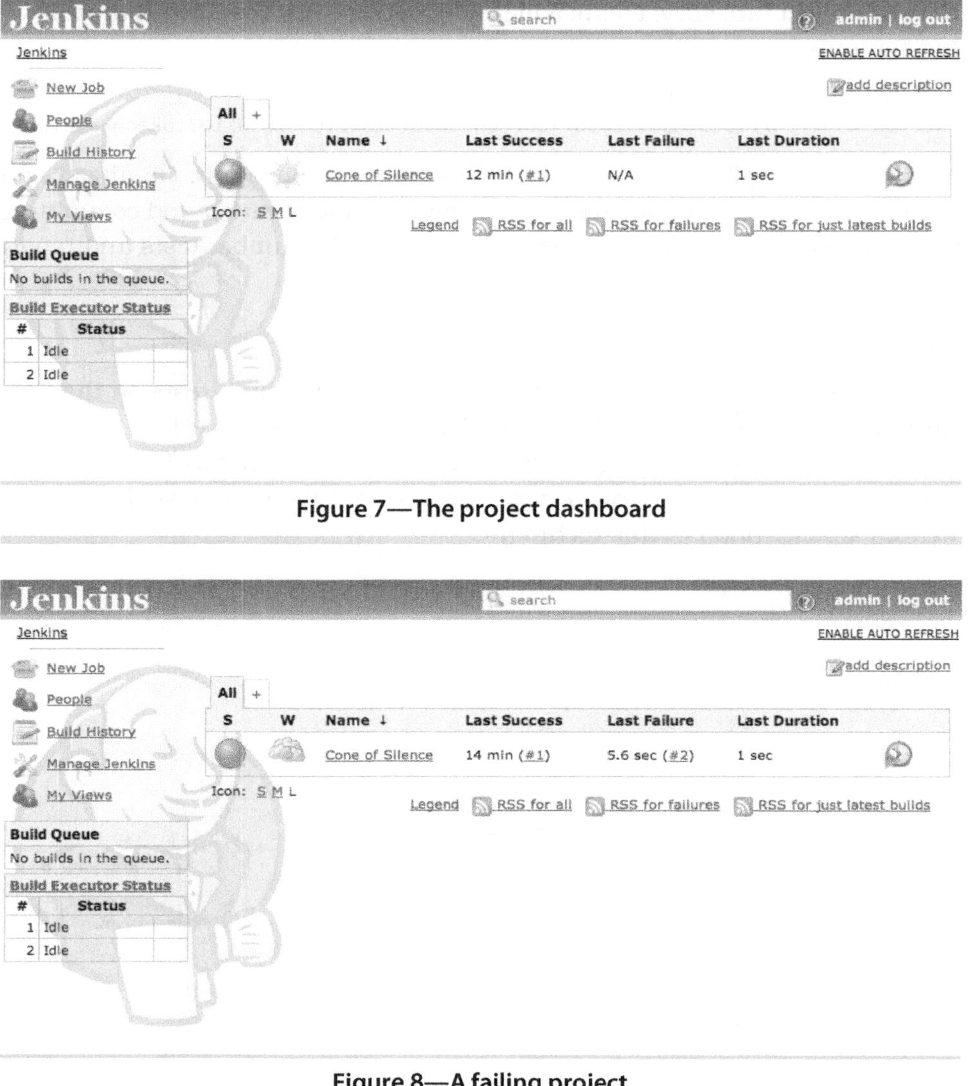

Figure 7—The project dashboard

Figure 8—A failing project

Back in your web browser, verify that Jenkins started a build when you hit the URL. Now, it's time to wire up Git to hit the same URL.

Post-commit Hook

Save your settings and go back to the dashboard. Now Jenkins is waiting patiently for notification that the source code has changed.

In your project directory, create a file called .git/hooks/post-commit with the following contents:

```
#!/bin/sh
exec curl http://localhost:8080/job/Cone%20of%20Silence/build?token=BackToBrooklyn
```

As the name implies, this script will run after every commit. Go ahead and try it by fixing the deliberate test failure you introduced earlier and committing your fix. Jenkins should immediately rerun your Cucumber tests and report success.

Further Exploration

This recipe assumes you want to run all of your Cucumber tests on the continuous integration server. However, if you need to skip certain scenarios (because they're still in progress or meant to be used only as benchmarks), you can tag specific scenarios for exclusion from the build. Joseph Wilk has written a description of this technique.[61]

61. http://blog.josephwilk.net/ruby/cucumber-tags-and-continuous-integration-oh-my.html

Recipe 11

Publish Your Documentation on Relish

Problem

You want to organize and share your .feature files in a readable format that allows navigation and screenshots.

Ingredients

- Relish,[62] a website where you can display your Cucumber files in an easy-to-navigate format
- Markdown[63] for displaying formatted text in your scenario descriptions

Solution

Cucumber files are designed to be read by everyone who has a say in your project: designers, developers, testers, planners, and so on. That's probably a big part of why you're using it.

But how do you actually share those files with your stakeholders? Do you email them a bunch of .feature files or have them check out your source repository? How do they know at a glance which files to read first? Sure, they'll probably know to find relevant information about your music recommendation engine in recommendation.feature, but there may also be related examples in sharing.feature.

Relish is a website that formats your Cucumber features nicely for your stakeholders to read and also provides additional navigation and documentation features.

In this recipe, we're going to write a couple of Cucumber scenarios and then upload them to a new project on Relish.

Writing the Features

Consider how you might write the specs for this book as a series of Cucumber examples (leaving aside how you'd actually implement the steps). You might

62. http://relishapp.com
63. http://daringfireball.net/projects/markdown

Disclosure

Relish is maintained by Matt Wynne, one of the contributors to this book. We chose to include this content because we genuinely feel that Relish is a useful tool for Cucumber users. To avoid giving you a sales pitch, we had Ian write this recipe in isolation.

The service charges a monthly fee for private projects but is free for public ones.

put summaries of the recipes in the first part of this book—the one on general tips—in features/tips.feature.

relish/simple/features/tips.feature

```
Feature: Tips and tricks

  This section contains general Cucumber techniques not tied to
  specific technologies or platforms.

  Scenario: Continuous integration

    A continuous integration server helps you catch regressions in
    your code by re-running your Cucumber examples whenever you push a
    new code change to the server.

    Given a continuous integration server
    When I push my code changes
    Then all my Cucumber features should run
```

Next, you might describe the web-related chapters of the book in features/web.feature.

relish/simple/features/web.feature

```
Feature: Testing web applications

  This section contains several tips for connecting to servers and
  processing HTML.

  Scenario: Parsing HTML tables

    Given an HTML table
    When I read the table recipe
    Then I should be able to parse my table easily
```

Now that you have some sample content, let's post it to Relish.

Starting with Relish

First, you'll need to get a Relish account by visiting the sign-up page.[64] Next, install the Relish gem, which contains the command-line program for posting documentation to the site.

```
$ gem install relish
```

Now, you can create a new Relish project using the account name you chose when you signed up. I used cuke-recipes as both the username and the project name.

```
$ relish projects:add cuke-recipes/cuke-recipes
```

If I had wanted this to be hidden from the public, I would have added :private to the end of the project name.

Make sure you're following the Cucumber convention of putting all your features in the features subdirectory so that Relish can find them. Publish your project to Relish by running the push command from your project directory.

```
$ relish push cuke-recipes/cuke-recipes
```

When that step finishes, your project will be visible at a dedicated URL based on your username and project name.[65] It should look something like Figure 9, *Relish without customizations*.

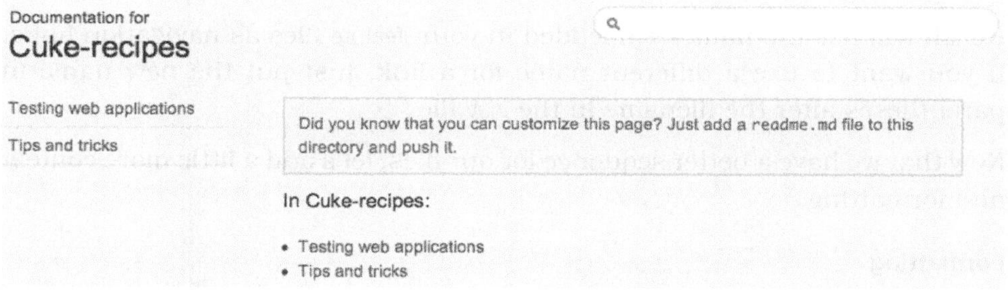

Figure 9—Relish without customizations

Notice that the project is somewhat disorganized so far. The web testing link comes before the general tips, and everything is just kind of dumped in our laps with no explanation. In the next section, we'll fix that by adding an overview as well as navigation information.

---

64. https://www.relishapp.com/users/sign_up
65. http://relishapp.com/cuke-recipes/cuke-recipes

Organization

First, let's add an overview telling the reader what the project is about. Create a file called features/README.md with the following contents:

relish/full/features/README.md

```
This book will show you how to get the most out of [Cucumber][1], from
specific situations to advanced test-writing advice.

[1]: http://cukes.info
```

I've thrown in a hyperlink in Markdown style, just so we can see how Relish renders formatted text.

When you push your directory to Relish again and hit Reload in your browser, you should see an introductory section about the project. Next, let's put the sections in a more logical order: general tips first, then web techniques. Create a file called features/.nav with the following list:

relish/full/features/.nav

```
- README.md (Overview)
- tips.feature
- web.feature
```

This file is a YAML-formatted[66] list of .feature files in the order you want them to appear in the nav bar on the left of your project's Relish page. A flat structure is fine for a project this simple, but you can nest lists if you need to do so.

Relish will use the names embedded in your .feature files as navigation links. If you want to use a different name for a link, just put the new name in parentheses after the filename in the .nav file.

Now that we have a better sequence for our files, let's add a little more context and formatting.

Formatting

As we saw with the README file, Relish understands Markdown. You can put any .md file in your features directory, and Relish will include it as another page in your project.

You can also embed Markdown directly in feature and scenario descriptions. To see how this works, add the following text to web.feature, just before the Scenario (the screenshot text should all go on one line):

66. http://yaml.org

```
Here's an example of [Jenkins][1], a popular CI server, in action:

![screenshot](https://wiki.jenkins-ci.org/download/attachments/
753667/jenkins-screenshot.png)

[1]: http://jenkins-ci.org
```

Now, when you repost your project and click the "Tips and tricks" link, you should see something like Figure 10, *Relish with navigation and formatting*, on page 59.

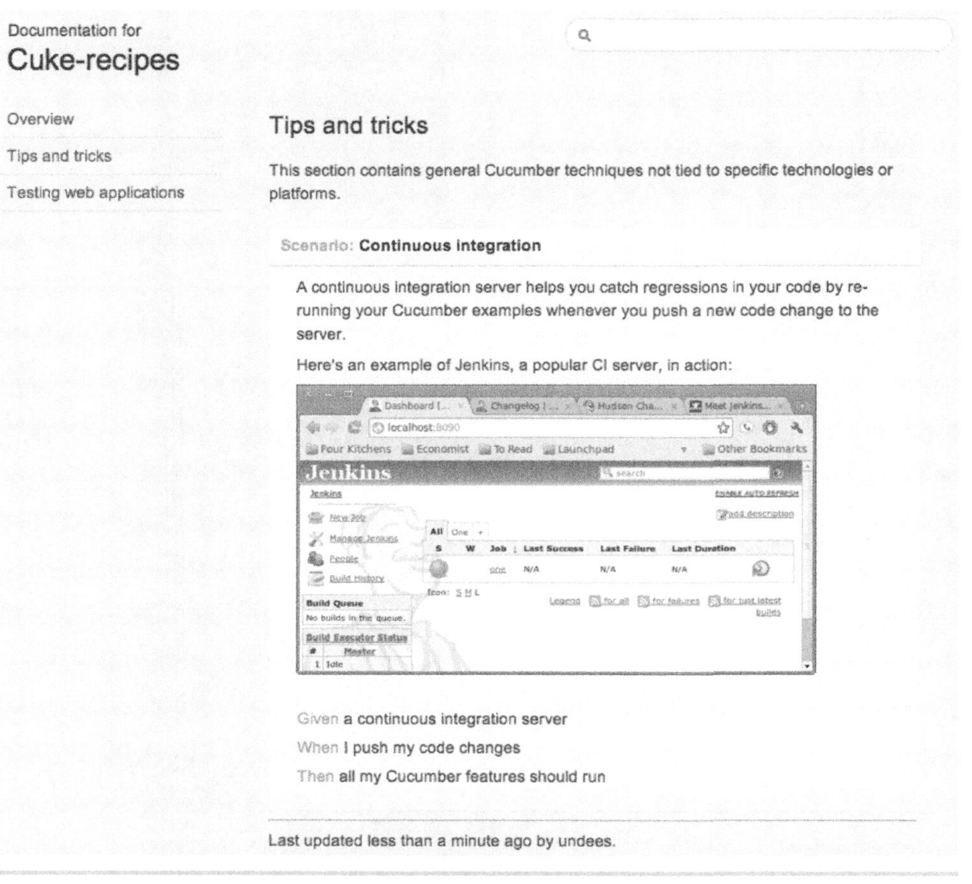

Figure 10—Relish with navigation and formatting

Further Exploration

Relish helps you publish your Cucumber examples as *living documentation*—in other words, as a spec that stays up-to-date as you work on your project.

The user manual is itself a Relish project,[67] which means that each aspect of the site's behavior you read about is backed up somewhere by a running Cucumber test. Take a look at the docs to learn about some of the advanced Relish features we haven't covered here, such as versioning your spec.

Note that Relish doesn't run your features for you; it's strictly for publishing your documentation in a readable, navigable format. To run your examples automatically on a server, see Recipe 10, *Add Cucumber to Your Continuous Integration Server*, on page 47.

67. https://www.relishapp.com/relish/relish/docs

Recipe 12

Test Through Multiple Interfaces Using Worlds

Problem

Your application has multiple public-facing interfaces, such as a graphical user interface (GUI) and an application programming interface (API). You'd like to test your code through both interfaces using the same set of Cucumber features.

Ingredients

- Multiple implementations of the World,[68] an object that Cucumber creates and passes into each test
- Selenium WebDriver[69] for testing a web app through the browser
- HTTParty[70] for testing an HTTP API
- The Sinatra web framework[71] to implement the example app

Solution

Many applications support more than one interface for controlling the underlying business logic. Your app might have a desktop GUI, a web interface, a REST API, some custom debugging hooks, or perhaps even all of these.

Wouldn't it be nice to write one set of Cucumber features that describe your application's behavior and then run those features against the GUI, the web interface, the API, and so on? That's exactly what Cucumber's World object enables you to do.

In this recipe, we're going to use the Sinatra web framework to build an application that has two interfaces: a web interface for humans and an HTTP API for machines. We'll write one World object to test each interface. The WebWorld object will use Selenium WebDriver to fire up a live browser and interact with

68. https://github.com/cucumber/cucumber/wiki/A-Whole-New-World
69. https://github.com/vertis/selenium-webdriver
70. https://github.com/jnunemaker/httparty
71. http://www.sinatrarb.com

the user-visible web page. The ApiWorld object will instead connect directly to the API using the HTTParty library.

Feature

This web app will be a simple one-function calculator. It will take the square root of whatever number we type into it. Here's the start of a feature describing the happy path, in features/square_root.feature:

world/features/square_root.feature

```
Feature: Square root

  Scenario: Positive number
    When I take the square root of 4.0
    Then I should get 2.0
```

The step definitions are going to be shared between both implementations of the tests. Only the World will change.

Before you write your first step definition, you might take a step back and see that both definitions will deal with floating-point numbers. The regular expressions for numbers can get kind of ugly. Let's use Cucumber's transforms[72] to put this processing in one place. Put the following code in features/step_definitions/square_root_steps.rb:

world/features/step_definitions/square_root_steps.rb

```
A_FLOAT = Transform(/(-?\d+(?:\.\d+)?)/) do |number|
  number.to_f
end
```

Now, you can use that transformation to implement the When step.

world/features/step_definitions/square_root_steps.rb

```
When /^I take the square root of (#{A_FLOAT})$/ do |number|
  take_square_root(number)
end
```

The Then step will compare the actual results to the expected ones. Because we're dealing with floating-point numbers, we'll use RSpec's ability to make approximate comparisons.

world/features/step_definitions/square_root_steps.rb

```
Then /^I should get (#{A_FLOAT})$/ do |expected|
  tolerance = expected.abs * 0.001
  square_root_result.should be_within(tolerance).of(expected)
end
```

72. https://www.relishapp.com/cucumber/cucumber/docs/transforms

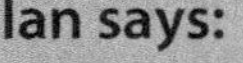

Ian says:

Testing Our Hardware

One of my co-workers used a technique like this one to test a piece of laboratory hardware he was working on. The device has two customer-visible interfaces: an embedded GUI and a text-based network API.

He began by writing step definitions specifically for the API and then adapted them to a second version that uses the GUI instead. By launching the test with different parameters, he could test the application logic through the GUI or the API.

He found it handy to have these features as a quick smoke test to make sure that both interfaces were returning the same data.

Where do those take_square_root() and square_root_result() methods come from? You'll implement those in the World objects.

Testing Through the API

For no particular reason, let's implement the API version of the test first. You'll need to install HTTParty.

```
$ gem install httparty
```

Now, put the following code in features/support/env.rb:

world/features/support/env.rb

```
require 'httparty'

class ApiWorld
  def take_square_root(number)
    response = HTTParty.get "http://localhost:4567/api/square_root/#{number}"
    @result = response.body.to_f
  end

  def square_root_result
    @result
  end

  def close
  end
end

After { close }
```

The step definitions require you to write two functions, take_square_root() and square_root_result(). With an HTTP API, the implementation is easy; we just hit the API endpoint and store the result.

We've added one more method, close(), and set up an After hook to call it automatically after each scenario. It doesn't need to do anything during API testing, but it will be handy for closing the browser when we're testing the user interface.

You'll notice this is not a RESTful API because we're using a dedicated /api URL that's separate from the web app. In an example this trivial, that's OK—it saves us a few lines of code. For a real web app, you get a lot of maintainability benefits from using one common set of URLs.

Testing Through the User Interface

All you need to do to test through the same user interface is reimplement the same set of methods from the ApiWorld object. Rather than hitting the API endpoint, you'll launch a browser and navigate to the page as a live user would. To do that, you'll need to install Selenium WebDriver.

```
$ gem install selenium-webdriver
```

Now, add the following code to env.rb:

world/features/support/env.rb

```ruby
require 'selenium-webdriver'

class WebWorld
  def initialize
    @browser = Selenium::WebDriver.for :firefox
  end

  def take_square_root(number)
    @browser.navigate.to "http://localhost:4567"
    @browser.find_element(:name => 'number').send_keys number.to_s
    @browser.find_element(:name => 'submit').click
  end

  def square_root_result
    @browser.find_element(:id => 'result').text.to_f
  end

  def close
    @browser.quit
  end
end
```

We're assuming the main page will have a form with a number field and a submit button. The results page will need to have an element with an ID of result.

How do we choose which World to use? The simplest way is an environment variable.

world/features/support/env.rb

```
if ENV['USE_GUI']
  World { WebWorld.new }
else
  World { ApiWorld.new }
end
```

Now that we have an idea of the URLs we want to use and the names of the form elements, we can build the web app.

Web App

For an app this simple, we'll build both the user interface and the API in the Sinatra web framework. Go ahead and install Sinatra.

```
$ gem install sinatra
```

Now, create a file called square_root.rb with the following contents:

world/square_root.rb

```
require 'sinatra'

get '/' do
  <<HERE
<!DOCTYPE html>
<html>
  <head>
    <title>Square root</title>
  </head>

  <body>
    Enter a number to take the square root:
    <form action="/square_root">
      <input name="number" type="text">
      <input name="submit" type="submit">
    </form>
  </body>
</html>
HERE
end
```

This displays a simple HTML form when someone visits the root of the web app. Clicking Submit will take the user to a path like /square_root?number=4. We need to implement that part of the web app as well.

world/square_root.rb

```
get '/square_root' do
  number = params[:number].to_f
  result = Math.sqrt(number)
  <<HERE
<!DOCTYPE html>
```

```
<html>
  <head>
    <title>Result</title>
  </head>

  <body>
    The square root of <span id="number">#{number}</span>
    is <span id="result">#{result}</span>.
  </body>
</html>
HERE
end
```

Finally, we can define the API endpoint.

world/square_root.rb

```
get '/api/square_root/:n' do |n|
  Math.sqrt(n.to_f).to_s
end
```

Notice that both the user interface and the API are calling the same implementation function: Math.sqrt(). Both interfaces are thin wrappers around the underlying logic.

You now have all you need to get the web app running. Launch the app like this:

```
$ ruby square_root.rb
```

Then, navigate to http://localhost:4567 and interact with the web form. If you're feeling adventurous, try using a command-line tool like cURL[73] to drive the API.

When you're ready to take your Cucumber tests for a spin, try testing through the API.

```
$ cucumber features
```

That should return fairly quickly, since you're not waiting for a browser to spin up. Now, to test through the user interface, all you need to do is set the USE_GUI environment variable.

```
$ USE_GUI=1 cucumber features
```

One final question: did you notice the parallels between our tests and our implementation? The tests express the same behavior (in the .feature file) and bring in two different World objects. The application uses the same business logic and wraps two different interfaces around it.

73. http://curl.haxx.se

Recipe 13

Manipulate Time

Problem

You want to test a long-running process, but you don't want your tests to be slow.

Ingredients

- Capybara[74] for testing web apps in multiple ways, both headless and in-browser
- Timecop[75] for faking the time of day in Ruby
- Sinatra[76] for building the sample app

Solution

One of the biggest time sinks in testing is waiting on your app. Whenever a program has to connect to a slow network, make a lengthy calculation, or wait for a specific time of day, you can speed up your tests dramatically by finding a way around the delay.

In this recipe, we're going to write a simple web app that has a fixed delay built in. We'll start with a slow test that waits for the app to finish its task. We'll then look at a couple of ways to speed up the clock, depending on how much of the app's logic is in JavaScript.

Traditional Web App

The app we're building will inflate and pop an imaginary balloon—something that takes several seconds. Here's the spec for the app; it goes in features/ balloon.feature:

time/web/features/balloon.feature

```
Feature: Balloon

  Scenario: Pop
    Given a balloon
    When I inflate it for 5 seconds
    Then it should pop
```

74. https://github.com/jnicklas/capybara
75. https://github.com/travisjeffery/timecop
76. http://www.sinatrarb.com

Assuming the web app has links called /inflate and /status and returns the text Inflating or Popped!, here's how we might implement those step definitions in features/step_definitions/balloon_steps.rb:

time/web/features/step_definitions/balloon_steps.rb

```
Given /^a balloon$/ do
  visit 'http://localhost:4567/inflate'
end

When /^I inflate it for (\d+) seconds$/ do |seconds|
  sleep seconds.to_f
  visit 'http://localhost:4567/status'
end

Then /^it should pop$/ do
  page.should have_content 'Popped!'
end
```

The visit and page methods are part of Capybara's API for web testing. To use them, you'll need to install Capybara.

```
$ gem install capybara
```

Now, configure Cucumber to use Capybara by adding the following setup to features/support/env.rb:

time/web/features/support/env.rb

```
require 'capybara/cucumber'
require 'timecop'
require './balloon'

Capybara.app = Sinatra::Application
```

All that's left is the app. Create a file called balloon.rb with the following contents:

time/web/balloon.rb

```
require 'sinatra'
enable :sessions
get '/inflate' do
  session[:start] = Time.now
  redirect to('/status')
end

get '/status' do
  now = Time.now
  elapsed = now - (session[:start] || now)
  elapsed >= 5 ? 'Popped!' : 'Inflating'
end
```

Now, when you run the test, it should pass. But it takes too long to complete because we have to wait for the app to get ready. How can we get around this?

We're testing this app in-process by calling its code directly through Ruby's Rack interface.[77] That means if we change the way Ruby handles time, the app will see it.

There are several ways to manipulate timestamps in Ruby. The one that fits our purposes best is a library called Timecop. Go ahead and install Timecop now.

```
$ gem install timecop
```

Now, replace the body of your When step with the following code:

time/web/features/step_definitions/balloon_steps.rb

```
Timecop.freeze(seconds.to_i) do

  visit 'http://localhost:4567/status'

end
```

Timecop's freeze() method causes Ruby's Time.now() to return a fixed, static value—in this case, a number of seconds into the future. The manipulation happens only during the execution of the block; afterward, Time.now() will behave normally. Now, when you rerun the tests, they should finish almost instantly.

Single-Page App

Solutions like Timecop work when our tests are running the same Ruby process as the app under test. But what about browser-based testing? And what about single-page, JavaScript-heavy web apps?

In this section, we'll convert our program to a single-page JavaScript application and then adapt the tests to the new architecture. First, replace the contents of balloon.rb with the following:

time/single_page/balloon.rb

```
require 'sinatra'

get '/inflate' do
  IO.read 'inflate.html'

end
```

Now, add a file called inflate.html with the following contents:

77. http://rack.github.com

time/single_page/inflate.html

```
<!DOCTYPE html>
<html>
  <head>
    <title>Balloon</title>
    <script
       type="text/javascript"
       src="https://ajax.googleapis.com/ajax/libs/jquery/1.8.2/jquery.min.js">
    </script>
    <script type="text/javascript">
      pop = function() {
        $('#status').text('Popped!');
      };
      popLater = function(ms) {
        setTimeout(pop, ms);
      };
      $(document).ready(function() {
        $('#go').click(function(e) {
          popLater(5000);
        });
      });
    </script>
  </head>
  <body>
    <p id="status">Ready</p>
    <input id="go" type="button" value="Go"></input>
  </body>
</html>
```

To test this app, we need to use a JavaScript-aware approach. Capybara supports a couple of different ways to drive JavaScript; the simplest to get started with is in-browser testing. Change your env.rb file to the following:

time/single_page/features/support/env.rb

```
require 'uri'
require 'capybara/cucumber'
Capybara.default_driver = :selenium
```

With this change, methods like visit() or page() will now go through a live browser instead of calling directly into Ruby code. Since we're controlling a browser now, we have access to a full JavaScript runtime. The only step you need to change in your step definitions is the When step.

time/single_page/features/step_definitions/balloon_steps.rb

```
When /^I inflate it for (\d+) seconds$/ do |seconds|
  page.execute_script <<HERE
popLater = function(ms) {
  pop();
};
HERE
```

Matt says:

Doing the Right Thing with Time

One of my clients was writing a mobile game in JavaScript for fans of a TV show to play while watching. On the show, people would bring in antiques from their basements for experts to evaluate. The surprise factor of the show stems from guessing and then finding out what an item is worth. The team wanted to build this excitement into the game.

When a person brings in, say, a vase from their attic, the game asks you how much you think it's worth and presents you with three choices. Later in the show, they reveal the actual value, and you get points for guessing correctly. You play a fresh round for each contestant on the show.

The game synchronizes itself to the show using an audio watermark plus specific timing information. During testing, the team used sample questions with ten-second spacing. They had been testing this manually, meaning they had to wait ten seconds each time they wanted to test a change.

We started by adding a single Cucumber scenario to automate a correct answer for the first question. Once we had the first passing automated test, we looked for a way to remove the delays. Ten seconds was long enough to wait for a single scenario, but multiplied up over a whole suite of features, it would have been ridiculous.

The app was event-based; after each question, it would set a timeout for the next event and then sleep. We extracted that tiny bit of logic into a function. For the tests, we overrode that function to move on to the next event immediately. It was a minor change, but now the test ran instantly.

As a happy side effect, the team realized they could put a secret button into the debug version of the app that allowed them to do the same thing. Now the manual tests could simulate going right through the whole 30-minute episode in just a few seconds.

Capybara's `execute_script()` function lets us run our own JavaScript code on the page. We can use this to override the `popLater()` function on the page and pop the balloon immediately.

To run the tests now, you'll need to launch the web server first. Run the following command and leave that terminal window open while you're testing:

```
$ ruby balloon.rb
```

Now, when you run your Cucumber tests, you should see Firefox launch and pop the balloon without a delay.

Recipe 14

Drive Cucumber's Wire Protocol

Problem

You're writing Cucumber tests to drive an application that doesn't provide an easy way to integrate Ruby, such as PHP, ActionScript, or C++.

Ingredients

- A .wire file for driving Cucumber's wire protocol[78]

Solution

In 2009, the Cucumber team was looking for a way to connect Cucumber to environments that don't have direct Ruby integration. They came up with the *wire protocol*, a simple text format through which Cucumber can talk to an external process over TCP and ask it things like, "Do you have any step definitions matching When I withdraw $100?"

Ian says:

Remote Testing

At work, some of our products have a user interface that happens to boot and run just fine on a regular Windows PC. This is great for testing, since we can install whatever test software we want without worrying about the resource constraints of embedded hardware.

But it would be nice to be able to test on the real hardware at some point. Thanks to the wire protocol, we were able to do so. A small "listener" program with very few dependencies ran on the device and drove the GUI. The Cucumber test suite ran on a PC and conducted the tests over the wire protocol.

The first customers of the protocol were developers using the Java and .NET runtimes. Although these environments now have more direct Cucumber support, the wire protocol is still useful for testing C++, PHP, and Flash applications.

78. https://github.com/cucumber/cucumber/wiki/wire-protocol

Each environment has its own installation and step definition techniques; you'll find a few of them in this book. But they all share one common way to connect from Cucumber. Create a file in your step_definitions folder with a .wire extension, and put the following text in it:

wire_client/step_definitions/cucumber.wire
```
host: localhost
port: 3901
```

Now, in addition to looking in the step_definitions directory to find implementations of your test steps, Cucumber will also send a query over the TCP port you designated.

If you want, you can also specify how long Cucumber will wait for the server to carry out each step.

wire_client/step_definitions/cucumber.wire
```
timeout:
  invoke: 1.0
```

The fact that Cucumber looks in two places (the local step_definitions directory and the wire protocol) comes with a warning and a benefit. First, the warning: if a step in your scenario happens to match both a local definition and a definition fetched from the wire protocol, Cucumber will bail out and warn you of the ambiguous match.

Now, the benefit: you can write compound steps locally that call multiple steps on the wire protocol server. This is particularly handy when the environment you're testing makes it difficult to add new step definitions (for example, if it requires a lengthy compile and link every time you tweak a definition).

For instance, imagine the remote server defines just a few generic, low-level steps like this one:

```
When I click the "([^"]+)" button
```

Your local step_definitions directory can then contain more application-specific step definitions like this one:

wire_client/step_definitions/publish_steps.rb
```
When /^I publish an article$/ do
  steps %{
    When I set the title to "First post!"
    When I set the body to "Hello world!"
    When I click the "Done" button
  }
end
```

Here, a single step calls out to a number of lower-level ones implemented on the server.

Further Exploration

In Recipe 33, *Test a PHP App with cuke4php*, on page 173, we use the wire protocol to drive a PHP application.

Recipe 15

Implement a Wire Protocol Listener

Problem

You want to test software running in an environment that doesn't have explicit Cucumber support, such as an embedded system.

Ingredients

- Cucumber's wire protocol,[79] which specifies how Cucumber can drive software tests over a network

Solution

The Cucumber project supports many programming languages—such as Ruby, Java, and JavaScript—directly. There are no special steps needed to get Cucumber to drive test code written in these languages. Without this support, you'd need to implement your own communication path between Cucumber and your software.

That's exactly what the wire protocol does. When you start a Cucumber test using the wire protocol, Cucumber connects to your app over TCP and sends it a series of messages: begin_scenario first, invoke to run a particular test step, and so on. All you have to do to have Cucumber drive your code is open up a network socket and listen for these incoming messages.

In this recipe, we're going to test a simple C-based embedded device—a thermostat—by teaching it the wire protocol.

Feature

Here's a simple test to see whether the air conditioning turns on when we first set the temperature. Place the following code in features/thermostat.feature:

wire_server/features/thermostat.feature

```
Feature: Thermostat

  Scenario: Air conditioning
    Given the room is at 80 F
    When I set the thermostat to 75 F
    Then the A/C should be on
```

79. https://github.com/cucumber/cucumber/wiki/wire-protocol

Normally, when you run this feature, Cucumber would look in the local step_definitions directory for Ruby code. Instead, we need to tell it to connect to the network. Create a file called step_definitions/cucumber.wire with the following contents:

wire_server/features/step_definitions/cucumber.wire
```
host: localhost
port: 3901
```

Now, when you run Cucumber, it will connect to localhost over port 3901 instead of looking for Ruby code.

Messages

The wire protocol will send several different kinds of messages to your test code.[80] The two most interesting ones are step_matches and invoke.

Let's look at step_matches first. When Cucumber sees the text Given the room is at 80 F, it needs to know two things.

- Are there any step definitions that match this line of text?
- Does this step definition take any arguments?

Cucumber will send a request to your app that looks like this:

```
["step_matches",{"name_to_match":"the room is at 80 F"}]
```

This data is in JavaScript Object Notation (JSON) format.[81] We need to construct a JSON reply in our thermostat code and send it back to Cucumber.

If we have a definition that matches the step, we reply with a unique ID for that step definition, plus the names and positions of any arguments. This step has one argument: the temperature, starting at the 15th position (counting from zero).

```
["success", [{"id"=>"0", "args"=>[{"val"=>"80", "pos"=>15}]}]]
```

The previous JSON says, "Yes, definition #0 matches this step. The text '80' starting at position 15 is the only argument." The ID can be anything unique; we'll use integers for this recipe.

For a step that has no arguments, you'd leave the args array empty. For a step that doesn't have a matching definition, you'd return the following message instead:

```
["success", []]
```

80. https://github.com/cucumber/cucumber/blob/master/legacy_features/wire_protocol.feature
81. http://json.org

Next, Cucumber will send your app the invoke message when it's time to actually run the step.

```
["invoke",{"id":"0","args":["80"]}]
```

This tells our code, "Run step definition #0 with a value of 80 for the argument." Based on whether the step passes or fails, we'd return a message like one of the following two:

```
["success"]
["fail",{"message":"Could not set temperature"}]
```

How might we implement this protocol? We could use a full-fledged solution like cucumber-cpp,[82] which takes care of the TCP server, JSON parsing, and regular-expression step matching.

If, however, we're running in a constrained environment with only C support, we might prefer to implement our own network listener. We'd like to show you just how easy it is to handle the wire protocol, so we're going to go with the roll-your-own approach here.

Network Server

A classic network server loop using the standard networking APIs looks pretty much the same everywhere: open up a connection using socket(), prepare it for listening with bind(), wait for incoming connections with accept(), and read data with recv().

Rather than reproducing all that boilerplate here, we're just going to adapt a stock implementation from the Web.[83] Download listener.c and save it in your project directory. Look for the text NOTE TO READERS; that's the marker for where we can inject the Cucumber code. Replace the body of the while loop just underneath that comment with the following code:

```
respond_to_cucumber(wStream, buf);
```

You'll need to declare this function near the top of listener.c, right after the last #include directive.

```
extern void respond_to_cucumber(FILE* stream, const char* message);
```

In a moment, we'll fill in this function. First, though, let's write our step definitions.

82. https://github.com/cucumber/cucumber-cpp
83. http://www.2600.com/code/212/listener.c

Step Definitions

Like any Ruby step definitions, our C definitions will connect a series of step names to chunks of code that implement those steps. We need some way to take arguments and some way to report passing or failing steps. We also need an API for our thermostat so that our test code can drive the hardware.

Let's start with the API. Create a new file called thermostat.h with the following declarations:

wire_server/thermostat.h
```
extern int ac_is_on();
extern void set_room_temp(int temperature);
extern void set_thermostat(int temperature);
```

Now, we can implement the three step definitions that call the API. Let's adopt the UNIX convention of returning 0 for a normal result and a nonzero value for a failure. Place the following code in a new file, cucumber.c:

wire_server/cucumber.c
```
#include <stdio.h>
#include <string.h>
#include "thermostat.h"
int the_room_is_at_f(const char* arg) {
    set_room_temp(atoi(arg));
    return 0;
}
int i_set_the_thermostat_to_f(const char* arg) {
    set_thermostat(atoi(arg));
    return 0;
}
int the_ac_should_be(const char* arg) {
    int want_ac_on = (0 == strcmp("on", arg));
    return ac_is_on() == want_ac_on ?
         0 :
        -1 ;
}
```

How do we map step names to their implementations? Regular Cucumber uses regular expressions; for simplicity's sake, we'll use C's scanf() format instead. The following code defines a couple of data types for matching steps to implementations:

wire_server/cucumber.c
```
typedef int (*callback_t)(const char* arg);
typedef struct stepdef {
    const char* pattern;
    callback_t callback;
} stepdef_t;
```

```
#define NUMDEFS 3
stepdef_t stepdefs[NUMDEFS] = {
    { "the room is at %31[^\"] F",          the_room_is_at_f          },
    { "I set the thermostat to %31[^\"] F", i_set_the_thermostat_to_f },
    { "the A/C should be %31[^\"]",          the_ac_should_be          },
};
```

The %31[^\"] markers mean, "Match any sequence of nonquote marks up to 31 characters long." This is a cheap way of extracting just the characters we need from a JSON string without actually parsing the JSON. For this simple project, that's good enough to meet our needs.

Message Handler

We could drop a simple JSON-handling library into our project. In fact, for an early version of this chapter's code, we used jsmn,[84] a minimalistic C JSON parser. However, if we're *really* strapped for computing resources, we can take advantage of the fact that Cucumber's JSON messages follow a strict convention.

So, instead of looking for the text step_matches as a string inside a JSON array, we could just look for it as a sequence of bytes starting at position 2 (skipping over the square bracket and opening quotation mark).

Add the following function definition to cucumber.c:

wire_server/cucumber.c

```
#define MSG_TYPE_IS(msg, type) \
    (0 == strncmp(msg + 2, type, sizeof(type) - 1))

void respond_to_cucumber(FILE* stream, const char* msg) {
    if (MSG_TYPE_IS(msg, "step_matches")) {
        respond_to_step_matches(stream, msg);
    } else if (MSG_TYPE_IS(msg, "invoke")) {
        respond_to_invoke(stream, msg);
    } else {
        respond_success(stream);
    }
}
```

For most wire protocol messages, we can blindly reply with a success response. We only need to specifically handle the steps_match and invoke messages.

To respond to the steps_match query, we just loop through the array of step definitions we built a moment ago until we find the one that matches.

84. http://zserge.bitbucket.org/jsmn.html

wire_server/cucumber.c

```
void respond_to_step_matches(FILE* stream, const char* msg) {
    int i;

    for (i = 0; i < NUMDEFS; ++i) {
        const char* step    = msg + 34;
        const char* pattern = stepdefs[i].pattern;
        char arg_val[32] = {0};
        if (sscanf(step, pattern, arg_val) > 0) {
            int arg_pos = strchr(pattern, '%') - pattern;
            respond_with_match(stream, i, arg_val, arg_pos);
            return;
        }
    }
    respond_success(stream); // no matches
}
```

We can only get away with blindly reading at fixed character offsets like this because we have complete control over the code sending the requests. Because we've omitted length checks for brevity, a malformed request could crash our server.

The implementation of respond_with_match() merely has to plug the various values into the JSON format expected by Cucumber.

wire_server/cucumber.c

```
void respond_with_match(FILE* stream, int id, const char* arg_val, int arg_pos) {
    fprintf(stream,
            "[\"success\","
            "[{\"id\":\"%d\", "
            "\"args\":[{\"val\":\"%s\", \"pos\":%d}]}]]\n",
            id,
            arg_val,
            arg_pos);
}
```

The other message we need to respond to is the invoke message. Cucumber hands us the step ID we need to run; all we need to do is find the argument, run the step, and send back a passing or failing answer.

wire_server/cucumber.c

```
void respond_to_invoke(FILE* stream, const char* msg) {
    const char* id_text  = msg + 17;
    const char* arg_text = msg + 29;

    int id = atoi(id_text);

    char arg_val[32] = {0};
    sscanf(arg_text, "%31[^\"]", arg_val);
```

```
        if (0 == stepdefs[id].callback(arg_val)) {
            respond_success(stream);
        } else {
            respond_failure(stream);
        }
}
```

Here are the definitions of respond_success() and respond_failure():

wire_server/cucumber.c

```
void respond_success(FILE* stream) {
    fputs("[\"success\",[]]\n", stream);
}
void respond_failure(FILE* stream) {
    fputs("[\"fail\",{\"message\":\"Step failed\"}]\n", stream);
}
```

With all the infrastructure in place, we can finally write our application code.

Application

First, let's create a few private definitions used only inside the thermostat code. Create a new file called thermostat.c with the following code:

wire_server/thermostat.c

```
#define INVALID 999999

static int room_temp    = INVALID;
static int desired_temp = INVALID;
static int ac_on        = 0;
static void update_ac() {
    if (room_temp    != INVALID &&
        desired_temp != INVALID) {
        ac_on = (room_temp > desired_temp);
    }
}
```

Once you've finished the private section, the public API—used by our step definitions and presumably the main thermostat control loop—is easy.

wire_server/thermostat.c

```
int ac_is_on() {
    return ac_on;
}
void set_room_temp(int temperature) {
    room_temp = temperature;
    update_ac();
}
void set_thermostat(int temperature) {
    desired_temp = temperature;
    update_ac();
}
```

Now that all the pieces are in place, we can finally build the software. Create a Makefile with the following contents:

wire_server/Makefile

```
default: thermostat

OBJS := thermostat.o cucumber.o listener.o

thermostat: $(OBJS)
	gcc -o thermostat $(OBJS)

%.o: %.c
	gcc -c $<
```

Build and run the server, passing it the same port number you used in your cucumber.wire file.

```
$ make
$ thermostat 3901
```

Leave the server running, and open a new terminal to run Cucumber.

```
$ cucumber features
```

You should see a report of passing tests. Try changing the logic of the thermostat code and see whether you can get a failing result.

Further Exploration

With a bit of work, you could make the code in this recipe flexible enough to allow multiple step arguments or robust enough to handle arbitrary JSON input. If you're coding on a system where C++ and the Boost library are an option, you might try cucucmber-cpp.[85] It's a bit of work to build but takes care of a lot of the parsing details for you.

85. http://spin.atomicobject.com/2012/05/23/acceptance-testing-c-with-cucumber-and-the-wire-protocol

CHAPTER 2

Java

In this chapter, we'll look at several techniques that are specific to the Java platform. We'll see how to test apps written in popular JVM languages, such as Clojure and Scala. We'll also discuss commonly used Java frameworks, such as Spring, Hibernate, and Swing.

Recipe 16

Use Cucumber Directly with JRuby

Problem

You want to test a project written in Java, Clojure, Scala, or another JVM language (or perhaps a mix of these languages). You want to keep your step definitions in Ruby for simplicity reasons.

Ingredients

- JRuby,[1] a pure-Java implementation of Ruby

Solution

Using JRuby is the simplest way to get started with Cucumber on the Java platform. There are no classes to write and no Maven artifacts to download. You just use Cucumber on JRuby the same way you'd use it on any other Ruby version.

Why write Ruby to test JVM code, instead of using Java or Scala or whatever the project is written in? There are a few reasons.

- You might be more productive writing step definitions in Ruby, particularly if the application you're testing was written in Java.
- Your application might be written in a mix of JVM languages. For these cases, you might choose Ruby as a common test language.
- You might actually be testing a Ruby program written for the JVM, such as the Redcar text editor.[2]

In this recipe, we're going to test Java's `BigInteger` data type just to get a feel for driving Java libraries from Cucumber. First, download and run the JRuby installer for your platform.[3] Then, as we discussed in Section 3, *Getting the Tools You'll Need*, on page xiv, you'll need to install the common Cucumber libraries into your new JRuby installation. To do this, preface the normal `gem` command with `jruby -S`.

1. http://jruby.org
2. http://redcareditor.com
3. http://jruby.org/download

```
$ jruby -S gem install cucumber rspec-expectations
```

We'll do a simple calculation just to exercise big integers. Let's add 1 to a row of a hundred 9s to see whether we get a 1 followed by a hundred 0s—also known as a *googol* (you have no idea how hard it is to type it that way now!). Put the following code in bigcalc.feature:

jruby/bigcalc.feature

```
Feature: Big calculations

  Scenario: Googol
    Given 100 "9"s
    When I add "1"
    Then I should see "1" with 100 "0"s
```

Let's bring Java's BigInteger class into the JRuby namespace so that we can access it easily. While this step isn't required, it makes access much more convenient—we can just refer to it as BigInteger rather than Java::JavaMath::BigInteger. To do so, create support/env.rb with the following code:

jruby/support/env.rb

```
require 'java'
java_import java.math.BigInteger
```

Now we can treat BigIntegers just like any Ruby objects. We can create them from strings, add them together, and compare the results. Here are the step definitions to go in step_definitions/bigcalc_steps.rb:

jruby/step_definitions/bigcalc_steps.rb

```
Given /^(\d+) "(.*?)"s$/ do |count, digit|
  @first = BigInteger.new(digit * count.to_i)
end

When /^I add "(.*?)"$/ do |digits|
  @second   = BigInteger.new(digits)
  @expected = @first.add @second
end

Then /^I should see "(.*?)" with (\d+) "(.*?)"s$/ do |lead, count, digit|
  @actual = BigInteger.new(lead + digit * count.to_i)
  @actual.should == @expected
end
```

Now, run the tests the usual way, using the cucumber command.

```
$ jruby -S cucumber bigcalc.feature
```

The test should pass. You're successfully calling into Java code from your Cucumber feature.

Further Exploration

JRuby is the easiest way to run Cucumber on the JVM. You use all the Ruby deployment tools you're used to, without needing any additional pieces. But there are always trade-offs. Every time you invoke JRuby from the command line, you pay a few extra seconds of test start-up time.

If you're testing JVM code written in something other than Ruby, you may not want to pay this start-up penalty. And you may not have any particular attachment to the Ruby language. In Recipe 17, *Use Cucumber with Java via Cucumber-JVM*, on page 87, we'll see an alternative that has a faster start-up time and lets you write glue code in any JVM language.

Recipe 17

Use Cucumber with Java via Cucumber-JVM

Problem

You need to test Java code using Cucumber syntax. You'd like to write your step definitions in pure Java, without bringing Ruby into the mix. And you need to connect it to your existing set of Java IDE and build tools.

Ingredients

- Cucumber-JVM,[4] a pure-Java (no Ruby) implementation of Cucumber
- IntelliJ IDEA Community Edition,[5] the open source edition of the beloved Java IDE
- JUnit[6] to serve as the test harness
- Maven[7] for dependency management

Solution

There are a few different ways to use Cucumber to test code written for the Java platform. The simplest is to use JRuby, an implementation of Ruby written in Java. But it's not the best fit for every project; it has a long start-up time, sparse tool support, and a single choice of step definition language (Ruby). Fortunately, there are alternatives with different trade-offs.

If your project uses a particular JVM language, such as Clojure, Scala, or Java, you'd probably prefer to write your Cucumber step definitions in that language, rather than JRuby. It's also nice to be able to plug Cucumber into whatever IDE and build ecosystem you're using.

Cucumber-JVM fills these needs. It's written entirely in Java, so there's no need to bring in Ruby code if you're not already writing Ruby. It's provided as a set of jars so that you can incorporate it into your workflow. It plugs into the JUnit test harness so you can run your Cucumber tests from your IDE.

---

4. https://github.com/cucumber/cucumber-jvm
5. http://www.jetbrains.com/idea/download
6. http://www.junit.org
7. http://maven.apache.org

For this recipe, we're going to write Cucumber features for a Java-powered soda machine. Remember those? In the 1990s, we were promised a bright future where all we'd have to do would be to wave a magic ring at a vending machine, and it would dispense a soda.[8] That bright future hasn't quite come to pass yet; we might as well build it ourselves.

We'll start with an empty project in IntelliJ IDEA, add Cucumber support using Maven, and then write and run a few features.

Setup

Download IntelliJ IDEA and install it onto your system. Install Maven, either directly from its download page[9] or by installing a Java implementation that includes it.[10]

Launch the IDE, click Create New Project, and choose "Create project from scratch." Type SodaMachine for the project name, and select Maven Module as the project type, as in Figure 11, *New Cucumber-JVM project*, on page 89. When the wizard prompts you for an archetype, leave it set to none.

IntelliJ IDEA will open your project's pom.xml file automatically.[11] Fill in the Cucumber-JVM and JUnit dependencies just before the closing </project> tag.

jvm/pom.xml

```
<dependencies>
    <dependency>
        <groupId>info.cukes</groupId>
        <artifactId>cucumber-java</artifactId>
        <version>1.0.11</version>
    </dependency>

    <dependency>
        <groupId>info.cukes</groupId>
        <artifactId>cucumber-junit</artifactId>
        <version>1.0.11</version>
    </dependency>

    <dependency>
        <groupId>junit</groupId>
        <artifactId>junit</artifactId>
        <version>4.10</version>
    </dependency>
</dependencies>
```

8. http://en.wikipedia.org/wiki/Jini
9. http://maven.apache.org/download.html
10. http://support.apple.com/kb/DL1421
11. http://maven.apache.org/guides/introduction/introduction-to-the-pom.html

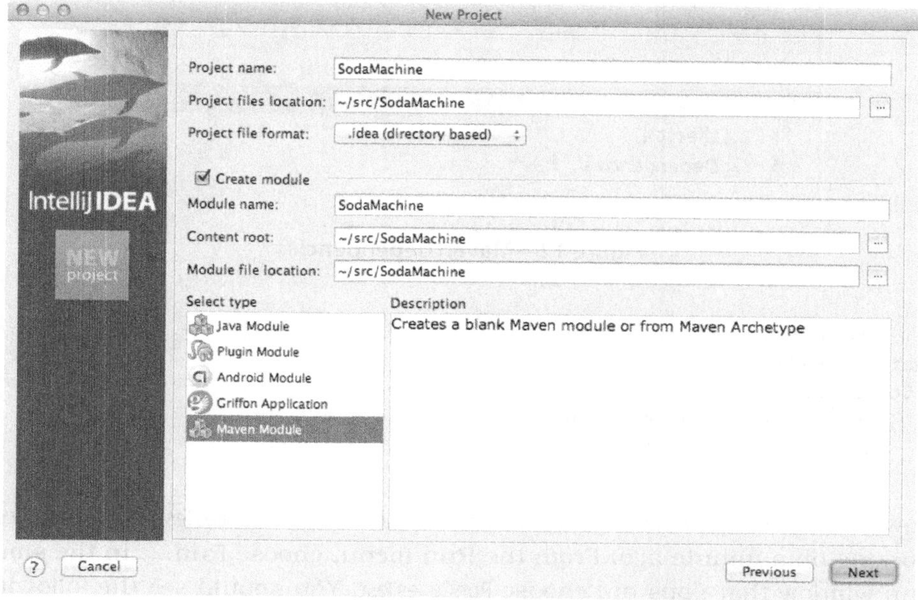

Figure 11—New Cucumber-JVM project

Select the View → Tool Windows → Maven Projects menu item. You should see your new Soda Machine 1.0 project. Click the Reimport All Maven Projects button—the one with two arrows, as in Figure 12, *Maven dependencies*, on page 90.

Now, you need to tell JUnit that it will be running Cucumber tests. Expand the directory tree in the Project window on the left to show the src/test/java folder. Right-click that folder, select New → Java Class, and give RunCukesTest for the class name. Replace the file's contents with the following code:

jvm/src/test/java/RunCukesTest.java

```
import cucumber.junit.Cucumber;
import org.junit.runner.RunWith;

@RunWith(Cucumber.class)
public class RunCukesTest {
}
```

Now IntelliJ IDEA is ready to run Cucumber. It's time to write some features.

Write Features

Create a directory in your project called src/test/resources, and create a plain-text file in it called SodaMachine.feature with the following contents:

Figure 12—Maven dependencies

jvm/src/test/resources/SodaMachine.feature

```
Feature: Soda machine
  Scenario: Get soda
    Given I have $2 in my account
    When I wave my magic ring at the machine
    Then I should get a soda
```

Now you're ready to run your feature. Open the RunCukesTest file you were working on a minute ago. From the Run menu, choose Run.... In the small Run window that pops up, choose RunCukesTest. You should see the following text in the output pane...

```
Test '.Scenario: Get soda.Given I have $2 in my account' ignored
Test '.Scenario: Get soda.When I wave my magic ring at the machine' ignored
Test '.Scenario: Get soda.Then I should get a soda' ignored

You can implement missing steps with the snippets below:
...
```

followed by the usual set of suggested step definitions. Go ahead and copy those so you can use them in your step definitions.

Implement Step Definitions

In the src/test/java directory, create a new StepDefinitions class with the following text copied and pasted from the output window:

jvm/src/test/java/StepDefinitions.java

```
import cucumber.annotation.en.*;
public class StepDefinitions {
    @Given("^I have \\$(\\d+) in my account$")
    public void I_have_$_in_my_account(int dollars) {
        // Express the Regexp above with the code you wish you had
    }

    @When("^I wave my magic ring at the machine$")
    public void I_wave_my_magic_ring_at_the_machine() {
        // Express the Regexp above with the code you wish you had
    }
```

```
    @Then("^I should get a soda$")
    public void I_should_get_a_soda() {
        // Express the Regexp above with the code you wish you had
    }
}
```

If you rerun your Cucumber tests, they should pass, and in the Run window IntelliJ IDEA should show something like Figure 13, *Completed test run*. The only thing left is to implement the soda machine. We'll leave that step as an exercise for the reader.

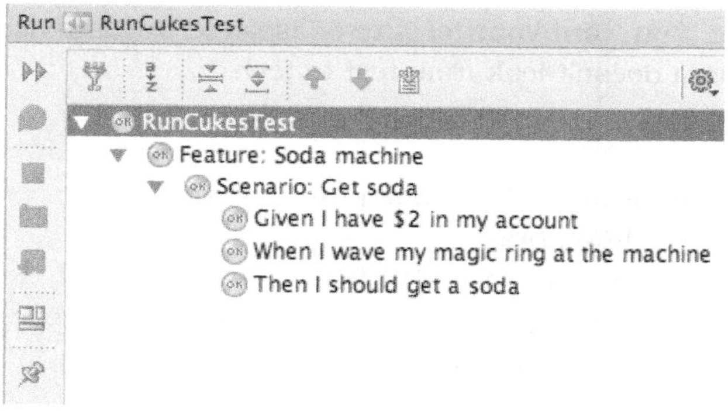

Figure 13—Completed test run

Further Exploration

In this recipe, we used IntelliJ IDEA to set up Cucumber-JVM. The approach is similar for other IDEs. To read one developer's experience in using Eclipse with Cucumber-JVM, see Zsolt Fabók's article called *Cucumber-JVM: Preparation.*[12]

12. http://www.zsoltfabok.com/blog/2011/12/cucumber-jvm-preparation/

Recipe 18

Drive a Spring + Hibernate Project

Problem

You want use Cucumber to test a Java application using Spring and Hibernate for persistence. You want your tests to be isolated by database transactions so that your data doesn't leak from test to test.

Ingredients

- The Spring application development framework[13]
- The Hibernate ORM library[14]
- A database system such as HSQLDB[15]
- Cucumber-JVM[16] to drive your Java code from Cucumber
- Maven[17] to install the libraries you'll need

Solution

Building an app with Spring can save you a lot of time, but you need to coordinate several moving parts: object-relational mappings, database transactions, and so on. In this recipe, we're going to put together a Cucumber test to drive just one aspect of a simple Spring model representing a book collection.

We're going to show all the Cucumber and Java code in this recipe, but for brevity's sake we're just going to show the most important parts of the XML configuration files.

The full configuration files are available online in the source code for this book.[18]

Here's the overall structure of the app we're building. We'll use the reverse URL of this book's blog,[19] es.cukerecip, as the Java package name.

13. http://www.springsource.org
14. http://www.hibernate.org
15. http://hsqldb.org
16. http://github.com/cucumber/cucumber-jvm
17. http://maven.apache.org
18. http://pragprog.com/titles/dhwcr/source_code
19. http://cukerecip.es

src/test/resources/es/cukerecip/book.feature Cucumber scenarios

src/test/resources Cucumber configuration files

src/test/java/es/cukerecip Cucumber step definitions in Java

src/main/java/es/cukerecip Java classes we're testing

pom.xml Application dependencies

src/main/resources Spring configuration

Let's visit these sections in greater detail.

Feature

Create a file called src/test/resources/es/cukerecip/books.feature with the following contents:

spring/src/test/resources/es/cukerecip/books.feature

```
@txn
Feature: Books
  Scenario: Save books
    Given a writer has contributed to the following books:
      | title              |
      | The Cucumber Book  |
      | Cucumber Recipes   |
```

The @txn tag indicates that we want this test to occur inside a database transaction so that the test data gets cleaned up automatically after each scenario.

In a real test, we'd do much more than just create a bunch of objects. Presumably, we'd want to do a query or edit and then make sure the results were what we expected. However, just this one step is going to keep us plenty busy for now.

Step Definitions

Now that the feature is written, it's time to move on to the step definitions. Create a file called src/test/java/es/cukerecip/Bookstepdefs.java with the following contents:

spring/src/test/java/es/cukerecip/BookStepdefs.java

```
package es.cukerecip;
import cucumber.api.java.en.Given;
import org.springframework.beans.factory.annotation.Autowired;
import java.util.List;
public class BookStepdefs {
    @Autowired
    private BookRepository bookRepository;
```

```
8      @Given("^a writer has contributed to the following books:$")
9      public void a_writer_has_contributed_to_the_following_books(
10         List<Book> books) throws Throwable {
11
12         for (Book b : books) {
13             bookRepository.save(b);
14         }
15     }
16 }
```

The Book and BookRepository classes are part of the Spring model we'll define in a moment. Notice the parameter type on line 9. Cucumber will transform the list of book titles from our .feature file into a Book objects for us.

You'll also need a class to kick off the tests. In the same directory, create RunCukesTest.java with the following code:

spring/src/test/java/es/cukerecip/RunCukesTest.java

```
package es.cukerecip;
import cucumber.api.junit.Cucumber;
import org.junit.runner.RunWith;
@RunWith(Cucumber.class)
@Cucumber.Options(glue = {"es.cukerecip", "cucumber.runtime.java.spring.hooks"})

public class RunCukesTest {
}
```

With the test code in place, it's time to turn to our models.

Models

The reason we're using an application framework like Spring in the first place is that we want to create simple Java classes and then decorate them with annotations to indicate how they should be stored in the database.

Create a file called src/main/java/es/cukerecip/Book.java with the following contents:

spring/src/main/java/es/cukerecip/Book.java

```
package es.cukerecip;
import javax.persistence.Entity;
import javax.persistence.GeneratedValue;
import javax.persistence.GenerationType;
import javax.persistence.Id;
import javax.persistence.ManyToOne;
@Entity
public class Book {
    @Id
    @GeneratedValue(strategy = GenerationType.AUTO)
    private Long id;
    private String title;
}
```

This indicates that each Book has a title and an autogenerated integer ID.

Now, we need a representation of a collection of books so that we can save new ones. We'll use an interface to describe this abstraction so that our Cucumber tests can save books without getting mired in persistence details.

spring/src/main/java/es/cukerecip/BookRepository.java

```
package es.cukerecip;
public interface BookRepository {
    void save(Book book);
}
```

The details belong in JpaBookRepository, which implements the BookRepository interface using the Java Persistence API (JPA).

spring/src/main/java/es/cukerecip/JpaBookRepository.java

```
package es.cukerecip;

import org.springframework.stereotype.Repository;
import org.springframework.transaction.annotation.Transactional;

import javax.persistence.EntityManager;
import javax.persistence.PersistenceContext;
import java.util.List;

@Repository
public class JpaBookRepository implements BookRepository {
    @PersistenceContext
    private EntityManager entityManager;

    @Transactional
    @Override
    public void save(Book book) {
        entityManager.persist(book);
    }
}
```

That's it for the code. Now, let's move on to configuration.

Dependencies

A typical Cucumber + Spring project has several dependencies. Table 1, *Project dependencies*, on page 96 lists the ones you'll need to put in your pom.xml file for Maven to install.

If you've never done this before, start with the minimal example[20] on Maven's website and then add a <dependencies> tag with one <dependency> in it for each row in the table.

20. http://maven.apache.org/guides/introduction/introduction-to-the-pom.html#Minimal_POM

groupId	artifactId	version
org.springframework	spring-tx	3.1.2.RELEASE
org.springframework	spring-orm	3.1.2.RELEASE
org.hibernate	hibernate-entitymanager	4.1.4.Final
org.hsqldb	hsqldb	2.2.8
info.cukes	cucumber-java	1.1.1
info.cukes	cucumber-spring	1.1.1
info.cukes	cucumber-junit	1.1.1
junit	junit	4.10

Table 1—Project dependencies

The next step is to configure Cucumber.

Configuration

We need to tell Cucumber where to look for our classes and other configuration files. Create a file called src/test/resources/cucumber.xml with the following contents:

spring/src/test/resources/cucumber.xml

```
<?xml version="1.0" encoding="UTF-8"?>
<beans xmlns="http://www.springframework.org/schema/beans"
       xmlns:xsi="http://www.w3.org/2001/XMLSchema-instance"
       xmlns:context="http://www.springframework.org/schema/context"
       xsi:schemaLocation="http://www.springframework.org/schema/beans
           http://www.springframework.org/schema/beans/spring-beans-3.0.xsd
           http://www.springframework.org/schema/context
           http://www.springframework.org/schema/context/spring-context-3.0.xsd">
    <context:component-scan base-package="es.cukerecip"/>
    <context:annotation-config/>

    <import resource="classpath*:/applicationContext.xml"/>
</beans>
```

This recipe uses the HSQLDB database, which supports both in-memory and on-disk representations; we'll use the in-memory option for speed and simplicity. Paste the following configuration into src/test/resources/jdbc.properties:

spring/src/test/resources/jdbc.properties

```
database.driver=org.hsqldb.jdbcDriver
database.url=jdbc:hsqldb:mem:user
database.user=sa
database.password=

hibernate.dialect=org.hibernate.dialect.HSQLDialect
hibernate.show_sql=true
```

The final configuration steps relate to application models you've written. Create a file called src/main/resources/applicationContext.xml with the following contents:

spring/src/main/resources/applicationContext.xml

```
<?xml version="1.0" encoding="UTF-8"?>
<beans xmlns="http://www.springframework.org/schema/beans"
       xmlns:xsi="http://www.w3.org/2001/XMLSchema-instance"
       xmlns:context="http://www.springframework.org/schema/context"
       xsi:schemaLocation="http://www.springframework.org/schema/beans
           http://www.springframework.org/schema/beans/spring-beans-3.0.xsd
           http://www.springframework.org/schema/context
           http://www.springframework.org/schema/context/spring-context-3.0.xsd">

    <context:component-scan base-package="es.cukerecip"/>

    <import resource="persistenceContext.xml"/>
</beans>
```

This will configure Spring to load our classes from the es.cukerecip package. It will also load the persistence configuration from persistenceContext.xml. On a typical project, this file can get quite involved. Let's just look at the most important part.

spring/src/main/resources/persistenceContext.xml

```
Line 1 <bean id="entityManagerFactory"
-            class="org.springframework.orm.jpa.LocalContainerEntityManagerFactoryBean">
-
-          <property name="packagesToScan" value="es.cukerecip"/>
5
-          <property name="dataSource" ref="dataSource"/>
-          <property name="jpaVendorAdapter">
-
-              <bean class="org.springframework.orm.jpa.vendor.HibernateJpaVendorAdapter">
10                 <property name="showSql" value="${hibernate.show_sql}"/>
-                  <property name="generateDdl" value="true"/>
-                  <property name="databasePlatform" value="${hibernate.dialect}"/>
-              </bean>
-
15         </property>
-      </bean>
```

On line 4, we direct Spring to look for model classes in the es.cukerecip package. On line 9, we configure Hibernate as the ORM for this project.

Now that all the code is written and the project is configured, you should be able to type mvn test into a terminal and watch the tests pass.

```
$ mvn test
...
-------------------------------------------------------
 T E S T S
-------------------------------------------------------
Running es.cukerecip.RunCukesTest
...
Results :

Tests run: 2, Failures: 0, Errors: 0, Skipped: 0
...
```

Recipe 19

Test a Grails App Using grails-cucumber

Problem

You're writing a web app using the Grails framework, and you want to use Cucumber to test it.

Ingredients

- Grails,[21] a web framework written in the Groovy language for the JVM
- grails-cucumber,[22] a testing plug-in that adds Cucumber support to Grails
- Cucumber-JVM,[23] the pure-Java implementation of Cucumber that makes grails-cucumber possible

Solution

Groovy is a programming language that aims to bring some of Ruby's expressiveness to the Java runtime. The syntax is quite flexible; you can often paste Java code directly into a .groovy file and then gradually add Groovy features as you go along.

Grails is a Rails-like web framework written in Groovy. In this recipe, we're going to build the world's least fun web game in Groovy and test it with Cucumber. To do that, we'll use the grails-cucumber plug-in. The project's wiki[24] explains both in-browser testing and direct testing; we'll use the latter for speed reasons.

Setup

First, download and extract the latest .zip file[25] from the Grails website. This distribution includes Groovy, so you don't need to add that separately. Now, add the Grails bin directory to your PATH. On Mac and Linux, you'd type the following:

```
$ export PATH=/path/to/grails/bin:$PATH
```

21. http://grails.org
22. https://github.com/hauner/grails-cucumber
23. https://github.com/cucumber/cucumber-jvm
24. https://github.com/hauner/grails-cucumber/wiki
25. http://grails.org/Download

Here's the Windows equivalent:

```
C:\> set PATH=C:\Path\To\Grails\bin;%PATH%
```

Next, create a Grails project for the game. Everything seems to be about Angry Birds these days. Let's make a copycat game called Furious Fowl.

```
$ grails new-app furious-fowl
```

To enable Cucumber support, add the following line to the plugins section of grails-app/conf/BuildConfig.groovy:

grails/grails-app/conf/BuildConfig.groovy

```
plugins {
    // ...

    test ":cucumber:0.6.0"
}
```

There's just one last piece of configuration. Grails's built-in test environment can set up fake HTTP requests and responses for you. All you need to do to get that working with Cucumber is add a file called test/functional/hooks/env.groovy with the following contents:

grails/test/functional/hooks/env.groovy

```
import static grails.plugin.cucumber.Hooks.hooks

hooks {
    integration ("@integration")
}
```

This will allow our step definitions to simulate HTTP requests.

Feature

Now the system is ready for the first feature. Place the following code in test/functional/Game.feature:

grails/test/functional/Game.feature

```
Feature: Furious Fowls game

  @integration
  Scenario: New game
    Given I see 3 buildings
    When I slingshot a bird
    Then I should see 2 buildings
```

The @integration tag signifies that we want to use the integration testing environment we set up in the previous section.

Go ahead and run your feature through grails-cucumber to make sure all the pieces are in place.

```
$ grails test-app :cucumber
```

You should see a failing test report indicating undefined steps, plus three snippets of Groovy code. These will become your step definitions. Copy them onto your clipboard; in the next section, we'll assemble them into working test steps.

Step Definitions

grails-cucumber looks for step definitions in the same directory as the .feature files. Create a new file called test/functional/GameSteps.groovy and paste your empty step definitions into it. Add the following highlighted lines to the top of the file:

grails/test/functional/GameSteps.groovy

```
import cucumber.runtime.PendingException

this.metaClass.mixin (cucumber.runtime.groovy.EN)

Given(~'^I see (\\d+) buildings\$') { int arg1 ->
    // ...
}

When(~'^I slingshot a bird\$') { ->
    // ...
}

Then(~'^I should see (\\d+) buildings\$') { int arg1 ->
    // ...
}
```

Let's take a moment to consider how the game will work in a browser. Players will visit the /game/index URL to start a new game. They'll be given a goal: knock down a certain number of buildings by slingshotting birds at them. Hitting the game/slinghot URL will launch a single bird and then redirect either to game/index or to game/victory, depending on whether any buildings are still standing.

We'll build in a simple test hook; passing in a number of buildings, as in game/index?buildings=3, will reset the game to a known state.

How do we hit a URL like game/index from our tests? Following the Grails convention, we'll look for a GameController class with an index method. We'll implement that class in a moment; for now, just code the tests as if it already exists.

grails/test/functional/GameSteps.groovy

```
import furious.fowl.GameController

GameController gameController

Given(~'^I see (\\d+) buildings\$') { int buildings ->
    gameController = new GameController ()
    gameController.params.buildings = buildings
    gameController.index ()
}
```

For the When step, all we have to do is visit the /game/slingshot URL.

grails/test/functional/GameSteps.groovy

```
When(~'^I slingshot a bird\$') { ->
    gameController.slingshot ()
}
```

The Then step will hit the game/index URL and verify that the number of buildings is right.

grails/test/functional/GameSteps.groovy

```
Then(~'^I should see (\\d+) buildings\$') { int buildings ->
➤   gameController.params.buildings = null
➤   gameController.response.reset ()

    gameController.index ()

    expected = "You see ${buildings} building(s)."
    assert gameController.response.text.contains(expected)
}
```

We've also had to add a little state management. We don't want to pass in the buildings=3 parameters left over from the Given step, so we clear them out at the top of the step definition.

Application Code

Now we're ready to add some actual application code. Create a Grails controller to hold the game code.

```
$ grails create-controller GameController
```

This will create a file called grails-app/controllers/furious/fowl/GameController.groovy. Open that file in your text editor and fill in the index method. Grails will automatically call this code when the player hits the /game/index URL.

grails/grails-app/controllers/furious/fowl/GameController.groovy

```
package furious.fowl
class GameController {
    def index() {
```

```
        if (params.buildings) {
            session.buildings = params.buildings as int
        }
        if (session.buildings <= 0) {
            session.buildings = 3
        }
        render "You see ${session.buildings} building(s)."
    }
}
```

This is the main landing page for the app. We grab the buildings=3 parameter from the URL (if it was passed in) and use session storage to keep track of the game state.

For the slingshot method, we simply knock down one building and redirect to game/victory or back to game/index.

grails/grails-app/controllers/furious/fowl/GameController.groovy

```
def slingshot() {
    session.buildings--
    def result = session.buildings > 0 ? 'index' : 'victory'
    redirect(action: result)
}
def victory() {
    render "You win!"
}
```

That's all you need to get the game running. When you retest the app, your Cucumber feature should pass. If you're curious to see what it's like to play Furious Fowl in your browser, type the following at the command line:

```
$ grails run-app
```

Now, you can visit the app's main URL[26] and knock down buildings to your heart's content.

26. http://localhost:8080/furious/fowl/game

Recipe 20

Test Scala Code

Problem

You want to test Scala code from Cucumber.

Ingredients

- Cucumber-JVM,[27] a Cucumber implementation in Java that can test code in any JVM language
- Cucumber-Scala, support for Scala that ships with Cucumber-JVM
- JUnit[28] for running your tests
- Maven[29] for installing these libraries

Solution

Cucumber-JVM is an implementation of the Cucumber test framework written in Java. With it, you can test code written in Scala and other popular JVM languages.

In this recipe, we're going to create a simple stock broker class in Scala and test it from Cucumber.

Setup

First, download and extract the latest Maven 3 .zip file for your platform.[30] Next, create pom.xml, the build script for your project, with the following structure:

```
<?xml version="1.0" encoding="UTF-8"?>
<project xmlns="http://maven.apache.org/POM/4.0.0"
         xmlns:xsi="http://www.w3.org/2001/XMLSchema-instance"
         xsi:schemaLocation="http://maven.apache.org/POM/4.0.0
                             http://maven.apache.org/xsd/maven-4.0.0.xsd">
    <modelVersion>4.0.0</modelVersion>
```

27. https://github.com/cucumber/cucumber-jvm
28. http://maven.apache.org
29. http://www.junit.org
30. http://maven.apache.org/download.html

```
    <groupId>StockBroker</groupId>
    <artifactId>StockBroker</artifactId>
    <version>1.0</version>

    <!-- project settings here -->

</project>
```

Your project will need Cucumber-JVM and Cucumber-Scala to recognize your test steps, JUnit to run them, and of course Scala itself. Add the following markup inside the <project> tag in pom.xml:

scala/pom.xml

```
<dependencies>
    <dependency>
        <groupId>info.cukes</groupId>
        <artifactId>cucumber-scala</artifactId>
        <version>1.0.14</version>
    </dependency>

    <dependency>
        <groupId>info.cukes</groupId>
        <artifactId>cucumber-junit</artifactId>
        <version>1.0.14</version>
    </dependency>

    <dependency>
        <groupId>junit</groupId>
        <artifactId>junit</artifactId>
        <version>4.10</version>
    </dependency>

    <dependency>
        <groupId>org.scala-lang</groupId>
        <artifactId>scala-library</artifactId>
        <version>2.10.0-M6</version>
        <scope>test</scope>
    </dependency>

    <dependency>
        <groupId>org.scala-lang</groupId>
        <artifactId>scala-compiler</artifactId>
        <version>2.10.0-M6</version>
        <scope>test</scope>
    </dependency>
</dependencies>
```

You'll also need to configure your project to compile Scala projects.

scala/pom.xml

```
<build>
    <plugins>
        <plugin>
            <groupId>org.scala-tools</groupId>
            <artifactId>maven-scala-plugin</artifactId>
            <version>2.15.2</version>
            <configuration>
                <!--encoding>UTF-8</encoding-->
                <excludes>
                    <exclude>**/*.java</exclude>
                </excludes>
            </configuration>
            <executions>
                <execution>
                    <goals>
                        <goal>add-source</goal>
                        <goal>compile</goal>
                        <goal>testCompile</goal>
                    </goals>
                </execution>
            </executions>
        </plugin>
    </plugins>
</build>
```

Now, we're ready to jump into writing features.

Feature

Place the following code in src/test/resources/StockBroker.feature:

scala/src/test/resources/StockBroker.feature

```
Feature: Stock broker

  Scenario: Buy low, sell high
    Given I have 100 shares of GOOG
    When I sell all my GOOG shares for $800.00/share
    Then I should have $80000.00
```

Before we can generate step definitions, we need to create a small class to serve as a test harness. Create a file called src/test/scala/RunCukesTest.scala with the following contents:

scala/src/test/scala/RunCukesTest.scala

```
import cucumber.junit.Cucumber
import org.junit.runner.RunWith

@RunWith(classOf[Cucumber])
class RunCukesTest
```

That's all we need to get the tests to run for the first time. Type in the following command:

```
$ mvn test
```

After a bunch of download and compilation messages whiz by, you should see a failing test report and a list of sample step definitions. Let's fill in those missing steps now.

Step Definitions

Create a file called src/test/scala/StockBrokerStepDefinitions.scala, and add the following text to it:

scala/src/test/scala/StockBrokerStepDefinitions.scala

```
import cucumber.runtime.{ScalaDsl, EN, PendingException}
import junit.framework.Assert._
import scala.collection.mutable.HashMap

class StockBrokerStepDefinitions extends ScalaDsl with EN {

  // step definitions go here
```

This will define the structure into which you'll fit your step definitions. Let's add the first of those now. Assuming our stock service will live inside a StockBroker class, here's how the Given step would look:

scala/src/test/scala/StockBrokerStepDefinitions.scala

```
var broker:StockBroker = null
Given("""^I have (\d+) shares of ([A-Z]+)"""){ (num:Double, name:String) =>
  val shares = new HashMap[String, Double]
  shares += name -> num
  broker = new StockBroker(shares)
}
```

The When step should cause our StockBroker instance to trigger a sale.

scala/src/test/scala/StockBrokerStepDefinitions.scala

```
When("""^I sell all my ([A-Z]+) shares for \$([0-9.]+)/share$"""){
  (name:String, price:BigDecimal) =>
  broker.sellAll(name, price)
}
```

Finally, we can compare the result with what we expected in the Then step.

scala/src/test/scala/StockBrokerStepDefinitions.scala

```
Then("""^I should have \$([0-9.]+)$"""){ (expected:BigDecimal) =>
  assertEquals(expected, broker.cash)
}
```

If you rerun the features now, you'll get an error message indicating that the StockBroker class doesn't exist. Let's fix that. Place the following code in src/main/scala/StockBroker.scala:

scala/src/main/scala/StockBroker.scala

```
import scala.collection.mutable.HashMap
class StockBroker(val shares:HashMap[String, Double]) {
  var cash:BigDecimal = 0.0
  def sellAll(name:String, price:BigDecimal) {
    cash = cash + shares(name) * price
    shares -= name
  }
}
```

Rerun your tests one last time; you should see a passing result.

Further Exploration

In this recipe, we tested a single, tiny Scala class from Cucumber. This is a bit overkill for such a small class; in the real world, you might drive an automation framework or an object that wrapped a network service.

For a test framework more suited to checking individual classes, see the ScalaCheck project.[31]

31. https://github.com/rickynils/scalacheck

Recipe 21

Test Clojure Code

Problem

You want to test your Clojure project using Cucumber. You have unit tests in place for individual pieces of Clojure code but want to write your higher-level integration tests in English.

Ingredients

- Leiningen[32] for installing Clojure and dependencies
- lein-cucumber[33] for connecting Cucumber to Clojure

Solution

Leiningen is a tool for automatically tracking and installing the dependencies for your Clojure project—including Clojure itself. If you're a Clojure developer, you're likely already using Leiningen. If you're new to Leiningen, all you have to do is download a single script[34] or Windows batch file.[35] For this recipe, we'll use Leiningen 2.0.

Once you've downloaded Leiningen and saved it somewhere that's on your PATH, create a new project for your Cucumber experimentation. I'm feeling hungry, so let's write a scenario describing a delicious pie.

```
$ lein new pie
$ cd pie
```

Open project.clj and add a reference to the lein-cucumber plug-in, as in the following code:

clojure/project.clj

```
(defproject pie "1.0.0-SNAPSHOT"
  :description "A delicious pie"
  :dependencies [[org.clojure/clojure "1.3.0"]]
  :plugins [[lein-cucumber "1.0.0"]])
```

32. http://leiningen.org
33. https://github.com/nilswloka/lein-cucumber
34. https://raw.github.com/technomancy/leiningen/preview/bin/lein
35. https://raw.github.com/technomancy/leiningen/preview/bin/lein.bat

Now, try running Cucumber with no steps defined, just to make sure all the pieces are working together.

```
$ lein deps
$ lein cucumber
```

This should report no assertions, because we haven't written any features. Let's do that now. Add the following text to features/pie.feature:

clojure/features/pie.feature

```
Feature: Pie

  Scenario: Baking
    Given the oven is preheated to 350
    When I bake the pie for 15 minutes
    Then it should taste delicious
```

Rerun lein cucumber, and Cucumber should inform you of the three undefined steps. Paste the boilerplate step definitions into features/step_definitions/pie_steps.clj, and modify them to look like the following:

clojure/features/step_definitions/pie_steps.clj

```
(use 'pie.core)
(Given #"^the oven is preheated to (\d+)$" [degrees]
       (preheat-oven degrees))
(When #"^I bake the pie for (\d+) minutes$" [minutes]
      (bake-for minutes))
(Then #"^it should taste delicious$" []
      (assert (= (pie-taste) 'delicious)))
```

Notice that we're using Clojure's built-in assert[36] to write our test expectations.

Now, open src/pie/core.clj, and add the Clojure code for the project.

clojure/src/pie/core.clj

```
(ns pie.core)
(defn preheat-oven [degrees]
  ;; activate Arduino-controlled thermostat
  )

(defn bake-for [minutes]
  ;; set timer
  )

(defn pie-taste []
  'delicious
  )
```

As a final step, rerun lein cucumber and verify that your tests are passing now.

36. http://clojure.github.com/clojure/clojure.core-api.html#clojure.core/assert

Recipe 22

Drive a Swing Interface with FEST

Problem

You want to test a Java program with a user interface implemented in Swing.

Ingredients

- JRuby,[37] a pure-Java implementation of Ruby
- FEST,[38] a Java library for driving Swing GUIs
- PresentationClock,[39] the example Java app we'll be testing

Solution

The Java testing community has created an amazing number of GUI automation libraries. They vary based on the type of user interfaces they can automate—Swing, SWT, JavaFX, and so on.

For this recipe, you'll be testing PresentationClock, a simple Swing app. The FEST automation library is a good fit for driving this program: it's actively maintained, well-documented,[40] and relatively easy to use.

You can operate FEST from Java using Cucumber-JVM or from JRuby using plain Cucumber. Here, we've opted for the latter.

Setup

Because this recipe is JRuby-specific, you'll need to download[41] and install the latest version.

You'll also need to perform the standard Cucumber setup from Section 3, *Getting the Tools You'll Need*, on page xiv.

```
$ jruby -S gem install cucumber rspec-expectations
```

37. http://jruby.org
38. http://fest.easytesting.org
39. http://presentclock.sf.net
40. http://fest.easytesting.org/swing/apidocs
41. http://jruby.org/download

Now, it's time to install FEST. Create a new folder for your project. Inside it, create a jars subdirectory. Download fest-swing-1.2.zip from the official site.[42] The .zip file contains a single .jar for FEST Swing, plus a lib directory full of additional .jar files. Copy the main .jar and the various lib dependencies into your jars folder.

We'll keep the PresentationClock .jar file in the same place. Download the application's .zip file from SourceForge[43] and then extract PresentationClock.jar into your existing jars directory.

Feature

Now that you have the tools installed, it's time to write a feature. This presentation timer has several components we could test; let's start with the reset button. Place the following code in features/timer.feature:

swing/features/reset.feature

```
Feature: Reset button

  Scenario: Reset while running
    Given 3 seconds have elapsed
    Then the clock should read "00:03"

    When I reset the clock
    Then the clock should read "00:00"
```

Run this test with the cucumber command, and then copy and paste the template step definitions into features/step_definitions/timer_steps.rb.

```
Given /^(\d+) seconds have elapsed$/ do |arg1|
  pending # express the regexp above with the code you wish you had
end
Then /^the clock should read "(.*?)"$/ do |arg1|
  pending # express the regexp above with the code you wish you had
end

When /^I reset the clock$/ do
  pending # express the regexp above with the code you wish you had
end
```

Before we fill in the bodies of these test steps, we need to connect FEST to the application's main window. Let's do that next.

42. http://code.google.com/p/fest/downloads/list

43. http://sourceforge.net/projects/presentclock/files/PresentationClock%202.0%20%282011-05-07%29

Glue Code

The main FEST code runs in a separate thread from your application so that your tests don't crash if the app fails to respond. This setup involves a little complexity at launch time, but it's nothing that the global hooks technique from Recipe 3, *Run Slow Setup/Teardown Code with Global Hooks*, on page 13 can't handle.

We'll follow the Cucumber custom of putting hooks in a file called features/support/env.rb. Create this file and add the following code at the top to bring in the parts of FEST that we need:

swing/features/support/env.rb

```
require 'java'

Dir['jars/*.jar'].each { |jar| require jar }

java_import org.freeshell.zs.presentationclock.PresentationClock
java_import org.fest.swing.edt.GuiActionRunner
java_import org.fest.swing.edt.GuiQuery
java_import org.fest.swing.fixture.FrameFixture
java_import org.fest.swing.core.matcher.JButtonMatcher
java_import org.fest.swing.core.matcher.JLabelMatcher
```

Now, we can add a global hook to launch the app before each test. To do this, we create a special class that launches the app in the correct thread and then tell FEST to use that class for initialization.

swing/features/support/env.rb

```
class AppStarter < GuiQuery
  # Launch the app in the Event Dispatch Thread (EDT),
  # which is the thread reserved for user interfaces.
  # FEST will call this method for us before the test.
  #
  def executeInEDT
    PresentationClock.new []
  end
end

module HasFrame
  runner   = GuiActionRunner.execute(AppStarter.new)
  @@window = FrameFixture.new(runner)

  # ... more methods go here ...
end

World(HasFrame)
```

The @@window variable is a *fixture*, which is FEST's main entry point for interacting with the app.

When the test is complete, you'll need to close the app and answer Yes to the confirmation dialog.

swing/features/support/env.rb
```
at_exit do
  title = 'Confirm Exit - PresentationClock'

  @@window.close
  @@window.option_pane.require_title(title).yes_button.click
end
```

This code snippet gives a good first taste of how to use the JFrameFixture instance. To look for a button, label, or option pane (i.e., confirmation dialog) belonging to the main window, you call methods named button(), label(), or option_pane().

Step Definitions

Now that the infrastructure for the test is in place, you can write the step definitions. These will go in features/step_definitions/timer_steps.rb. The Given and When steps are easy; you simply have to reset the timer and wait.

swing/features/step_definitions/timer_steps.rb
```
Given /^(\d+) seconds have elapsed$/ do |seconds|
  reset
  sleep seconds.to_f
end

When /^I reset the clock$/ do
  reset
end
```

The implementation of reset() goes in the same HasFrame module where you put the setup code. All you need to do is find the Reset button and click it. The easiest way to find a button is via its internal name property. Unfortunately, this app didn't assign names to its controls. You'll need to search for the button's on-screen text instead.

swing/features/support/env.rb
```
def reset
  button = @@window.button(JButtonMatcher.with_text 'Reset')
  button.click
end
```

This approach isn't ideal; if the button's text changes (in a new version or international translation of the app), you'll need to modify the test. But it's the best we can do in this particular case.

The final step is to check the contents of the clock's readout.

swing/features/step_definitions/timer_steps.rb

```
Then /^the clock should read "(.*?)"$/ do |expected|
  look_for_text expected
end
```

The app implements this display as a JLabel, and fortunately there are only two labels in the interface. You can just search for the one showing the expected time.

swing/features/support/env.rb

```
def look_for_text(expected)
  @@window.label JLabelMatcher.with_text(expected)
end
```

If the label we're searching for doesn't exist, Cucumber will log a test failure, and FEST will print a list of all the controls in the interface.

Further Exploration

This recipe searched for on-screen controls by their contents. A much more stable method for identifying a Swing control is via its internal name. Since PresentationClock's source is available, you might experiment with modifying its Java code to add name properties to the Reset button and time readout. The step definitions become much simpler (e.g., @window.button('ResetButton').click).

You've also probably grown tired of waiting three seconds for the clock to count up to 00:03 during the Cucumber run. Using the techniques in Recipe 13, *Manipulate Time*, on page 67, you can trim out this delay and speed up the test.

[illegible]

```
[illegible]
end
```

[illegible]

```
[illegible]
def [illegible]_text_selected)
  [illegible]
end
```

If the label [illegible] doesn't exist, [illegible] and RSpec will [illegible] of the controls [illegible]

Further Exploration

[illegible]

[illegible]

CHAPTER 3

.NET and Windows

This chapter contains recipes related to testing C-based and .NET-based Windows apps using Cucumber. It also covers a few tips for running Cucumber on Windows, such as how to make sure that pass/fail colors show up correctly in reports.

Recipe 23

Get Good Text Output on Windows

Problem

You're running Cucumber on Windows and want the console output to be green or red based on the pass/fail status of the steps. You also want non-U.S. characters to show up correctly in the output.

Ingredients

- ANSICON, a Windows helper for ANSI colored output[1]
- Windows's built-in `chcp` command for setting the code page[2]
- The Consolas[3] or Lucida Console[4] font (both of which ship with recent Windows versions) for correctly displaying Unicode characters
- Ruby 1.9.*x*, which handles Unicode better than 1.8.*x*

Solution

Most command-line environments support cursor movement and text coloring through *ANSI escape codes*,[5] sequences of special characters that a program can print as part of its output. DOS used to support these codes, but Windows does not. Fortunately, the open source ANSICON program provides this missing support.

Another area where Windows command-line programs take a bit of extra configuration is the display of international text. To show these kinds of characters directly, you need to make sure the Command Prompt app is using a font that can render them and then select a *code page* that includes them.

Neither of these two configurations is particularly taxing to implement. Let's start with the pass/fail colors.

1. https://github.com/adoxa/ansicon
2. http://technet.microsoft.com/en-us/library/bb490874.aspx
3. http://www.microsoft.com/typography/fonts/family.aspx?FID=300
4. http://www.microsoft.com/typography/fonts/family.aspx?FID=18
5. http://en.wikipedia.org/wiki/ANSI_escape_code

Pass/Fail Colors

First, we'll try running a simple scenario with passed, failed, and pending steps. As we'll see, Cucumber itself will provide guidance on how to customize the output format. Save the following example in windows.feature:

windows_console/windows.feature
```
Feature: Windows console

  Scenario: Pass/fail colors
    Given I am on Windows
    When I run Cucumber
    Then I should see colors
```

Go ahead and run that once, and then paste the boilerplate step definitions into step_definitions/windows_steps.rb. Make a couple of the steps pass or fail so that we'll get some variety in the output. I happened to make the first step pass, the second one fail, and the third one stay pending.

Now, run your steps again. Notice that the output begins with the following line:

```
*** WARNING: You must use ANSICON 1.31 or higher
(http://adoxa.110mb.com/ansicon) to get coloured output on
Windows
```

The sentiment is right, but the 110mb.com domain is blocked by a lot of corporate firewalls. Fortunately, the project's download page on GitHub also has the files.[6] Download the latest .zip file from there, and extract it to somewhere that's on your PATH. (Or you can just put all the files in the current project directory for this experiment.)

Now, type the following at the command prompt:

```
C:\MyProject> ansicon
```

The screen should clear and leave you back at the prompt. Now, rerun your features. The result should look something like the output shown in Figure 14, *Pass/fail coloring results*, on page 120.

Now that we have pass/fail coloring working, let's turn our attention to international text.

International Text

Add the following scenario to your Cucumber file:

---

6. https://github.com/adoxa/ansicon/downloads

```
C:\MyProject>cucumber windows.feature
Feature: Windows console

  Scenario: Pass/fail colors # windows.feature:3
    Given I am on Windows    # step_definitions/windows_steps.rb:1
    When I run Cucumber      # step_definitions/windows_steps.rb:5
      This is what a failing step looks like (RuntimeError)
      ./step_definitions/windows_steps.rb:6
      windows.feature:5:in `When I run Cucumber'
    Then I should see colors # step_definitions/windows_steps.rb:13

Failing Scenarios:
cucumber windows.feature:3 # Scenario: Pass/fail colors

1 scenario (1 failed)
3 steps (1 failed, 1 skipped, 1 passed)
0m0.145s
```

Figure 14—Pass/fail coloring results

windows_console/windows.feature

```
Scenario: European characters
  Given I am on Windows
  When my step contains an accented é
  Then it should show up in the output
```

This time when you save the file, direct your text editor to use the UTF-8 encoding. This process is different for every editor. Yours may support an option in the Save As dialog, as in Figure 15, *Selecting an encoding*. Or it may take a special comment at the top of the file, like mine does.

windows_console/windows.feature

```
# -*- coding: utf-8 -*-
```

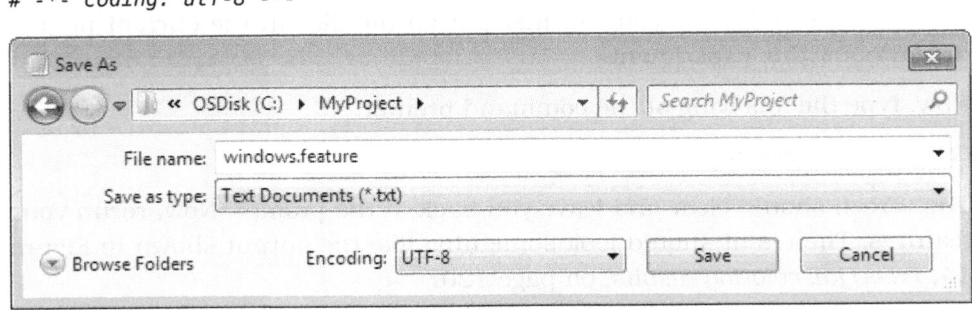

Figure 15—Selecting an encoding

When you rerun the test with a properly UTF-8 encoded file, you might see corrupted characters in the `When` step, something like this:

```
When my step contains an accented ├─
```

Cucumber is trying to print UTF-8 characters, but the Command Prompt app still expects characters encoded in the default code page for your computer. You need to set the code page to 65001 (UTF-8) by using the `chcp` command built into Windows.

```
C:\MyProject> chcp 65001
```

Now that Cucumber and the terminal are both speaking the same encoding, there's just one last step. The default font for the Command Prompt app is a raster font that doesn't have glyphs for many characters. If you click the icon in the upper-left corner of the Command Prompt window and choose Properties, you should see something like Figure 16, *Selecting a Unicode-capable font*. From here, you can change the font to one of the other built-in monospace typefaces that has a wider character range, such as Consolas or Lucida Console.

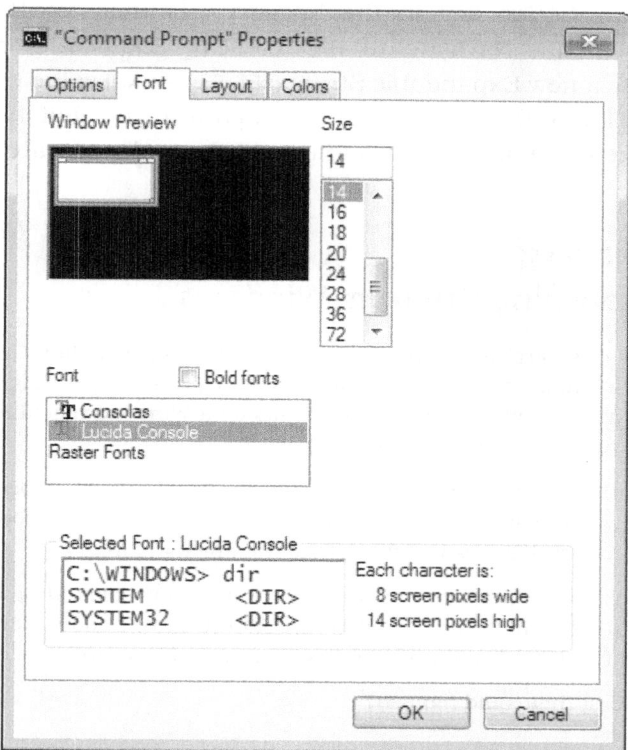

Figure 16—Selecting a Unicode-capable font

After you've changed the code page and the font, rerun your Cucumber feature. You should now see the accented é.

The ANSICON coloring and code page selection will last only until you close the current Command Prompt window. Let's make these settings the default for future sessions.

Making It Permanent

To make your customizations permanent, add them to a batch file you can call automatically. The exact path isn't important; I've used C:\Tools\AutoRun.cmd for this example.

windows_console/AutoRun.cmd

```
@if "%ANSICON_VER%"=="" (
    C:\Path\To\ansicon.exe
)
@chcp 65001
```

Once your batch file is in place, you can configure Windows to run it automatically using an AutoRun key in the Registry.[7] Launch regedit.exe from the Start→Run... menu. Navigate to HKEY_CURRENT_USER\Software\Microsoft\Command Processor. Create a new Expandable String (REG_SZ_EXPAND) value inside this key, called AutoRun. Fill in the value with the full path to your batch file. If there's already a value there, place your addition at the end, separated by a double ampersand.

Matt says:

Branching Out from Windows

The founders of several of the projects we've discussed, including Cucumber and Ruby, use something other than Windows as their primary operating system. This means that the experience of using these tools on a Windows machine tends to be less polished than on Linux or OS X.

The situation is improving somewhat through the heroic efforts of people like Luis Lavena. Still, after years working exclusively on the Microsoft platform, I found a much smoother developer experience after switching away from it.

You don't have to reconfigure your machine or turn your computing habits inside out to get started with Cucumber on Linux. All you have to do is download a free virtualization tool like VirtualBox[a] and install a copy of Ubuntu.[b]

What's the worst that could happen?

---

a. https://www.virtualbox.org
b. http://www.ubuntu.com

---

7. http://superuser.com/questions/54919/how-do-i-run-a-command-when-opening-cmd-exe-with-shortcut

Now, Cucumber will be set up correctly every time you open a Command Prompt window.

Further Exploration

Luis Lavena wrote an excellent introduction to ANSI escape codes, how to generate them directly in your output, and how to enable them in Windows.[8]

8. http://blog.mmediasys.com/2010/11/24/we-all-love-colors

Recipe 24

Test .NET Code with SpecFlow

Problem

You want to execute .NET code from a Cucumber test. For example, you might be writing integration tests for an ASP.NET web application or GUI tests for a desktop app. Because your GUI test framework or your web components are written in C#, you need to be able to call them from the .NET universe.

Ingredients

- Microsoft Visual Studio Professional[9] 2010 or 2012 for building the examples
- SpecFlow for parsing Cucumber syntax[10]
- A test runner such as NUnit,[11] xUnit.net,[12] or SpecRun[13]
- The NuGet package manager[14] to install SpecFlow and the test runner

Solution

SpecFlow is an open source test framework that recognizes Cucumber's Gherkin syntax (in fact, it uses the same Gherkin parser) but connects to C# behind the scenes instead of Ruby. With SpecFlow, you can continue to write tests in plain English the way you're used to with Cucumber, while taking advantage of the world of .NET libraries.

This recipe shows the basics of getting up and running with SpecFlow. First, we'll go through the basics of installing SpecFlow and its dependencies. Then, we'll set up an empty C# project and configure it to work with SpecFlow.

The project workflow should feel familiar if you've used Cucumber before. You'll start by writing features in plain English and then add step definitions to drive the app under test. The main difference is that the step definitions will be in C# syntax instead of Ruby.

---

9. https://www.microsoft.com/visualstudio/eng/downloads
10. http://www.specflow.org
11. http://www.nunit.org
12. http://xunit.codeplex.com
13. http://www.specrun.com
14. http://nuget.org

Setup

We're assuming you have Visual Studio Professional installed. It's possible to use SpecFlow with the free Visual C# Express environment, but the process is less automated.

To install NuGet into Visual Studio, choose Tools → Extensions and Updates → Online Gallery. Use the search field to find NuGet Package Manager. Click NuGet's Download button.

Using the same process, find and install the SpecFlow extension. This will add templates to Visual Studio for .feature files and step definitions.

Restart Visual Studio so that the extensions can finish installing. Now you're ready to create a SpecFlow project.

Create a Project

In Cucumber, we tend to keep your step definitions and glue code in directories called step_definitions and support, respectively. With SpecFlow, we'll put all that code in a C# project instead.

Go ahead and create the structure for that project. Launch Visual Studio. Choose File → New Project → Visual C# → Class Library. Name your project Calculator.Specs, as shown here:

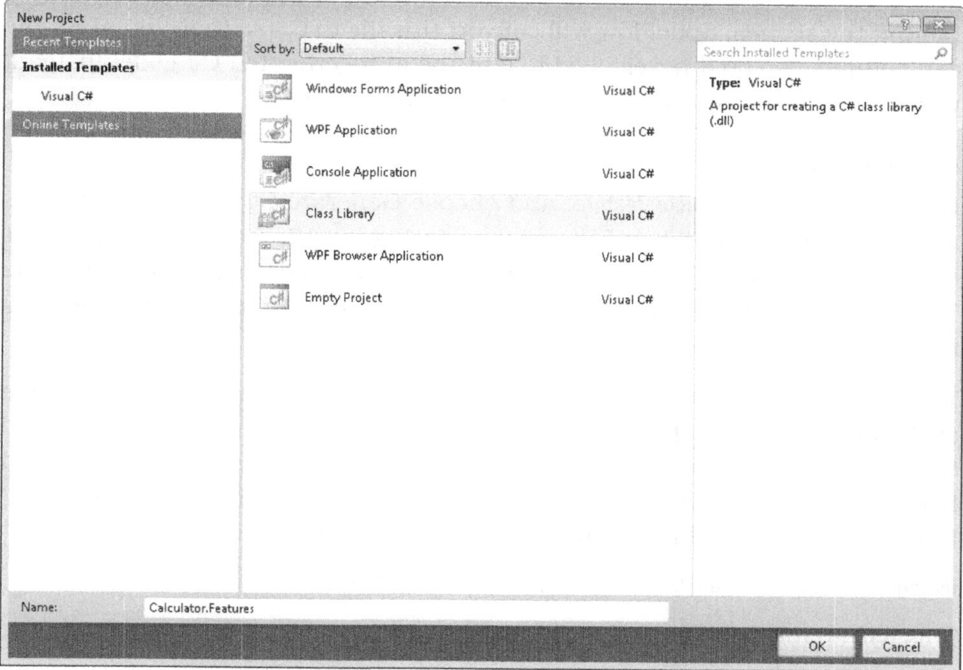

You can use any test runner for this project. We'll use the evaluation version of SpecRun here. Choose Project → Manage NuGet Packages → Online, and then use the search field to find and install the SpecFlow.SpecRun package. This will download both SpecRun and SpecFlow and add their references to your project.

Save your solution file to disk. Now, it's time to add some Cucumber tests.

Add a Feature

Choose Project → Add New Item... → Visual C# Items → SpecFlow Feature File. Name your new file Addition.feature. Fill it with the following text:

spec_flow/Addition.feature

```
Feature: Addition

In order to know my total grocery bill
As a shopper
I want to add numbers

  Scenario: Add two numbers

    Given I have cleared the calculator
    When I enter 2
    And I add 2
    Then the result should be 4
```

Behind the scenes, SpecFlow will convert this file to C# so that Visual Studio can compile it. You'll never need to edit the autogenerated C# code; instead, you'll work in the .feature file or in step definition files.

Add Step Definitions

Right-click inside Addition.feature, and choose Generate Step Definitions. This will bring up a dialog box like the one in Figure 17, *Generating SpecFlow definitions*, on page 127. Leave all the checkboxes checked, and click Generate. Visual Studio will prompt you for a filename; the default of AdditionSteps.cs is fine.

You'll need some way to write pass/fail assertions. Some test runners, such as NUnit, come with their own. Here, we'll use the ones built into Visual Studio's unit test framework. In the menu bar, select Project → Add Reference... → .NET, and choose Microsoft.VisualStudio.QualityTools.UnitTest-Framework. Then, add the following line at the top of Addition.feature:

```
using Microsoft.VisualStudio.TestTools.UnitTesting;
```

This will enable you to write things like Assert.AreEqual() in your step definitions.

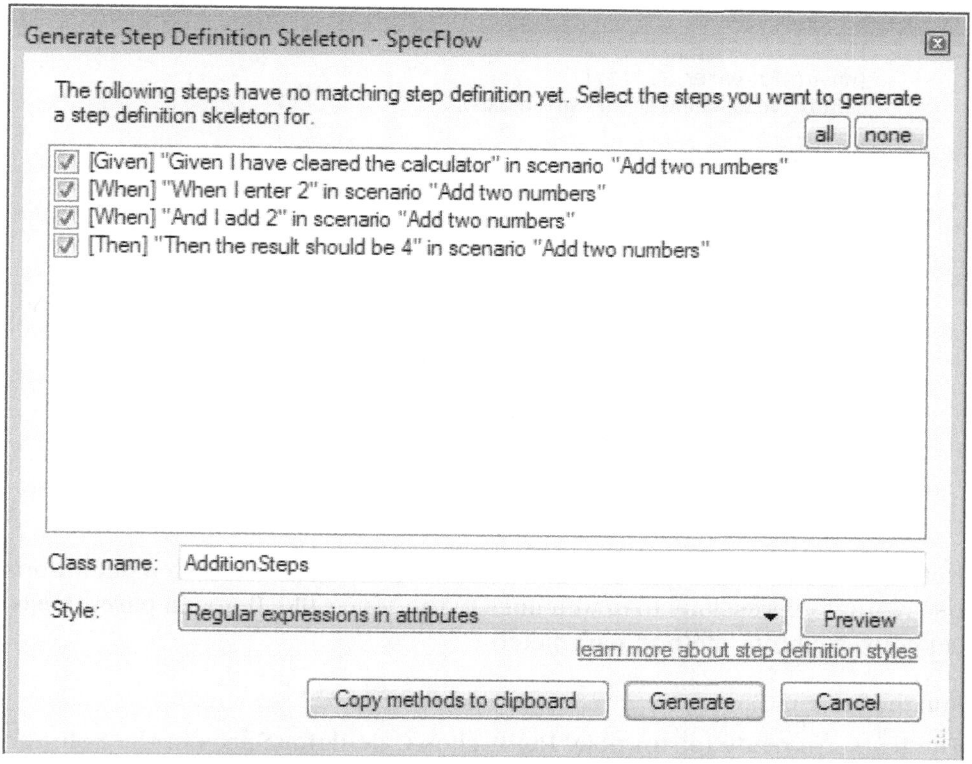

Generate Step Definition Skeleton - SpecFlow

The following steps have no matching step definition yet. Select the steps you want to generate a step definition skeleton for.

all none

[Given] "Given I have cleared the calculator" in scenario "Add two numbers"
[When] "When I enter 2" in scenario "Add two numbers"
[When] "And I add 2" in scenario "Add two numbers"
[Then] "Then the result should be 4" in scenario "Add two numbers"

Class name: AdditionSteps

Style: Regular expressions in attributes Preview

learn more about step definition styles

Copy methods to clipboard Generate Cancel

Figure 17—Generating SpecFlow definitions

Now, the project is ready for us to fill in the step definitions. On a real project, you'd be calling into other C# code here. Indeed, in Recipe 25, *Drive a Windows App Using White*, on page 130, you'll do exactly that. For now, though, you can just add some placeholder C# to get the tests to pass.

spec_flow/AdditionSteps.cs

```
using System;
using TechTalk.SpecFlow;
using Microsoft.VisualStudio.TestTools.UnitTesting;

namespace Calculator.Specs
{
    [Binding]
    public class AdditionSteps
    {
        private int result;
        [Given(@"I have cleared the calculator")]
        public void GivenIHaveClearedTheCalculator()
        {
```

```
            result = 0;
        }
        [When(@"I enter (.*)")]
        public void WhenIEnter(int number)
        {
            result = number;
        }
        [When(@"I add (.*)")]
        public void WhenIAdd(int number)
        {
            result += number;
        }
        [Then(@"the result should be (.*)")]
        public void ThenTheResultShouldBe(int expected)
        {
            Assert.AreEqual(expected, result);
        }
    }
}
```

Notice that, just like their Cucumber counterparts, SpecFlow step definitions use regular expressions to match lines in the .feature file. Items in parentheses get converted into method parameters.

Run the Tests

The tests are ready to run now. Right-click Calculator.Specs in the Solution Explorer, and choose Run SpecFlow Scenarios. You should see something like the following:

```
Test run started

Scenario: Add two numbers (in Calculator.Specs, Addition)...
  Done on thread #0: Succeeded.

Done.
Result: all tests passed
  Total: 1
  Succeeded: 1
  Ignored: 0
  Pending: 0
  Skipped: 0
  Failed: 0

  Execution Time: 00:00:00.6960000
```

SpecRun also generates an HTML report, which you can view by Ctrl+clicking its filename in the output window; see Figure 18, *A SpecFlow report*, on page 129.

Calculator.Specs Test Execution Report

- Project: Calculator.Specs
- Configuration: Default
- Test Assemblies: Calculator.Specs.dll
- Start Time: 11/14/2012 8:51:19 AM
- Duration: 00:00:00.6960000
- Test Threads: 1

Result: all tests passed

Success rate	Tests	Succeeded	Failed	Pending	Ignored	Skipped
100%	1	1	0	0	0	0

Test Timeline Summary

thread
#0

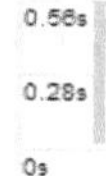

Test Result View

0.56s
0.28s
0s

Feature Summary

Feature	Success rate	Tests	Succeeded	Failed	Pending	Ignored	Skipped
Addition	100%	1	1	0	0	0	0

Figure 18—A SpecFlow report

Further Exploration

The example step definitions we saw here were just placeholder code. To see what those definitions would look like driving a real GUI, see Recipe 25, *Drive a Windows App Using White*, on page 130.

In this recipe, you used Visual Studio Professional to automate much of the project setup process. If you're using the free Visual C# Express build environment, you can still use SpecFlow; see Allister Scott's article called *C# ATDD on a Shoestring*.[15]

15. http://watirmelon.com/2011/02/18/c-sharp-atdd-on-a-shoestring

Recipe 25

Drive a Windows App Using White

Problem

You want to drive a Windows application through its user interface. You have a battery of integration-level tests that bypass the GUI (I hope!) but also want a quick smoke test to exercise the entire program on your continuous integration server whenever someone makes a change.

Ingredients

- The White library for GUI testing[16]
- UIA Verify for exploring the structure of your GUI[17]
- The setup and code from Recipe 24, *Test .NET Code with SpecFlow*, on page 124, including the following:
  - Microsoft Visual Studio Professional
  - SpecFlow
  - SpecRun

Solution

In Recipe 24, *Test .NET Code with SpecFlow*, on page 124, we used the SpecFlow test framework to write step definitions in C# and drive .NET code. By itself, SpecFlow doesn't care what kind of project you're automating: a GUI, a web app, a command-line app, or just an individual C# class. You'll typically combine SpecFlow with a specific library for the kind of app you're testing, such as a GUI automation library to test a regular Windows app.

This is where White comes in. The White library is a body of C# code that can simulate user input to drive Windows applications. The app under test can be a C program written to the classic Windows API or a C# program using WinForms or WPF.

This recipe will add GUI test steps to the calculator example from Recipe 24, *Test .NET Code with SpecFlow*, on page 124 to drive the Windows calculator.

16. http://teststack.github.com/White
17. http://uiautomationverify.codeplex.com

Setup

First, you'll need to add White to your project. From the Project menu, choose Manage NuGet Packages → Online. Use the search field to find and install TestStack.White.

Next, you'll need to figure out the unique IDs of the various buttons you'll be clicking. You'll need the UIA Verify tool for this. Download and extract the official .zip file, but don't start the tool yet.[18]

Launch the Calculator app from the Windows Start menu. Now, run VisualUIAVerify.exe from where you extracted it in the previous step. You should see something like Figure 19, *Identifying controls with UIA Verify*.

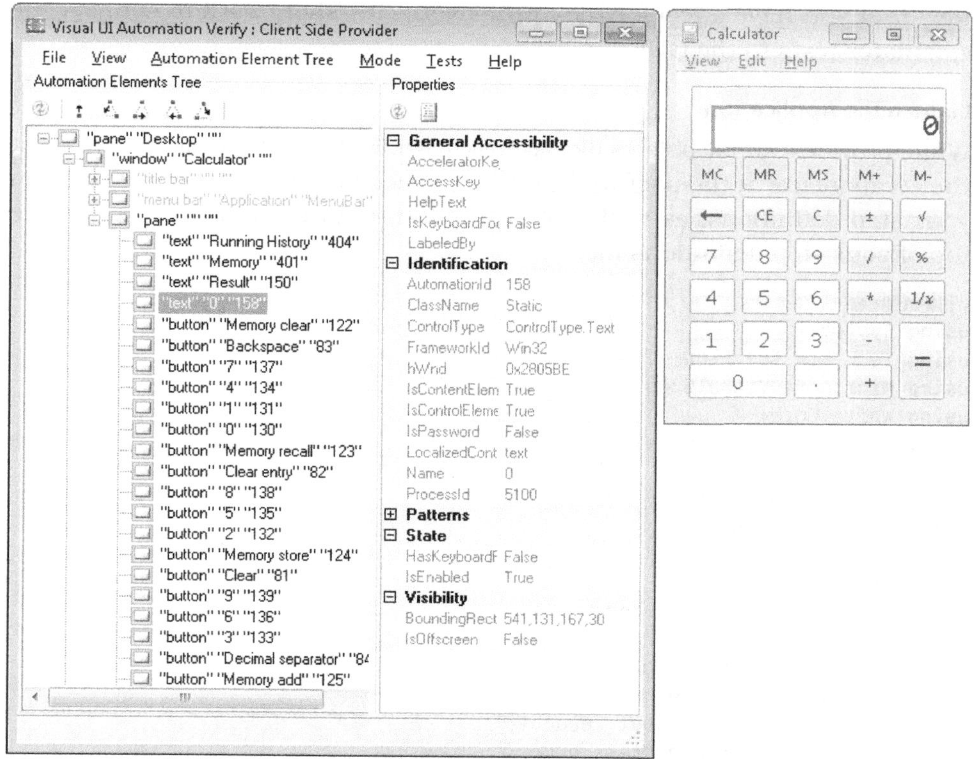

Figure 19—Identifying controls with UIA Verify

The list on the left contains the top-level windows visible on your system's desktop. When you drill down into the list and click a control, UIA Verify

18. http://uiautomationverify.codeplex.com/releases

highlights the control on the screen and shows its properties on the right side of the window.

The easiest way to locate a control in White is by name (i.e., text caption). A brief exploration around the controls reveals that the digit keys have captions of 0 through 9, and the math keys you're using are labeled Add and Equals.

The results readout is a bit different, though; its caption changes with each computation. Instead of using a name that's subject to change, you'll use its automation ID. For .NET apps, this string is a meaningful value assigned by the developer. Since calc.exe is a C application, it uses numeric control IDs. The readout has an ID of 158; make a note of that value for later.

Now that you have a feel for the app's layout, it's short work to connect the calculator tests to the GUI.

Launch the Application

White provides simple objects like Application, Window, Button, and Label to represent the components of the user interface. You'll need to declare a few of those in your step definitions, as well as bringing in the White.Core namespace at the top of your step definitions file.

white_c/AdditionSteps.cs

```
using System;
using TechTalk.SpecFlow;
using Microsoft.VisualStudio.TestTools.UnitTesting;
using White.Core;
using White.Core.UIItems.WindowItems;
using White.Core.UIItems;
using White.Core.UIItems.Finders;
namespace Calculator.Specs
{
    [Binding]
    public class AdditionSteps
    {
        private static Application app;
        private static Window window;
        private static Label readout;
        // ... hooks and steps go here ...
    }
}
```

At the beginning of the test, you'll launch the target program. It'd be nice to have to do this relatively slow operation just once, before the first test runs. SpecFlow's hook mechanism, modeled after Cucumber's, makes this easy.[19]

19. https://github.com/techtalk/SpecFlow/wiki/Hooks

white_c/AdditionSteps.cs
```
private const string IDC_READOUT = "158";

[BeforeTestRun]
public static void BeforeTestRun()
{
    app = Application.Launch("calc");
    window = app.GetWindow("Calculator");
    readout = (Label)window.Get(SearchCriteria.ByAutomationId(IDC_READOUT));
}

[AfterTestRun]
public static void AfterTestRun()
{
    window.Close();
}
```

Notice that this code also looks for the results readout by its automation ID and keeps a reference to it for later. IDC_READOUT is just the control ID you discovered earlier with the UIA Verify tool. (The IDC_... convention comes from old-school Windows apps.)

Drive the GUI

Now, you're ready to implement the step definitions. In your implementations, you'll find and click various buttons in the user interface. How? You'll do it by chaining together pieces of the White API to locate controls on the screen. You've already seen two such pieces: the Get() function and the SearchCriteria type. These operations can be chained together in endless combinations to look for specific captions, automation IDs, parent windows, control types, and so forth.

For the specific case of locating a control by type and name, White provides a handy shortcut—a template version of Get().

white_c/AdditionSteps.cs
```
[Given(@"I have cleared the calculator")]
public void GivenIHaveClearedTheCalculator()
{
    window.Get<Button>("Clear").Click();
}
```

You can use the same technique to find and press the buttons representing numbers and math operations.

white_c/AdditionSteps.cs
```
[When(@"I enter (.*)")]
public void WhenIEnter(int number)
{
```

```
    foreach (char digit in number.ToString())
    {
        window.Get<Button>(digit.ToString()).Click();
    }
}

[When(@"I add (.*)")]
public void WhenIAdd(int number)
{
    window.Get<Button>("Add").Click();
    WhenIEnter(number);
}
```

The final step is to compare the Text property of the readout and make sure the computation is correct.

white_c/AdditionSteps.cs

```
[Then(@"the result should be (.*)")]
public void ThenTheResultShouldBe(int expected)
{
    window.Get<Button>("Equals").Click();
    var result = int.Parse(readout.Text);
    Assert.AreEqual(expected, result);
}
```

Now, you should see a passing result when you right-click the solution and choose Run SpecFlow Scenarios.

Further Exploration

White provides a library of specific actions you can simulate on each of the common Windows controls: checkboxes, drop-downs, and so forth. Most of these are fairly guessable from the type of control; for example, the CheckBox class has a Checked property.

In cases where the method names aren't quite as obvious for the control type, you can glance through the project's catalog of common actions.[20] This list isn't exhaustive, and on real projects I've occasionally found myself needing to look up the available methods myself in the White source code.[21]

20. http://white.codeplex.com/wikipage?title=UI%20Items
21. https://github.com/TestStack/White/tree/master/src/TestStack.White/UIItems

Recipe 26

Test Windows GUIs with AutoIt

Problem

You want to test a Windows user interface from pure Ruby, rather than using a compiled .NET language.

Ingredients

- AutoIt,[22] a freeware Windows automation suite
- Ruby's built-in Win32OLE libary[23] to control AutoIt
- Unit Converter,[24] an example app to test

Solution

Windows power users have used AutoIt for years to perform little daily tasks around their systems. Among other things, AutoIt can launch programs, find windows, and click controls. In this recipe, we'll write one test case for a simple Windows unit conversion program.

Setup

First, you'll need to install AutoIt. Download and run the latest AutoIt Full Installation package from the official site.[25] This will register AutoIt's ActiveX control with the system so that we can access it from Ruby. If you're prompted to choose between x86 and x64, select the former.

Now, download Unit Converter and extract the .exe somewhere on your system; for this recipe, we've put it in C:\Converter.

That's it for the setup; we can move on to writing the feature.

Feature and Step Definitions

Here's one simple scenario for a unit converter; put it in features\units.feature:

22. http://www.autoitscript.com/site/autoit
23. http://www.ruby-doc.org/stdlib-1.9.3/libdoc/win32ole/rdoc/WIN32OLE.html
24. http://sourceforge.net/projects/unitconversion
25. http://www.autoitscript.com/site/autoit/downloads

win_gui/features/units.feature

```
Feature: Unit conversion

  Scenario: Miles to kilometers
    When I convert 26.2 miles to kilometers
    Then the result should be 42.1648 kilometers
```

Write the step definitions as if you have an API for the app with methods like convert_mi_to_km() and result(). (You'll create those in a later step.) Place the following code in features\step_definitions\unit_steps.rb:

win_gui/features/step_definitions/unit_steps.rb

```
Line 1 A_FLOAT = Transform(/(-?\d+(?:\.\d+)?)/) do |number|
     -   number.to_f
     - end
     -
     5 When /^I convert (#{A_FLOAT}) miles to kilometers$/ do |miles|
     -   convert_miles_to_km miles
     - end
     -
     - Then /^the result should be (#{A_FLOAT}) kilometers$/ do |expected|
    10   result.should be_within(0.0001).of(expected)
     - end
```

Notice that we're leaning on Cucumber's data-transformation capabilities[26] in line 1 so that we can reuse the digit-matching regular expression across the When and Then steps.

Controls

Before we get to the glue code that links the step definitions to the GUI controls, we need to know how to find the controls. The most reliable way is to use their automation IDs. You can find these IDs using the Window Info tool that ships with AutoIt.

Choose Start → All Programs → AutoIt v3 → AutoIt Window Info (x86). Launch the Unit Converter tool as well. Bring up the two windows side by side, as in Figure 20, *Finding controls in AutoIt*, on page 137.

Drag the crosshair from the Window Info tool into the edit control in UnitConverter. Make a note of the Advanced Mode value in the Control tab; this string, [NAME:txtbxA], is AutoIt's name for the textbox (based on the automation ID).

After a little browsing, you should find the following values:

26. https://github.com/cucumber/cucumber/wiki/Step-Argument-Transforms

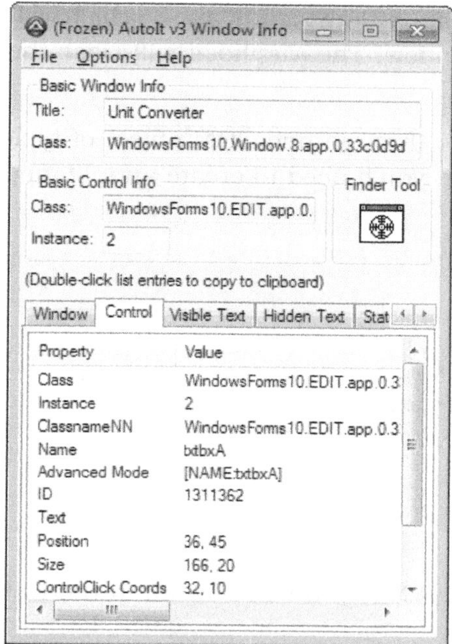

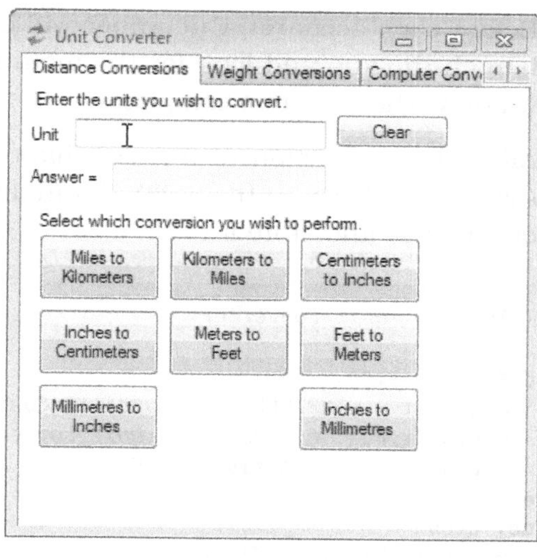

Figure 20—Finding controls in AutoIt

Control	AutoIt identifier
Unit textbox	[NAME:txtbxA]
Miles to Kilometers button	[NAME:m2k]
Answer textbox	[NAME:txtbxAnsA]

Now, we're ready to call into AutoIt to find those controls.

Glue Code

Create a file called features\support\env.rb with the following structure:

win_gui/features/support/env.rb

```
require 'win32ole'
class UnitWorld
  # ... definitions will go here ...
end
World { UnitWorld.new }
After do
  close
end
```

Before each scenario, Cucumber will create a UnitWorld instance, which will launch the app and look for the main window. The After hook will close the window when the test completes.

All of the interaction with AutoIt happens through one COM object of type AutoitX3.Control. So, in the UnitWorld initializer, you'll need to create an instance of this type and store it.

win_gui/features/support/env.rb
```
TITLE   = 'Unit Converter'

def initialize
  @auto_it = WIN32OLE.new 'AutoitX3.Control'
  @auto_it.Run 'C:\Converter\Unit Converter.exe'
  @auto_it.WinWaitActive TITLE
end
def close
  @auto_it.WinClose TITLE
end
```

Using the control names you discovered earlier, you can now fill in the last portion of the API.

win_gui/features/support/env.rb
```
INPUT   = '[NAME:txtbxA]'
CONVERT = '[NAME:m2k]'
RESULT  = '[NAME:txtbxAnsA]'

def convert_miles_to_km(miles)
  @auto_it.ControlSetText TITLE, '', INPUT, miles.to_s
  @auto_it.ControlClick   TITLE, '', CONVERT
end
def result
  @auto_it.ControlGetText(TITLE, '', RESULT).to_f
end
```

Now, exit Unit Converter and run cucumber from the command line. You should see the app launch, respond to the simulated user input, and exit again.

Further Exploration

AutoIt is the granddaddy of free-as-in-beer Windows GUI automation toolkits. But if you're looking for something a little more Ruby-oriented, you might give win_gui[27] or Win32-Autogui[28] a try. These libraries aren't as powerful out of the box, but they're more extensible.

27. https://github.com/arvicco/win_gui
28. https://github.com/robertwahler/win32-autogui

Recipe 27

Test on Windows Phone

Problem

You want to test a Windows Phone app using Cucumber syntax.

Ingredients

- Visual Studio Professional 2010 Service Pack 1[29] or newer
- The Windows Phone SDK 7.1[30]
- The Windows Phone Test Framework[31] by Expensify
- SpecFlow[32] for parsing Cucumber syntax
- NUnit[33] to run the tests
- The NuGet package manager[34] to install the testing tools

Solution

Writing Cucumber-style tests for Windows Phone involves orchestrating a few different pieces that work together. A test runner starts and stops the test. SpecFlow parses your plain-English test steps and matches them to your C# step definitions. A server embedded into your app listens for incoming commands and simulates screen taps.

The Windows Phone Test Framework by Expensify combines these various tools into a couple of easy-to-install packages. In this recipe, we'll use the framework to test a simple Windows Phone app in the emulator.

Setup

Most of the setup in this recipe happens after you've created your project. But there are two Visual Studio add-ons you'll need to install globally first. In Visual Studio, navigate to Tools → Extensions and Updates → Online

29. http://www.microsoft.com/en-us/download/details.aspx?id=23691
30. http://www.microsoft.com/en-us/download/details.aspx?id=27570
31. https://github.com/Expensify/WindowsPhoneTestFramework
32. http://www.specflow.org
33. http://www.nunit.org
34. http://www.nuget.org

Gallery. Search for and install both the NuGet Package Manager and the SpecFlow extension.

Now, you'll need to make sure the test framework can connect to the application you're testing. Type the following line into the Command Prompt window, substituting your domain and username at the end:

```
C:\> netsh http add urlacl url=http://+:8085/ user=DOMAIN\username
```

Windows should display the message `URL reservation successfully added` and return you to the command prompt. Once this step is complete, you can move on to creating your project.

Create an Application

Let's write a simple app that tells us whether a given word is a palindrome. In Visual Studio, choose Choose File → New Project → Silverlight for Windows Phone → Windows Phone Application. Name the app Palindromer.

Using the menu, choose Project → Manage NuGet Packages → Online. Search for *wp7test*. This will return two packages: the App component you embed into your application and the BDD component you use inside your tests. We'll get to the BDD version later; here, install just the App package, as in Figure 21, *Installing the Windows Phone test framework*.

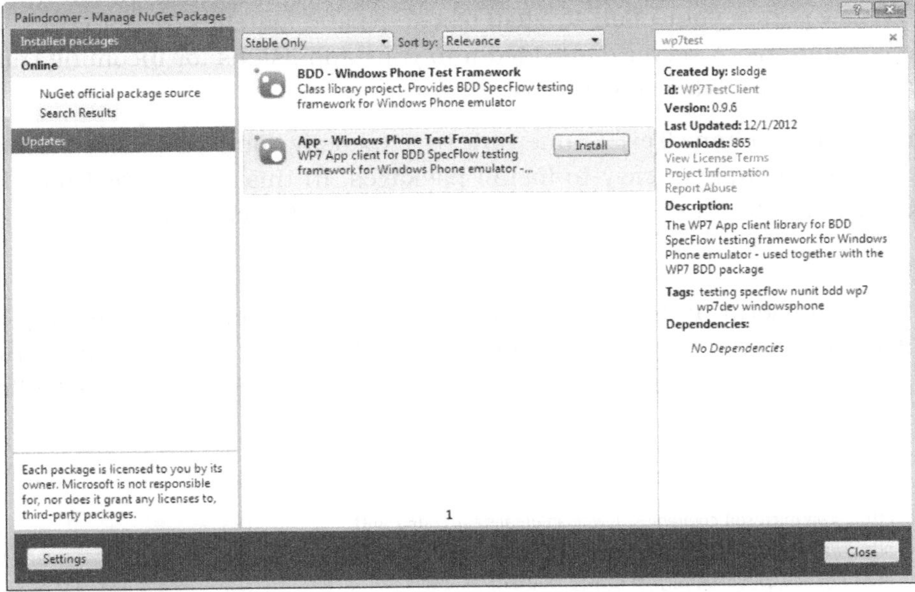

Figure 21—Installing the Windows Phone test framework

Now that the test framework is embedded into your app, you'll need to add code to start the server when the app launches. Open App.xaml.cs, and make the following changes:

windows_phone/Palindromer/App.xaml.cs

```
using WindowsPhoneTestFramework.Client.AutomationClient;
namespace Palindromer
{
    public partial class App : Application
    {
        public App()
        {
            // Make these the last lines of the App() constructor
#if DEBUG
            Automation.Instance.Initialise();
#endif
        }
    }
}
```

Now, you're ready to create the skeleton of your tests.

Create a Test Project

Right-click your solution and choose Add → New Project. Choose Visual C# → Windows → Class Library. Note that this is a regular desktop C# assembly, not a mobile one. Name your project Palindromer.Spec.

Now, install the Windows Phone Test Framework into your test project. Navigate to Project → Manage NuGet Packages → Online. Search for "wp7test" like you did before, but this time install the BDD version of the package.

This framework uses a 32-bit COM extension to control the Windows Phone emulator. To use it, mark your test project as a 32-bit assembly. Choose Build → Configuration Manager → Palindromer.Spec → Platform → <New...>; then select x86. See Figure 22, *Selecting the processor type*, on page 142.

The final step in creating the test project is to connect it to your phone project. Open Palindromer\Properties\WMAppmanifest.xml, and look for the <App ProductID="..."> tag. Copy the product ID to the clipboard.

Now, open Palindromer.Spec\App.config. When you installed the Windows Phone Test Framework, it automatically created four keys for you to fill out inside the <appSettings> section. Paste the project ID into the ApplicationId key.

You'll also need to fill in the paths to your application's icon and .xap (build archive) files, plus the app name. When you're done, the section will look something like the following:

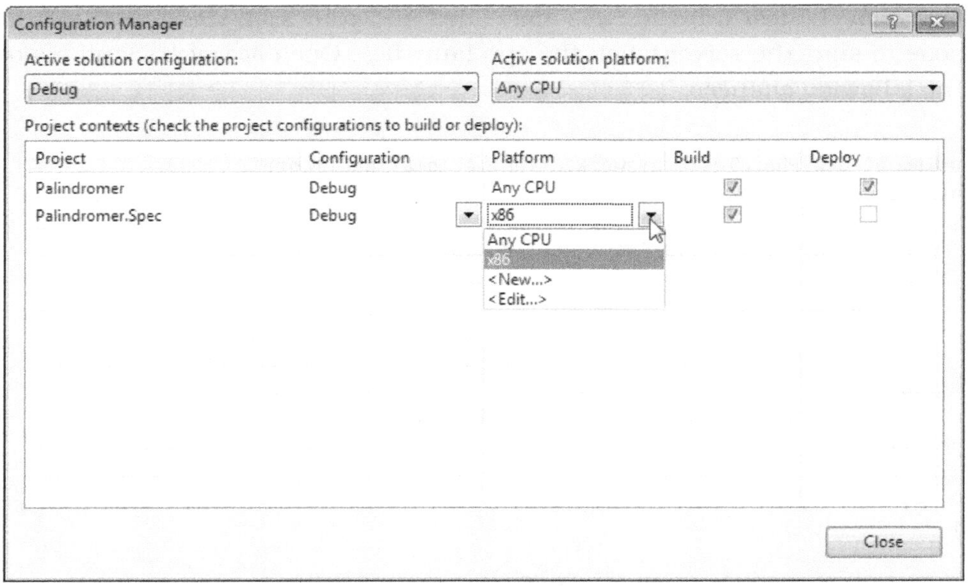

Figure 22—Selecting the processor type

```
<add key="EmuSteps.Application.WindowsPhone.ApplicationId"
     value="{cc535914-aa51-459e-aa9b-0d7afc01afe0}" />
<add key="EmuSteps.Application.WindowsPhone.ApplicationIconPath"
     value="C:\Palindromer\Palindromer\ApplicationIcon.png" />
<add key="EmuSteps.Application.WindowsPhone.ApplicationPackagePath"
     value="C:\Palindromer\Palindromer\Bin\Debug\Palindromer.xap" />
<add key="EmuSteps.Application.WindowsPhone.ApplicationName"
     value="Palindromer" />
```

Once the project is configured, you can create and run a simple test on it.

First Run

Before we get to the real tests, let's drop in a tiny .feature file that will do nothing but bring up the application. Right-click the Palindromer.Spec file, and choose Add → New Item → Visual C# Items → SpecFlow Feature File. Name the file Palindromer.feature, and put the following text into it:

```
Feature: Palindromer

  Scenario: Make a palindrome
    Given my app is clean installed and running
```

The Windows Phone Test Framework includes several stock step definitions for launching the app, tapping controls, and so on. For the most part, we'll be avoiding these and just writing our own—but the one for launching the app comes in handy here.

If you're using a test runner such as SpecRun or Resharper, you can run the tests directly in Visual Studio by right-clicking your project and choosing Run SpecFlow Scenarios. As of this writing, the NUnit support is less integrated. For NUnit, you'll need to start everything from the command line in your project directory.

```
C:\Palindromer> packages\NUnit.2.5.10.11092\tools\nunit-console-x86.exe ^
                Palindromer.Spec\bin\x86\Debug\Palindromer.Spec.dll
```

You should see the emulator launch and bring up the app.

Feature

Now that the app and the test framework are talking to each other, it's time to write a real feature. Add the following text inside your existing scenario, right after the Given line:

```
When I enter the word "tattarrattat"
Then it should be recognized as a palindrome
```

If you rerun your tests, you should get a warning that there are two missing step definitions. It's time to fix that.

Step Definitions

Right-click the Palindromer.Spec project, and choose Add → New Item → SpecFlow Step Definition. Name the file PalindromerSteps.cs, and make the following changes to it:

windows_phone/Palindromer.Spec/PalindromerSteps.cs

```
➤ using WindowsPhoneTestFramework.Test.EmuSteps;

namespace Palindromer.Spec
{
    [Binding]
➤   public class PalindromerSteps : EmuDefinitionBase
    {
        // ... step definitions go here ...
    }
}
```

This will give us access to the API for driving the app. Now, we can use that API to write our step definitions. Let's assume the user will be typing into a control called wordTextBox and reading the result in another one called resultTextBlock. Here's how we'd express that using the Windows Phone Test Framework:

windows_phone/Palindromer.Spec/PalindromerSteps.cs

```
[When(@"I type the word ""([^""]*)""")]
public void WhenITypeTheWord(string word)
{
    Assert.IsTrue(
        Emu.ApplicationAutomationController.SetTextOnControl(
            "wordTextBox", word));
}
[Then(@"it should be recognized as a palindrome")]
public void ThenItShouldBeRecognizedAsAPalindrome()
{
    string result;
    Assert.IsTrue(
        Emu.ApplicationAutomationController.TryGetTextFromControl(
            "resultTextBlock", out result));
    Assert.AreEqual("... is a palindrome", result);
}
```

For more examples of how to use this API, see the source code to the framework's prebuilt step definitions.[35]

Go ahead and rerun the tests. They should fail at this point, because the app's behavior isn't implemented yet. Let's move on to that step.

Modifying the App

In the Palindromer project, double-click MainPage.xaml. This will bring up the GUI editor. Drag a TextBox and a TextBlock from the Toolbox into the main window, and position them as in Figure 23, *Laying out the app*. Name them wordTextBox and resultTextBlock, respectively. Fill the TextBlock with the text ... is not a palindrome.

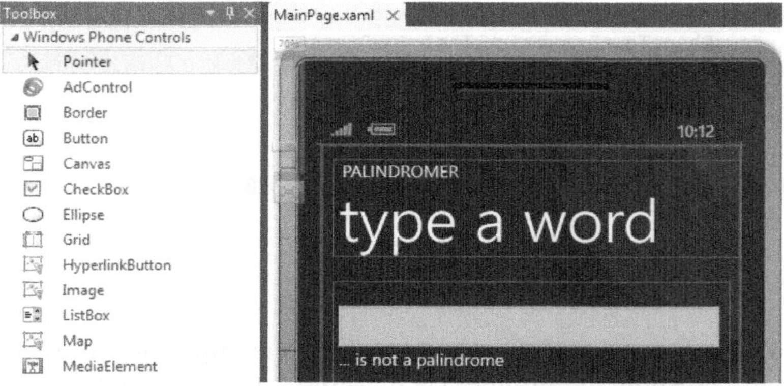

Figure 23—Laying out the app

35. https://github.com/Expensify/WindowsPhoneTestFramework/blob/master/Test/EmuSteps/StepDefinitions

We need to check the text for palindromes whenever the user changes it. Click the wordTextBox control to select it. Next, in the Properties window, click the Events tab, and then double-click the white space next to the TextChanged event. See Figure 24, *Creating an event handler*.

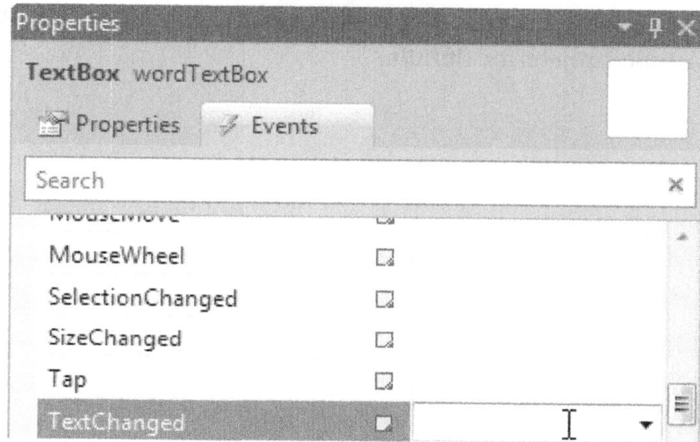

Figure 24—Creating an event handler

This will bring up the code editor. Paste the following text into the body of the function:

windows_phone/Palindromer/MainPage.xaml.cs
```
private void wordTextBox_TextChanged(object sender, TextChangedEventArgs e)
{
    var word = wordTextBox.Text;
    var reversed = new string(word.Reverse().ToArray());
    var isPalindrome = (word.Length > 0 && word.Equals(reversed));

    resultTextBlock.Text =
        "... " +
        (isPalindrome ? "is" : "is not") +
        " a palindrome";
}
```

Rerun the tests one final time. They should now pass.

Further Exploration

In this recipe, we wrote and tested a simple app in the emulator. The Windows Phone Test Framework supplies a handy program called EmuHost.exe for launching the app and poking at controls while you're still writing your step definitions. Run packages\WP7Test.0.9.6\tools\EmuHost.exe, and type help to learn more.

Although we just tested on the emulator here, the Windows Phone Test Framework contains some limited support for running on a live device. While it can't simulate gestures such as taps and flicks, it can set and get the values of controls.

The SpecFlow project contains its own take on driving Windows Phone apps; see their example project for details.[36]

36. https://github.com/techtalk/SpecFlow-Examples/tree/master/BowlingKata/BowlingKata-WindowsPhone7-MsTest

CHAPTER 4

Mobile and Web

In this chapter, we'll see how to get started with Cucumber on mobile devices running Android or iOS. We'll also take a look at a few nuances of web testing, including Flash, JavaScript, and PHP.

Recipe 28

Test on iOS Using Frank

Problem

You want to test an iPhone or iPad app easily from Cucumber.

Ingredients

- Frank,[1] an adapter that connects your iOS app to Cucumber

Solution

There are several GUI automation libraries for iPhone and iPad apps, each with its trade-offs. Some are ready to use right away, with no modification to your application code—but they work only with the iOS simulator. Others can test real devices but require you to create a special debug build of your app and add some automation hooks to it.

The approaches are not mutually exclusive. You can start with a simpler library and then move to a more flexible one later. For this recipe, we'll use Frank, a library that automatically creates a testing build of your app.

Frank consists of two parts.

- A network server that you compile into your iOS app during testing (but not for release)
- A Ruby library that translates your Cucumber test steps into commands for the server to carry out GUI interactions

In this recipe, we're going to retrofit Frank into an existing open source iOS app and then write a Cucumber test for the app. Specifically, we're going to test iOS Calculator,[2] an open source alternative to the calculator that ships with iOS.

Setup

The Frank project provides excellent installation instructions.[3] Here's how to apply them to the calculator app. First, install the gem.

1. http://www.testingwithfrank.com
2. https://github.com/mglagola/iOS-Calculator
3. http://www.testingwithfrank.com/installing.html

```
$ gem install frank-cucumber
```

Grab the source code to iOS Calculator.

```
$ git clone https://github.com/mglagola/iOS-Calculator.git
```

Next, run the following command inside the iOS-Calculator directory:

```
$ frank setup
```

This will add test hooks to the project. We want Frank's network server to be part of our iOS app, but only during testing—not during the final build. Fortunately, Frank confines its changes to a separate build.

We should be able to build the Frank-enabled app now. From the command line, run the following command:

```
$ frank build
```

Once the build completes, let's do a quick smoke check to make sure all the parts are working. From the Frank subdirectory, run the cucumber command. After a few seconds, the app should launch in the simulator and then rotate through all the display orientations.

If the simulator launches but shows a blank screen instead of the app, you'll need to choose Reset Content and Settings... from the iOS Simulator menu and try again (this will remove any other apps you've installed on the simulator as well).

Once we're confident we can connect to the app from Cucumber, we can delve into finding and clicking controls.

Finding Controls

Frank embeds a nifty web server called Symbiote into your iOS app to display information about the various on-screen controls. With the app running in the simulator, type the following command into Terminal:

```
$ frank inspect
```

This will launch your browser and navigate to the simulator's address.[4] You should see something like Figure 25, *Inspecting the UI in Symbiote*, on page 150.

On the left, Symbiote shows a nested list of all the controls in the app. If you hover over one of these with the mouse cursor, the control will light up green in the screenshot on the right. Clicking a control name on the left will bring up several details about it, including accessibility information.

4. http://localhost:37265/

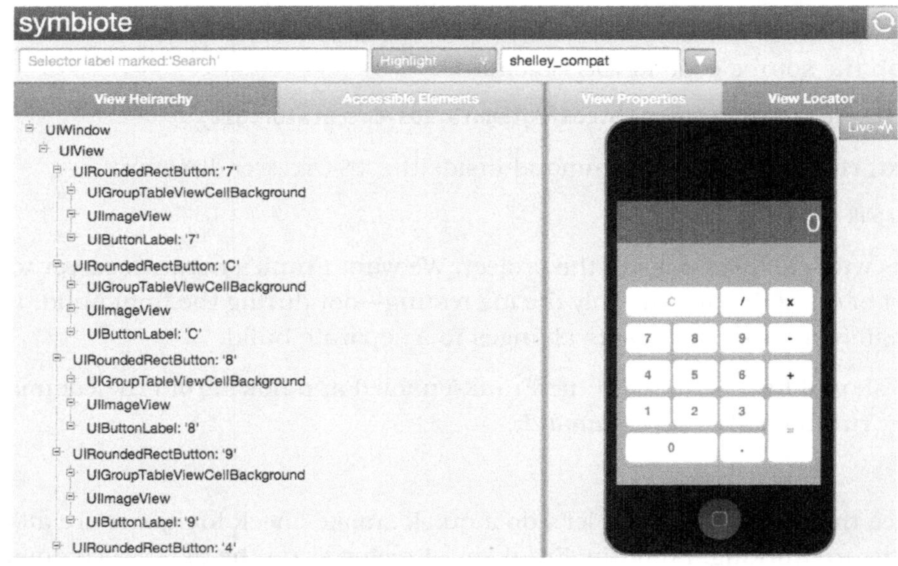

Figure 25—Inspecting the UI in Symbiote

Symbiote can also highlight controls directly in the simulator. Type *button marked:'C'* into the Selector search box in your browser and click the Highlight button. The Clear button should turn green momentarily in the running calculator app.

You can type the same kind of search terms into Ruby to fill in your Cucumber step definitions. Before we get to the scenario and steps, let's get some practice locating controls in Ruby.

Frank is designed to work with Cucumber, but it also comes with a console for stand-alone exploration. Let's use it to click a button in the app.

```
$ frank console
connecting to app... connected
[1] pry(#<Frank::Console>)> touch "button marked:'8'"
=> nil
```

When you type the touch() command and press Enter, Frank will type an 8 into the calculator.

The search syntax we've been using is called Shelley, and it's modeled after the UIQuery language used in an older project called UISpec. To learn more about Shelley, see the syntax page on the Frank site.[5]

5. http://testingwithfrank.com/selector_syntax.html

Go ahead and experiment with finding and clicking other controls. Since we'll be using the label (readout) and the various numeric buttons, you might start with those controls.

Feature

Although Frank provided us with a lovely features directory with sample step definitions, we're going to start from scratch for this project. Create a new directory, and put the following code in features/calculator.feature:

frank/features/calculator.feature

```
Feature: Calculator

  Scenario: Square
    Given I have cleared the calculator
    When I press "8"
    And I press "x="
    Then the result should be "64"
```

Now, add the required Frank configuration to features/support/env.rb.

frank/features/support/env.rb

```
require 'frank-cucumber'
Frank::Cucumber::FrankHelper.use_shelley_from_now_on
```

We're using an environment variable to find the compiled app, so you'll need to set that up at the command line. The binary lives in Frank/frankified_build inside the calculator project directory.

```
$ export APP_BUNDLE_PATH=\
  /path/to/iOS-Calculator/Frank/frankified_build/Frankified.app
```

On to the step definitions. For the Given step, we want to click the Clear button on the calculator. Put the following code in features/step_definitions/calculator_steps.rb:

frank/features/step_definitions/calculator_steps.rb

```
Given /^I have cleared the calculator$/ do
  touch "button marked:'C'"
end
```

This step takes the same search notation you used earlier with Symbiote and passes it to the touch() method. The When step is similar, except that we're looping over several keystrokes instead of a single one.

frank/features/step_definitions/calculator_steps.rb

```
When /^I press "(.+)"$/ do |keys|
  keys.each_char do |k|
    touch "button marked:'#{k}"
  end
end
```

To check the calculator's result, we call Frank's check_element_exists() method to find a text label with the value we expect.

frank/features/step_definitions/calculator_steps.rb

```
Then /^the result should be "(.+)"$/ do |expected|
  check_element_exists "label marked:'#{expected}"
end
```

Now, when you rerun your Cucumber scenario from the command line, you should see the app reacting.

Launching the App

So far, we've been interacting with an already-running app. How do we launch the app before the test and shut it down afterward so that we're always starting in a known state?

Frank comes with a built-in API call named launch_app() to start the simulator and a stock Cucumber step to exit. Place the following code in features/support/env.rb:

frank/features/support/env.rb

```
Before do
  app_path = ENV['APP_BUNDLE_PATH'] || raise('APP_BUNDLE_PATH undefined')
  launch_app app_path
end
After do
  step 'I quit the simulator'
end
```

Rerun your Cucumber scenario. The simulator should now launch and quit on its own.

Further Exploration

In this recipe, we were able to drive the calculator app solely by tapping the screen and searching for UI elements. For more advanced interactions, Frank supplies a frankly_map() method that sends any Objective-C message directly to a control.

```
selector = "view marked:'Some View Name'"
check_element_exists selector
frankly_map selector, 'someObjCMessage:', some_parameter
```

The quickest way to test an iOS app is to run it in the simulator on your development machine, as we've done here. Because Frank embeds a simple HTTP server into your app, it's also possible to test on a live device using the same techniques —you'd just use the IP address of your device instead of localhost.

Recipe 29

Test Android Apps with Calabash

Problem

You want to test an Android application using Cucumber.

Ingredients

- Calabash,[6] an open source library for testing mobile apps
- The Android SDK[7] for building and running the example application
- Eclipse[8] for sketching the user interface

Solution

Calabash is a library that connects Cucumber to Android or iOS apps. The Android flavor works by embedding a TCP server into your application and then controlling it remotely from your computer using the Robotium GUI automation tool.[9]

In this recipe, we'll write a simple bookmarking application and test it with Calabash. You can perform the tasks either in Eclipse or on the command line; we'll show Eclipse here.

Setup

To build and run the example code, you'll need to install the Android SDK. This process takes a couple of steps. First, extract the .zip file for your platform and make a note of the directory. Then, launch the installer (called SDK Manager.exe on Windows and tools/android on other systems). Select the checkboxes for the Tools group and the latest Android SDK, as in Figure 26, *Installing the Android SDK*, on page 154. Click the install button, and wait for the process to complete.

For the next step, configure the Eclipse IDE for Android development. Download and install the Eclipse Classic package[10] for your system. Launch

6. http://calaba.sh
7. http://developer.android.com/sdk
8. http://eclipse.org
9. http://code.google.com/p/robotium
10. http://www.eclipse.org/downloads

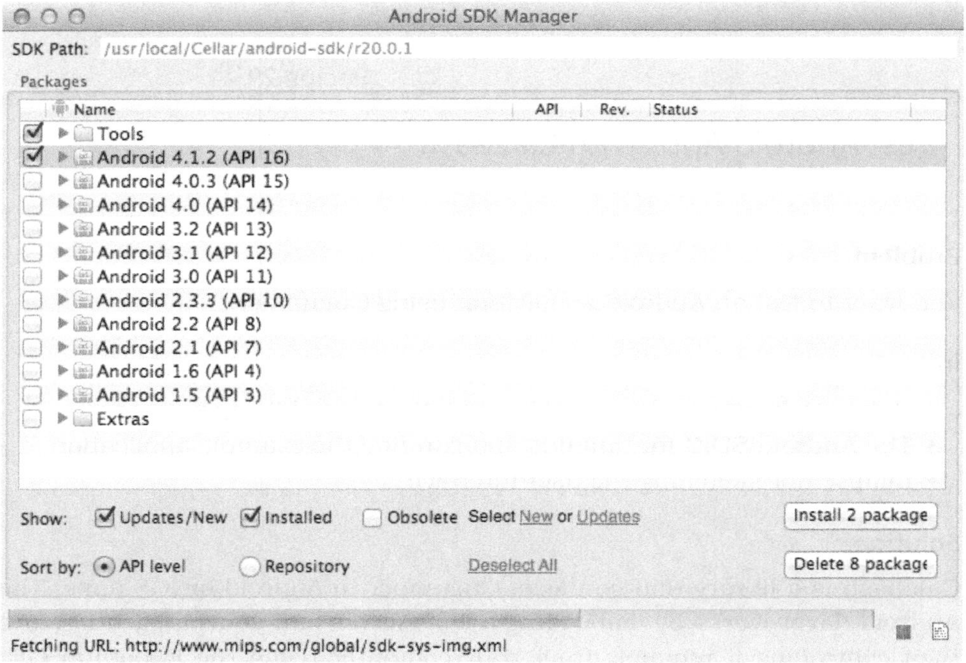

Figure 26—Installing the Android SDK

Eclipse, and choose the Help → Install New Software menu item. Type https://dl-ssl.google.com/android/eclipse into the Work with: field, and press Enter.

The list of Eclipse add-ons should update with a couple of Android packages; see Figure 27, *Installing the Android Developer Tools*, on page 155. Select the Developer Tools package, and click your way through the rest of the wizard.

You'll need to restart Eclipse. When you do, the IDE will prompt you to install or use an SDK. Choose Use existing SDKs, and navigate to the location where you extracted the zip file earlier.

The last step for setting up Eclipse is to prepare the Android simulator. Choose Window → AVD Manager from the menu. Create a new device targeted at the ARM processor with the latest Android SDK; see Figure 28, *Creating an emulated device*, on page 156.

Once you have Eclipse and the Android SDK set up, installing Calabash is easy.

```
$ gem install calabash-android
```

Now, you're ready to write some features.

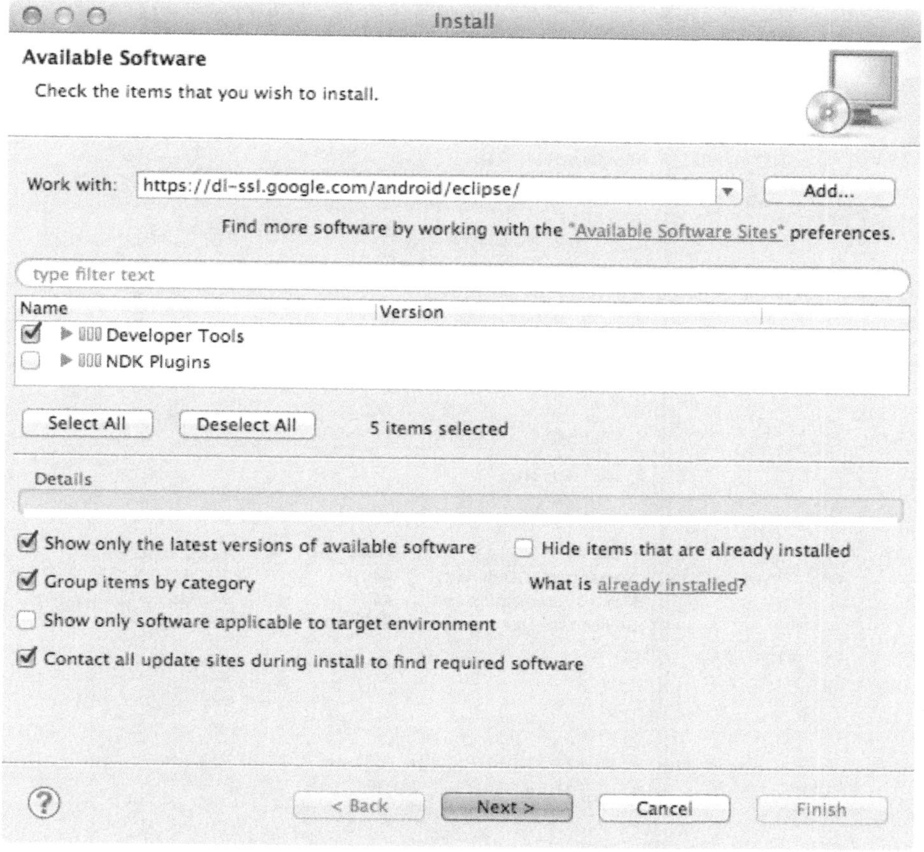

Figure 27—Installing the Android Developer Tools

Feature

We're going to build a simple app for bookmarking websites. The user interface will have a text field, an Add button, and a list control. When you type a URL and click Add, the new URL will show up on the list.

Here's how you might describe this behavior using a Cucumber feature:

android/features/bookmark.feature

```
Feature: Bookmarks

  Scenario: Bookmark a URL
    When I bookmark "http://pragprog.com"
    Then I should see the following bookmarks:
      | url                 |
      | http://pragprog.com |
```

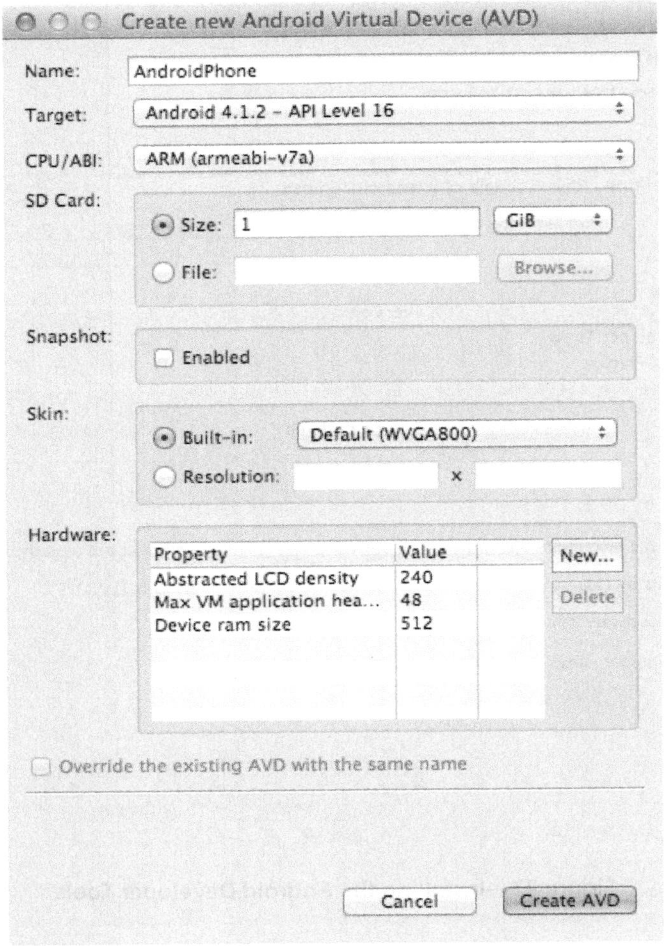

Figure 28—Creating an emulated device

Before we run this through Cucumber, let's create the empty skeleton of an Android application.

App Skeleton

In Eclipse, choose File → New Project from the menu. Select the Android Application Project type. Type Bookmarkerist for the project name, and leave the other options at their default values. Hit Next until the wizard prompts you to create an activity. Choose the BlankActivity option. Click your way through the rest of the wizard, leaving the settings at their defaults.

For Calabash to connect to Bookmarkerist, we'll need to add Internet access to the requested permissions. Double-click AndroidManifest.xml, navigate to the Permissions tab, click Add → Uses Permission, and choose android.permission.INTERNET from the list.

We haven't added any behavior yet, but this skeleton of an app should be just enough to connect to from Calabash. Click the Run button in the toolbar, and wait for the application to start in the simulator. This may take several minutes.

Once the app is running, navigate to your project directory on the command line, and type the following command:

```
$ calabash-android gen
```

This generates a features directory with some hooks and step definitions built in. Delete features/my_first.feature, and add a new file called features/bookmark.feature with the code from *Feature*, on page 155.

```
$ calabash-android run bin/Bookmarkerist.apk
```

Calabash will attach its TCP server to the app and then attempt to control it. Of course, we don't have any step definitions yet. Writing those will require names for our GUI controls, so let's do a little work on the app next.

App Behavior

In the file browser on the left, double-click res\layout\activity_main.xml.

This will launch a GUI editor. From the palette on the left, drag an EditText, a Button, and a ListView into the layout area, as in Figure 29, *Laying out the controls*, on page 158.

Name the controls url, addUrl, and bookmarks, respectively. Right-click ListView, and choose Preview List Content → Simple List Item.

Next, you'll write code to implement the controls' behavior. Open src/com/example/bookmarkerist/MainActivity.java, and edit the beginning of the class to look like the following:

android/src/com/example/bookmarkerist/MainActivity.java

```
public class MainActivity extends Activity {
    ArrayAdapter<String> adapter;
    ListView bookmarks;
    EditText url;
    @Override
    public void onCreate(Bundle savedInstanceState) {
        super.onCreate(savedInstanceState);
        setContentView(R.layout.activity_main);
```

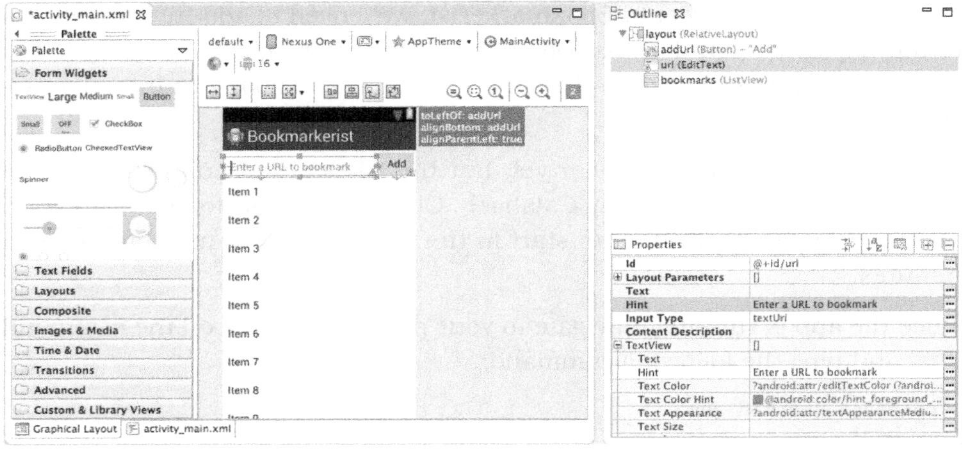

Figure 29—Laying out the controls

```
        url = (EditText)findViewById(R.id.url);
        adapter = new ArrayAdapter<String>(
            this, android.R.layout.simple_list_item_1);
        bookmarks = (ListView)findViewById(R.id.bookmarks);
        bookmarks.setAdapter(adapter);
    }
    public void addBookmark(View v) {
        adapter.add(url.getText().toString());
        adapter.notifyDataSetChanged();
        url.setText("");
    }
    // ... rest of class ...
}
```

A couple of the declarations at the top of the class will have red exclamation points next to them in Eclipse. Click each of these in turn, and choose Import *«class»* to generate import statements. Rerun the app in the simulator.

Step Definitions

Now, it's time to implement the step definitions. Calabash comes with a library of step definitions such as When I press the "Add" button. But we prefer not to have the details of user interface elements in our top-level Cucumber features. Instead, you can use the source code to these built-ins as a guide.[11]

Create a new file called features/step_definitions/bookmark_steps.rb with the following code:

11. https://github.com/calabash/calabash-android/tree/master/ruby-gem/lib/calabash-android/steps

android/features/step_definitions/bookmark_steps.rb

```
When /^I bookmark "(.*?)"$/ do |url|
  performAction 'enter_text_into_numbered_field', url, 1
  performAction 'click_on_view_by_id', 'addUrl'
end
```

The performAction calls use the Robotium API to interact with controls in the app. You can reference controls by their order in the UI or by the ID you gave them in Eclipse. Here, we click the first (and only) text field in the app and then click the addUrl button.

The Then step just needs to fetch the list of bookmarks from the GUI.

android/features/step_definitions/bookmark_steps.rb

```
Then /^I should see the following bookmarks:$/ do |expected|
  performAction 'wait_for_text', 'Enter a URL to bookmark', 5
  result = performAction 'get_list_item_text'
  actual = result['bonusInformation']
  actual.each_with_index do | row_data, index |
    row_data = JSON.parse row_data
    actual[index] = row_data
  end
  expected.map_headers! 'url' => 'text1'
  expected.diff! actual
end
```

The list contents come back to us as an array of JSON strings. Here, we assemble them into a table that Cucumber can understand. Android calls the list contents text1, but we'd rather use the more reader-friendly name of url. The techniques in Recipe 1, *Compare and Transform Tables of Data*, on page 2 allow us to map from one name to the other.

Try rerunning the Calabash steps again. You won't see the app launch in the simulator, but your Cucumber steps will connect to it behind the scenes. The result should be a series of passing tests.

Further Exploration

Calabash also comes in an iOS flavor.[12] While we prefer an iOS-specific solution if you're specifically targeting iOS, it may be worth giving calabash-ios a shot if you're writing for both platforms.

While Calabash is an open source project, the company behind it also offers a paid service where they run your tests on a variety of devices in their lab.[13]

12. https://github.com/calabash/calabash-ios
13. https://www.lesspainful.com

Recipe 30

Parse HTML Tables

Problem

You're testing a web page containing tabular data (or any repeating data, really), and you need to compare the contents to a table in your Cucumber scenario.

Ingredients

- Capybara[14] for testing web applications
- Capybara's arsenal of *finders*[15] for traversing patterns in HTML
- XPath[16] for describing the locations of objects on the page

Solution

Capybara is a Ruby web testing library. It provides a simple API for visiting web pages and parsing the results. Behind the scenes, Capybara will either launch a real browser (for non-Ruby web apps) or call directly into the server code (for Ruby apps built on Rails, Sinatra, or any other Rack framework).

In this recipe, you'll serve a simple static site using the Sinatra framework and then use Capybara to find the right table on the page and extract the contents. Imagine you have a web page containing team rankings for a lawn darts league, something like this:

Leagues Administration

Ranking	Team
1	Earache My Eye
2	Front Yardigans

You'd like to match the results against the ones you expect your algorithm to return. Any web testing library can scrape a bunch of raw HTML off the page and hand it to you for processing. But then it'd be up to you to use a DOM parsing library to loop through that HTML and extract the team names.

Capybara's finders can spare you that agony. Let's see how.

14. http://jnicklas.github.com/capybara
15. http://rubydoc.info/github/jnicklas/capybara/master/Capybara/Node/Finders:find
16. http://www.w3.org/TR/xpath

The Application

For this recipe, we'll serve the data as a static HTML file. Put the following markup in public/lawn_darts.html:

html_tables/public/lawn_darts.html
```
<!doctype html>
<title>Lawn Darts</title>
<table>
  <tr>
    <td><a href="#">Leagues</a></td>
    <td><a href="#">Administration</a></td>
  </tr>
</table>

<table>
  <tr>
    <th>Ranking</th>
    <th>Team</th>
  </tr>
  <tr>
    <td>1</td>
    <td>Earache My Eye</td>
  </tr>
  <tr>
    <td>2</td>
    <td>Front Yardigans</td>
  </tr>
</table>
```

Notice that this markup is devoid of id or name attributes, CSS classes, or anything else that we could easily grab hold of from our tests. If we have control over the HTML generation code, we should inject some kind of identifiers to make elements easy to find.

For this recipe, we're going to assume (as is the case on some real-world projects) that you're stuck with the markup you get. As we'll see, the tests won't be fiendishly complicated—the secret is to isolate the brittle parts (which might break if the design changes) in a single part of the code.

You could use Capybara with this file right now by connecting it to the Selenium browser-based framework. But let's wrap a trivial Ruby application around it instead so that we can test through the much faster Rack interface.

First, install the Rack-based Sinatra web framework.

```
$ gem install sinatra
```

Now, create a file called lawn_darts_app.rb with the following contents:

html_tables/lawn_darts_app.rb
```
require 'sinatra/base'

class LawnDartsApp < Sinatra::Base
end
```

Now that we have a Ruby web interface, we can drive this static site from Cucumber.

Test Setup

Here's a Cucumber scenario that will check the contents of the table containing our teams. This code goes in features/league.feature.

html_tables/features/league.feature
```
Feature: Lawn darts league

  Scenario: View teams
    When I view the league page
    Then I should see the following teams:
      | Ranking | Team            |
      |       1 | Earache My Eye  |
      |       2 | Front Yardigans |
```

Because this test uses Capybara, now is a good time to install it.

```
$ gem install capybara
```

You'll need to connect Cucumber to Capybara by putting the following code in features/support/env.rb:

html_tables/features/support/env.rb
```
require 'capybara/cucumber'
require './lawn_darts_app'

Capybara.app = LawnDartsApp
```

Now that Cucumber can drive the site, it's time to add step definitions to retrieve and process the HTML.

Scraping HTML

In the first step definition, Capybara needs visit the league page. Create a file called features/step_definitions/league_steps.rb with the following contents:

html_tables/features/step_definitions/league_steps.rb
```
When /^I view the league page$/ do
  visit '/lawn_darts.html'
end
```

Once we've hit the page, Capybara has the contents ready for us to slice and dice. We'll do that in the Then step.

html_tables/features/step_definitions/league_steps.rb

```
Line 1 Then /^I should see the following teams:$/ do |expected|
     2   rows   = find('table:nth-of-type(2)').all('tr')
     3   actual = rows.map { |r| r.all('th,td').map { |c| c.text } }
     4   expected.diff! actual
     5 end
```

Let's walk through that step line by line. At line 2, Capybara's find() method retrieves the table element that contains the teams. This is actually the second table on the page (the first one contains navigation links), so we need to use XPath's nth-of-type modifier.

Once we have the table, we call the all() method on it to retrieve all the <tr> elements on the page.

Each <tr> element may contain multiple cells in the form of <th> or <td> elements. On line 3, we loop through each row's cells and retrieve the contents.

Finally, on line 4, we use Cucumber's diff!() method to compare the actual table against the expected value and report a test failure if there are any differences.

As we've seen, comparing HTML tables is just a matter of combining two simple pieces. A web scraping library like Capybara does the initial work of converting the HTML into a standard Ruby array. Cucumber takes over from there and compares the native Ruby data to what's in the scenario.

Further Exploration

In this recipe, we tested a Ruby-based web app through a Ruby-specific test interface. For non-Ruby apps, you can use Capybara with a web browser through the Selenium layer; see Recipe 3, *Run Slow Setup/Teardown Code with Global Hooks*, on page 13 for an example that uses Selenium.

For more information about comparing tables in Cucumber, see Recipe 1, *Compare and Transform Tables of Data*, on page 2.

Recipe 31

Drive JavaScript/CoffeeScript Using Cucumber-JS

Problem

You're testing JavaScript code that's running either on the server side in a framework like Node.js or in the browser. You'd like to use the familiar Cucumber syntax to drive your JavaScript (or possibly CoffeeScript) code.

Ingredients

- Cucumber-JS,[17] an implementation of Cucumber written in JavaScript
- Node.js (or just Node),[18] a JavaScript application framework
- Node Package Manager,[19] the main way of installing libraries into Node
- CoffeeScript,[20] a more elegant syntax for JavaScript

Solution

JavaScript runs in a lot of environments, from GUI code in the browser to back-end server frameworks like Node.js. In this recipe, we're going to write a simple Cucumber test for some JavaScript code (CoffeeScript, actually—more on that in a moment).

You'll run the test in Cucumber-JS, a pure-JavaScript implementation of Cucumber. Cucumber-JS should run fine anywhere JavaScript runs, meaning that you could run your tests in a browser or in a local copy of Node.js on your development machine. For simplicity and rapid turnaround, we'll choose the latter.

Cucumber-JS works just fine with vanilla JavaScript. But it also has explicit support for CoffeeScript, Jeremy Ashkenas' delightful reimagining of JavaScript. CoffeeScript provides a lightweight syntax optimized for maintainability but compiles down to simple JavaScript.

We'll go ahead and use CoffeeScript for the code in this section, because it really is that easy to plug it in.

---

17. https://github.com/cucumber/cucumber-js
18. http://nodejs.org
19. https://npmjs.org
20. http://www.coffeescript.org

Feature

For this recipe, we'll test a control panel that has a single button and a readout. In a salute to *The Hitchhiker's Guide to the Galaxy [Ada95]*, the control panel will chide anyone who clicks the button. First, though, we'll need to get our dependencies installed.

Setting up Cucumber-JS for feature development is really easy. First, download and run the Node installer for your platform.[21] This will also put NPM on your system. You can then use NPM to install Cucumber-JS.

```
$ npm install -g cucumber
```

Now, put the following code in features/control_panel.feature:

javascript/features/control_panel.feature

```
Feature: Control panel

  Scenario: Press a button
    Given the sign is unlit
    When I press the button
    Then the sign should light up with
      """
      Please do not press this button again
      """
```

If you try to run this feature from the command line...

```
$ cucumber.js
```

you'll get the standard message about missing step definitions, but with the sample code excerpts in JavaScript rather than Ruby. Let's fill in those definitions now.

Step Definitions

Just as with regular Cucumber, you'll typically keep step definitions in the features/step_definitions directory. The only difference is that you'll use .js or .coffee files instead of .rb ones.

The general outline of a step definition would look like this in JavaScript:

```
var stepDefinitions = function() {
  this.Given(/^the sign is unlit/, function(callback) {
    this.controlPanel.deactivateSign();
    callback();
  });
};
module.exports = stepDefinitions;
```

21. http://nodejs.org/download

To define a step, you call the Given(), When(), or Then() method and pass it a function containing your step definition. Your function will get called whenever Cucumber-JS encounters a matching step in a feature file. If you need to share something between steps—such as the controlPanel instance—you store it as a property of the this object.

The main difference from regular Cucumber is that each step definition also gets a callback parameter, which you must remember to call after your step runs—this is Cucumber-JS's cue to move on to the next test step.

Here's the CoffeeScript equivalent of the previous code; from here on out, all the examples will be in CoffeeScript.

javascript/features/step_definitions/control_panel_steps.coffee

```
stepDefinitions = () ->
  @Given /^the sign is unlit/, (callback) ->
    @controlPanel.deactivateSign()
    callback()

module.exports = stepDefinitions
```

We're using an object called @controlPanel. Where does that get created? It gets created in the World, which we initialize in features/support/support/World.coffee.

javascript/features/support/World.coffee

```
{ControlPanel} = require './ControlPanel'
World = (callback) ->
  @controlPanel = new ControlPanel
  callback()
exports.World = World
```

We'll define the ControlPanel in a moment. First, let's round out the step definitions. Unlike classic Cucumber, you have to bring the World into your step definitions explicitly. Add the following code just inside your stepDefinitions function:

javascript/features/step_definitions/control_panel_steps.coffee

```
@World = require('../support/World').World
```

Now, we're ready to move on to the When and Then steps.

javascript/features/step_definitions/control_panel_steps.coffee

```
@When /^I press the button$/, (callback) ->
  @controlPanel.pressButton()
  callback()

@Then /^the sign should light up with/, (expected, callback) ->
  strictEqual @controlPanel.signMessage(), expected
  callback()
```

To check that the sign is displaying the correct text, we're using the strictEqual assertion from Node's assert library. We need to bring that function into our step definition file's namespace before we can call it. This code goes at the very top of your step definitions file:

javascript/features/step_definitions/control_panel_steps.coffee
```
{strictEqual} = require 'assert'
```

With the tests in place, we can move on to the actual project code.

Implementation

Here's an implementation of the CoffeeScript object that will get your tests passing. For this project, we'll just keep this code in the support directory, in a file called ControlPanel.coffee.

javascript/features/support/ControlPanel.coffee
```
class ControlPanel
  constructor: ->
    @message = ''

  signMessage: ->
    @message

  deactivateSign: ->
    @message = ''

  pressButton: ->
    @message = 'Please do not press this button again'

exports.ControlPanel = ControlPanel
```

Now, when you rerun your tests, they should pass.

Further Exploration

Once your tests are passing on your development machine, where do you go from here? That depends on the environment your JavaScript code will eventually be running in.

If you're writing a pure-JavaScript app using a framework like Express,[22] you can use a headless (simulated) browser to test your app directly in Node.[23] If your app is a mix of JavaScript on the client side and something like Ruby or PHP on the server, you can test your JavaScript features directly in a real web browser.[24]

---

22. http://expressjs.com
23. https://github.com/olivoil/NodeBDD
24. https://github.com/jbpros/cukecipes

Recipe 32

Test a Web App Using Watir

Problem

You want to test a web application across several browsers, including Chrome, Firefox, Safari, Internet Explorer, and Opera.

Ingredients

- Watir (Web Application Testing in Ruby),[25] a programmer-friendly in-browser test library
- WebDriver,[26] a cross-platform API for controlling web browsers
- Watir WebDriver,[27] a Watir implementation that uses WebDriver under the hood
- Nokogiri,[28] a Ruby library for parsing HTML results
- (Mac users) SafariWatir[29] for testing in Safari
- (Chrome users) ChromeDriver,[30] a stand-alone program that helps Watir control Google Chrome

Solution

Watir is a Ruby browser automation library focused on ease of use. Watir started its life as a simple, Ruby-focused library—in contrast to Selenium, which supported multiple programming languages but was harder to use from Ruby. The main downside of Watir at the time was that you needed additional tools to support browsers other than Internet Explorer.

The two toolkits have grown toward each other in recent years. Selenium has adopted a new, easier-to-use API. Watir now supports multiple browsers much

25. http://www.watir.com
26. http://webdriver.googlecode.com
27. http://www.watirwebdriver.com
28. http://nokogiri.org
29. http://wiki.openqa.org/display/WTR/SafariWatir
30. http://chromedriver.googlecode.com

more seamlessly—in a delightful twist, it does so by using Selenium under the hood.

In this recipe, we're going to write a simple browser-based test using Watir.

Setup

First, let's get Watir installed on your system. On Windows, you'd start with the watir gem.

```
C:\> gem install watir
```

On any operating system (including Windows), you'll need the watir-webdriver gem if you want to test browsers other than Internet Explorer.

```
$ gem install watir-webdriver
```

Finally, on the Mac, you'll likely want safariwatir.

```
$ gem install safariwatir
```

If you plan on testing with Chrome, you'll need ChromeDriver[31] as well. This is just a stand-alone program that you copy into a directory on your PATH.

On its own, Watir does a great job of controlling the browser: following links, filling in text fields, and so on. But it doesn't have many tools for checking results—for verifying that what's on the page is what you expect to see.

For extracting specific HTML elements to check in our test, we'll turn to Nokogiri, one of Ruby's most beloved HTML parsers. Nokogiri relies on two C libraries called libxml2 and libxslt, both of which are available on multiple platforms.[32]

To install these C libraries on Ubuntu Linux, you would run the following command:

```
$ sudo apt-get install libxml2-dev libxslt1-dev
```

Here's the Mac equivalent if you're using Homebrew:

```
$ brew install libxml2 libxslt
```

On Windows, you don't need to do anything; Nokogiri comes bundled with the required XML libraries.

Once you take care of the dependencies, installing Nokogiri is straightforward.

```
$ gem install nokogiri
```

---

31. http://code.google.com/p/chromedriver/downloads/list
32. http://xmlsoft.org/

Whew! All this setup just for a simple web test. The payoff comes when we see how easy it is to drive a web browser.

Driving the Browser

Let's write a test that visits your Pragmatic Bookshelf account and makes sure you have access to a list of your purchased books. Place the following code in features/bookshelf.feature:

watir/features/bookshelf.feature

```
Feature: Bookshelf

  Scenario: Purchased books
    Given I am logged in
    When I view my account
    Then I should see a sorted list of purchased books
```

We'll need to launch the browser once at the beginning of the test run and shut it down as Cucumber is exiting. To do this, we'll use the technique from Recipe 3, *Run Slow Setup/Teardown Code with Global Hooks*, on page 13. Add the following code to features/support/env.rb. Feel free to substitute :firefox, :safari, :ie, or :opera for the browser.

watir/features/support/env.rb

```
require 'watir-webdriver'
require 'nokogiri'

module HasBrowser
  @@browser = Watir::Browser.new :chrome
  at_exit { @@browser.close }

  def browser
    @@browser
  end
end

World HasBrowser
```

Now, let's turn our attention to the step definitions. The first thing our implementation needs to do is visit the account page and log in.

Rather than keeping your Pragmatic credentials in a source file that may get checked into revision control, let's stash them in a pair of environment variables we can read from our step definitions. Run the following code in your Mac or Linux shell, using your actual email address and password:

```
$ export PRAG_EMAIL=somebody@example.com
$ export PRAG_PASSWORD=sekrit
```

Here's the Windows version of the same commands:

```
C:\> SET PRAG_EMAIL=somebody@example.com
C:\> SET PRAG_PASSWORD=sekrit
```

With Watir, you can find HTML elements on a page using their name attribute, their CSS class or ID, or an XPath expression. For this step, we need to find the text fields named email and password. Here's the first step definition in features/step_definitions/bookshelf_steps.rb:

watir/features/step_definitions/bookshelf_steps.rb

```
EmailField    = '//div[@id="content"]//input[@name="email"]'
PasswordField = '//div[@id="content"]//input[@name="password"]'
SubmitButton  = '//div[@id="content"]//button[@type="submit"]'
Given /^I am logged in$/ do
  browser.goto 'http://pragprog.com/login'
  browser.text_field(:xpath => EmailField   ).set ENV['PRAG_EMAIL']
  browser.text_field(:xpath => PasswordField).set ENV['PRAG_PASSWORD']
  browser.button(:xpath => SubmitButton).click
end
```

Watir will wait until the form finishes submitting and the account page loads. From there, visiting the bookshelf page is easy.

watir/features/step_definitions/bookshelf_steps.rb

```
When /^I view my account$/ do
  browser.goto 'http://pragprog.com/my_bookshelf'
end
```

The last remaining task is to go through the HTML on the bookshelf page and make sure it contains the correct book titles.

Parsing the Results

Here's a simplified version of the HTML containing the book titles:

```
<table id="bookshelf">
  <tr>
    <td class="description">
      <h4>The Cucumber Book</h4>
    </td>
  </tr>
</table>
```

There are a couple of ways to identify the <h4> element containing the title. We could use an XPath expression or CSS selectors. XPath is a little more flexible, but CSS is good enough for this simple example. Here's how to look for an <h4> inside a <td> inside a table row.

watir/features/step_definitions/bookshelf_steps.rb

```
Then /^I should see a sorted list of purchased books$/ do
  doc = Nokogiri::HTML browser.html
  titles = doc.css('table#bookshelf tr td.description p.title').map &:text
  titles.should_not be_empty
  titles.should == titles.sort_by(&:upcase)
end
```

Now, run your features. You should see your browser launch, fill in the form fields, visit the bookshelf page, and exit. For extra credit, try swapping browsers by changing the browser name in env.rb.

Matt says:

Choosing Between Watir and Capybara

We wanted to include this chapter in the original *Cucumber Book* because Watir is such a popular tool in the testing community, but we ran out of time to write it. We did, however, write about Capybara. (Capybara is also featured in the book you're reading now; see Recipe 13, *Manipulate Time*, on page 67; Recipe 4, *Refactor to Extract Your Own Application Driver DSL*, on page 18; and Recipe 30, *Parse HTML Tables*, on page 160.)

Now that you've seen examples of both Watir and Capybara, how do you choose between them? It's largely a matter of personal taste. The two APIs are quite different.

Watir focuses more on the Document Object Model (DOM)—the structure of the page—whereas Capybara mirrors the kinds of actions that a real user would take (such as filling in fields or selecting checkboxes). Both allow you to use CSS or XPath selectors when you need to reach beneath the covers to do something difficult. Capybara does better at handling the timing issues that crop up during the testing of asynchronous JavaScript code.

I recommend running a timeboxed experiment (for a week or two, say) where you try both. Make your decision at the end of the experiment once you have some practical experience with both of them.

Further Exploration

The Watir family of tools has excellent documentation: detailed instructions for multiple platforms, getting-started examples, API descriptions, and so on. In particular, the open source Watir book[33] is an enjoyable reference.

33. http://watir.com/book

Recipe 33

Test a PHP App with cuke4php

Problem

You want to be able to run quick tests of your PHP app without the overhead of launching a browser.

Ingredients

- PHP 5.3.*x*[34]
- Cuke4php,[35] a tool for writing step definitions in PHP
- Cucumber's wire protocol,[36] used behind the scenes by Cuke4php
- The PHPUnit test framework[37] for assertions
- (Optional) An environment for running full browser tests afterward: Selenium, Firefox, and a web server

Solution

You're probably testing your PHP app at a few different layers. At the bottom layer, you may be using PHPUnit to test individual classes and functions. At the top layer, you might have something like Selenium for testing the app in a live browser.

Cuke4php sits somewhere in the middle. It lets you test the business logic of your app in plain English (like Cucumber). But it does so by driving your PHP code through a Cucumber-specific protocol, rather than going through the browser. The result is a fast integration test that you can quickly run on your code base before sharing changes with your colleagues.

This style of testing is much easier if your app's user interface is just a thin layer over the business logic, that is, if your user-facing .php files contain only display information. For this recipe, we'll create such an app: a temperature converter. The main index.php file will be mostly HTML markup, with just a little code to direct the user's choices into kelvinator.php, where the real work happens.

---

34. http://www.php.net/downloads.php
35. https://github.com/olbrich/cuke4php/wiki
36. https://github.com/cucumber/cucumber/wiki/Wire-Protocol
37. https://github.com/sebastianbergmann/phpunit

Setup

For this recipe, you'll need to have PHP already on your system.[38] Installation varies widely by platform, so there's no single recipe I can provide here.

First, install PHPUnit. The easiest way to do this is using the PEAR packaging tool. If you don't already have PEAR, download http://pear.php.net/go-pear.phar and run the following:

```
$ php go-pear.phar
```

With PEAR ready to go, you can use it to fetch and install PHPUnit.

```
$ pear config-set auto_discover 1
$ pear install pear.phpunit.de/PHPunit
```

At this point, you may want to do a quick sanity check on the installation. Add the PHPUnit directory (PEAR will tell you this when you install) to your PATH environment variable. Then, type in a simple PHPUnit test case and save it as test.php.

php/test.php

```
<?php
class SimpleTest extends PHPUnit_Framework_TestCase {
    public function testMath() {
        $this->assertEquals(2 + 2, 4);
    }
}
?>
```

Now, run the test.

```
$ phpunit test.php
PHPUnit 3.6.10 by Sebastian Bergmann.

.

Time: 0 seconds, Memory: 4.50Mb

OK (1 test, 1 assertion)
```

The last piece of the puzzle is Cuke4php. This is a collection of PHP and Ruby code, packaged as a Ruby gem.

```
$ gem install cuke4php
```

Now, you're ready to test some PHP.

---

38. http://php.net/manual/en/install.php

Feature

Let's start with a Cucumber description of our temperature converter. Add the following code to features/kelvinator.feature:

php/features/kelvinator.feature

```
Feature: Kelvinator

  Scenario: Centigrade to Kelvin
    Given a temperature of 100 degrees centigrade
    When I convert it to Kelvin
    Then the result should be 373 degrees Kelvin
```

Normally, this is the point at which you'd run the unimplemented features and generate some boilerplate step definitions. But because we're testing PHP, you'll need to do a little configuration first.

Cuke4php is actually a server that runs your PHP code in a stand-alone process. Cucumber connects through that server through its wire protocol. You'll need to add a file in the features/step_definitions directory called Cuke4PHP.wire with the following contents:

php/features/step_definitions/Cuke4PHP.wire

```
host: localhost
port: <%= ENV['CUKE4PHP_PORT'] %>
```

Don't worry about setting that environment variable; Cuke4php will do that for you.

Step Definitions

Just as you would do when running Cucumber with Ruby, run Cuke4php without any step definitions to generate some boilerplate code. Notice we're using the cuke4php command, rather than plain cucumber. The new command sets up environment variables, fires up a server to run PHP, and then hands off to the real Cucumber.

Here's what the output should look like, complete with boilerplate step definitions at the bottom:

```
$ cuke4php features
Feature: Kelvinator

  Scenario: Centigrade to Kelvin                    # features/kelvinator.feature:3
    Given a temperature of 100 degrees centigrade # features/kelvinator.feature:4
    When I convert it to Kelvin                   # features/kelvinator.feature:5
    Then the result should be 373 degrees Kelvin  # features/kelvinator.feature:6

1 scenario (1 undefined)
3 steps (3 undefined)
```

```
0m0.012s

You can implement step definitions for undefined steps with these snippets:


/**
* Given /^a temperature of 100 degrees centigrade$/
**/
public function stepATemperatureOf100DegreesCentigrade() {
    self::markPending();
}


/**
* When /^I convert it to Kelvin$/
**/
public function stepIConvertItToKelvin() {
    self::markPending();
}


/**
* Then /^the result should be 373 degrees Kelvin$/
**/
public function stepTheResultShouldBe373DegreesKelvin() {
    self::markPending();
}
```

Rather than handing us Ruby snippets, Cuke4php has supplied PHP ones. Create a new file called features/step_definitions/KelvinatorSteps.php with the following structure:

php/features/step_definitions/KelvinatorSteps.php

```
<?php
class KelvinatorSteps extends CucumberSteps {
    // Your step definitions will go here
}
?>
```

Now, paste the empty step definitions from the command line into the body of your KelvinatorSteps class. When you rerun the tests, the steps should be marked as pending, rather than undefined.

Drive the Tested Code

Just like classic Cucumber, Cuke4php matches step definitions via regular expression. The only difference is that with PHP, you just put the regex in a comment block before your step definition, rather than passing it in as a parameter. Let's work on the Given step first.

php/features/step_definitions/KelvinatorSteps.php

```
1 /**
2 * Given /^a temperature of (\d+) degrees centigrade$/
3 **/
4 public function stepATemperatureOfDegreesCentigrade($centigrade) {
5     $this->aGlobals['centigrade'] = $centigrade;
6 }
```

We've only needed to change three things from the boilerplate code snippet to get this step definition working. First, we've changed the specific temperature in the regular expression on line 2 to capture any sequence of digits. Next, we've added a $centigrade parameter to the function at line 4. Finally, at line 5, we're storing the temperature in a shared array called aGlobals that Cuke4php furnishes for keeping data around between steps.

The When step is much simpler; it doesn't need any changes to the regex or the signature. All it needs to do is store the converted temperature for later comparison.

php/features/step_definitions/KelvinatorSteps.php

```
/**
 * When /^I convert it to Kelvin$/
 **/
public function stepIConvertItToKelvin() {
    $this->aGlobals['kelvin'] = kelvinate(
        $this->aGlobals['centigrade']);
}
```

The final step definition needs to compare the Kelvin value calculated by your app against the value you expect.

php/features/step_definitions/KelvinatorSteps.php

```
1 /**
2  * Then /^the result should be (\d+) degrees Kelvin$/
3  **/
4 public function stepTheResultShouldBe3DegreesKelvin($expected) {
5     self::assertEquals($this->aGlobals['kelvin'], $expected);
6 }
```

As with the Given step, you'll need to add a capture group to the regular expression and a parameter to the function. The assertion on line 5 comes straight from PHPUnit; you can use any of their rich library of assertions.[39]

Implement the Tested Code

Now that we have failing tests, it's time to implement the application. Put the following code in kelvinator.php:

39. http://www.phpunit.de/manual/3.4/en/appendixes.assertions.html

php/kelvinator.php

```
<?php
function kelvinate($centigrade) {
    return $centigrade + 273;
}
?>
```

The top-level application will be in index.php. It's just a thin wrapper around the logic you've already written.

php/index.php

```
<!doctype html>
<html>
  <head>
    <meta charset="utf-8">
    <title>Kelvinator</title>
  </head>

  <body>
    <h1>Kelvinator</h1>
<?
    if (array_key_exists("centigrade", $_GET)) {
      require("kelvinator.php");
      $centigrade = $_GET["centigrade"];
      $kelvin = kelvinate($centigrade);
?>
    <p><?= $centigrade ?> °C is <span id="kelvin"><?= $kelvin ?> °K</span></p>
<?
    } else {
?>
    <form action="index.php" method="GET">
      <input name="centigrade" type="text">
      <label for="centigrade">°C</label>
      <input type="submit" value="Kelvinate!">
    </form>
<?
    }
?>
  </body>

</html>
```

Actually, the main file could be even thinner than this. You could put the decision of whether to render the form in a different .php file so that it's easier to test. But that's a lot of moving parts for what's supposed to be short recipe, so we'll just keep it simple for now.

You'll need to teach your step definitions where the kelvinate() function lives. Add a require() line to KelvinatorSteps.php, just before your class definition.

php/features/step_definitions/KelvinatorSteps.php
```
require('kelvinator.php');
```

Now, when you rerun cuke4php, you should see passing tests.

Test in the Browser

We've just seen how Cuke4php can test application-level logic without a browser. This can be useful for testing on your development machine, where fast turnaround time is of paramount importance.

But at some point, you probably want to test the app in a real browser as well—perhaps on a powerful, centralized build server. If your user interface is just a thin wrapper around your application logic, you may even be able to reuse some of your Cuke4php tests as full-on Cucumber tests. That's what we'll to do in this section.

At this point, you'll need to launch a web server and put index.php and kelvinator.php where your server can see them. On a Mac, you can just copy the two files to the Sites folder in your home directory and then turn on Personal Web Sharing in your System Preferences.

You'll be using the Selenium WebDriver library for this part of the recipe, so install that now if you don't already have it.

```
$ gem install selenium-webdriver
```

We're going to keep the Ruby definitions in a separate directory from the PHP implementations. browser seems like a good name for this directory. Create a file called browser/env.rb, and put the following code in it:

php/browser/env.rb
```
require 'selenium-webdriver'

module HasBrowser
  @@browser = Selenium::WebDriver.for :firefox
  at_exit { @@browser.quit }

  def browser
    @@browser
  end
end

World(HasBrowser)
```

This code starts Firefox at the beginning of the test and shuts it down at the end, using the techniques from Recipe 3, *Run Slow Setup/Teardown Code with Global Hooks*, on page 13.

Now, you're ready to fill in the Ruby step definitions in browser/kelvinator_steps.rb. You may need to adjust the path on line 6 if you're serving the PHP from somewhere other than your home user account.

php/browser/kelvinator_steps.rb

```
1  Given /^a temperature of (\d+) degrees centigrade$/ do |centigrade|
2    @centigrade = centigrade.to_i
3  end
4  
5  When /^I convert it to Kelvin$/ do
6    browser.navigate.to "http://localhost/~#{ENV['USER']}/index.php"
7    input = browser.find_element :name, 'centigrade'
8    input.send_keys @centigrade.to_s
9    input.submit
10 
11   output = browser.find_element :id, 'kelvin'
12   @kelvin = output.text.to_i
13 end
14 
15 Then /^the result should be (\d+) degrees Kelvin$/ do |expected|
16   @kelvin.should == expected.to_i
17 end
```

You'll notice that the behavior inside the steps is similar. The Given step remembers the input temperature, the When step drives the application to perform the conversion, and the Then step compares the result. The only difference is that you're driving the full application through the browser, rather than undercutting the user interface.

To run these tests using the full browser, pass the browser directory to Cucumber on the command line.

```
$ cucumber -rbrowser features
```

You should now see the same tests run, using Firefox instead of the Cucumber wire protocol. The test will be quite a bit slower: five to ten times on my machine.

Further Exploration

When you take the "thin user interface" technique to its logical extreme, you get the Presenter First style of application,[40] where literally every GUI action is a trivial function call. The result is that you can test even your high-level user-facing code without having to fire up a graphical application or web server.

40. https://en.wikipedia.org/wiki/Presenter_First

Recipe 34

Play Back Canned Network Data Using VCR

Problem

You're testing an app that relies on one or more third-party, HTTP-based APIs. You're worried about what will happen to your test results if one of the APIs you use times out or starts returning different data than what you expected.

Ingredients

- VCR,[41] a library that can record a live HTTP interaction and then play it back during testing
- WebMock[42] for simulating web traffic

Solution

Before we start writing the code for this recipe, let's talk about application styles. There's a whole class of apps whose usefulness comes from the way they tie together data sources from around the Web. Consider, for instance, the Influence Explorer civic project from Sunlight Labs.[43] This site combines campaign finance disclosures and open U.S. purchasing data (among other sources) to provide a public service: examining the lobbying habits of companies that are awarded federal contracts.

There are some challenges in testing this style of program. If one of the data sources goes down, a naïvely written test may slow down or hang altogether. If an assumption about the domain turns out to be false ("Company X always lobbies more than Company Y on copyright issues"), tests could suddenly start failing months down the road.

How do we deal with these risks while still using realistic data? One way is to capture a live interaction once with your data sources and then play the canned data back during testing. That's exactly what Myron Marston's VCR library does for you.

---

41. https://github.com/myronmarston/vcr
42. https://github.com/bblimke/webmock
43. http://influenceexplorer.com

In this recipe, we're going to build a simple library that retrieves stock prices from the Internet and test it with Cucumber and VCR.

Library

Our library is going to take two stock symbols from the user, look up both their prices, and report which one has the higher share price. We'll call it Stock vs. Stock. We could use this library to build a simple command-line program or a "fight"-style web app like Googlefight.[44]

Let's start with the tests, in stocks.feature.

vcr/features/stocks.feature

```
Feature: Stock vs. Stock

  @vcr
  Scenario: Compare two stocks
    When I compare GOOG and GRPN
    Then GOOG should win
```

Note the @vcr tag. Later, we'll use that tag to tell VCR which tests need to be fed canned data.

The step definitions are just going to pass the stock symbols to our yet-to-be-written library. These will go in features/step_definitions/stock_steps.rb.

vcr/features/step_definitions/stock_steps.rb

```
When /^I compare (\w+) and (\w+)$/ do |sym1, sym2|
  @winner = StockVsStock.fight sym1, sym2
end

Then /^(\w+) should win$/ do |expected|
  @winner.should == expected
end
```

VCR supports a number of different Ruby I/O libraries, including the standard Net::HTTP module that ships with Ruby. That's the one we'll base our library on. Put the following code in lib/stock_vs_stock.rb:

vcr/lib/stock_vs_stock.rb

```
require 'open-uri'
class StockVsStock
  def self.fight sym1, sym2
    uri = URI.parse("http://download.finance.yahoo.com/d/quotes.csv?" +
                    "s=#{sym1}+#{sym2}&f=l1s")
    response = uri.read
    rows     = response.split
    results  = rows.map do |row|
```

44. http://googlefight.com

```
      price, symbol = row.split(',')
      [price.to_f, symbol[1..-2]]
    end
    winning_row = results.sort.last
    winning_row[1] # just the symbol
  end
end
```

This code uses CSV data provided by Yahoo! Finance[45] to look up both symbols. We parse the results into an array of price/symbol pairs and then sort them and return the winner.

You'll need to require() the new code from support/env.rb, the standard place for importing libraries into Cucumber tests.

vcr/features/support/env.rb

```
$LOAD_PATH << 'lib'
require 'stock_vs_stock'
```

Now, run your features.

```
$ cucumber features
```

The tests should pass. This is all well and good for today's valuations, but what happens if Groupon surges in the future and overtakes Google? Our test will suddenly fail, even if our logic is still correct.

Future-Proofing with VCR

This is where VCR comes in. First, install the gem.

```
$ gem install vcr
```

You'll also need to install one of the many fake networking libraries available for Ruby. For this recipe, we'll use WebMock.

```
$ gem install webmock
```

Now, we can configure Cucumber to use VCR. Add the following code to features/support/env.rb:

vcr/features/support/env.rb

```
require 'vcr'
VCR.configure do |c|
  c.cassette_library_dir = 'fixtures/vcr_cassettes'
  c.hook_into :webmock
end
```

We'll also need to tell VCR to watch for the @vcr tag we created earlier.

45. http://finance.yahoo.com

vcr/features/support/env.rb
```
VCR.cucumber_tags do |t|
  t.tag '@vcr', :use_scenario_name => true
end
```

Run your features again. VCR will record the HTTP traffic and save it in a YAML file deep inside the fixtures directory. Now, on subsequent runs, Cucumber will use that canned data instead of hitting the network. Try disconnecting your network and running one final time; the tests should still pass.

Further Exploration

VCR has a lot of additional features. You can set up your canned data to refresh periodically. You can mask out confidential data like passwords from appearing in the YAML files. For more information about these topics, see the official documentation.[46]

For a great demonstration of setting up VCR with a new project, see Gary Bernhardt's excellent screencast on the subject.[47]

46. https://www.relishapp.com/myronmarston/vcr/docs
47. https://www.destroyallsoftware.com/screencasts/catalog/sucks-rocks-3-the-search-engine

Recipe 35

Drive a Flash App Using Cuke4AS3

Problem

You're writing a Flash or Adobe Air application using ActionScript, and you want to describe and then drive out its behavior using Cucumber.

Ingredients

- Cucumber installed in your system Ruby (i.e., not using RVM)
- Adobe Flex SDK
- Adobe Air runtime
- Cuke4AS3[48]
- Your text editor or IDE of choice. We've tried to keep this recipe simple enough that you should be able to follow along using a simple text editor. Obviously, if you're happier with an IDE, feel free to use that.
- A nice cup of tea

Solution

Getting Cuke4AS3 running is fairly involved, so we're going to assume you have a reasonable level of experience with ActionScript programming and concentrate on explaining how to automate your ActionScript project using Cuke4AS3.

We're going to start by installing a few things to get all the infrastructure in place that you need to run a Cucumber scenario. Then we'll build a very simple Flash game, driving the development of the solution from Cucumber.

Setup

Cuke4AS3 doesn't currently work with RVM, so you'll need to make sure you have installed Cucumber in your system Ruby. If you are using RVM, just switch to the system Ruby and then install Cucumber.

```
$ rvm use system
$ gem install cucumber
```

If you're not using RVM, just install Cucumber as normal.

48. http://github.com/flashquartermaster/Cuke4AS3

You'll need the Flex SDK[49] installed to be able to compile your ActionScript app. If you're using Homebrew on Mac OS X, you can install the Flex SDK with brew install flex_sdk. Also, make sure you've installed the Adobe Air runtime[50] so that you can run the Cuke4AS3 developer console.

Now download Cuke4AS3's All_I_need_to_get_started.zip[51] package. Unpack it, and you should find three versions of the Cuke4AS3DeveloperUI: an .exe for Windows, a .dmg for Mac OS X, and a .deb for Linux. Run the installer for your platform.

You should now see the Cuke4AS3 developer UI open. The developer UI will take care of compiling our ActionScript app, starting a wire protocol server, and running Cucumber. We'd better get started!

A Walking Skeleton

We'll start by creating the bare bones of a Cuke4AS3 suite before we add our first scenario and start actually driving out some code in the solution.

Create an src directory in the root of your project folder. In that folder, create the familiar features folder and within that a step_definitions folder.

Now you need to create three files in the src/features/step_definitions folder. First create the .wire file that tells Cucumber how to connect to Cuke4AS3 to run our step definitions. Then create a step definitions file and finally a special file called Cuke4AS3_Suite.as that tells Cuke4AS3 where to find our steps. Please take care to spell the name of this file exactly as we have done.

The wire file is simple and just looks like this:

flash/src/features/step_definitions/Cuke4AS3.wire

```
host: localhost
port: 54321
```

You'll start with a blank step definitions file and add step definitions once you've written your scenario. Create a file called src/features/step_definitions/Steps.as with just an empty class in it.

```
package features.step_definitions
{
    public class Steps
    {
    }
}
```

49. http://www.adobe.com/devnet/flex/flex-sdk-download.html
50. http://get.adobe.com/air/
51. Found in https://github.com/flashquartermaster/Cuke4AS3/downloads

We'll add some real step definitions to this once we have a failing scenario.

Finally, you need the Cuke4AS3_Suite.as file.

flash/src/features/step_definitions/Cuke4AS3_Suite.as

```
package features.step_definitions
{
    import features.step_definitions.Steps;
    import flash.display.Sprite;

    public class Cuke4AS3_Suite extends Sprite
    {
        public function Cuke4AS3_Suite()
        {
            var steps:Steps;
        }
    }
}
```

That's it. Your project directory should now look like this:

```
└── src
    └── features
        └── step_definitions
            ├── Cuke4AS3.wire
            ├── Cuke4AS3_Suite.as
            └── Steps.as
```

Now you should be able to run Cucumber against your ActionScript step definitions. It's time to fire up the Cuke4AS3 developer console.

Configuring the Cuke4AS3 Developer Console

The Cuke4AS3 developer console needs a few configuration settings to be able to work. Open the Cuke4AS3 developer console, switch to the configuration tab, and enter the following three settings:

Source: This tells Cuke4AS3 where to find your features directory. Point this to the src folder of your project directory.

Mxmlc: This is the path to your mxmlc executable from the Flash SDK. Cuke4AS3 will use this to compile your ActionScript step definitions.

On Mac OS X and Linux, you should be able to just type `$ which mxmlc` at a command prompt to get this setting.

If you're using Flash Builder 4.5, then it is likely to be the following:

Windows	C:\Program Files\Adobe\Adobe Flash Builder 4.5\sdks\4.5.0\bin\mxmlc.exe
OS X	/Applications/Adobe Flash Builder 4.5/sdks/4.5.0/bin/mxmlc

If you are using FlashDevelop, then it is likely to be the following:

```
C:\Program Files\FlashDevelop\Tools\flexsdk\bin\mxmlc.exe
```

Cucumber: This is the path to your cucumber executable. On Mac OS X and Linux, you should be able to find this setting by running the following at a command prompt:

```
$ which cucumber
```

Windows users should look in the bin directory of their Ruby installation and add a path to their Ruby binary, something like C:\Ruby192\bin\ruby.exe. Then, in the Cucumber Arguments box, put the path to your cucumber binary, which should be in the same folder, as in C:\Ruby192\bin\cucumber.

Now click the Save button so you never have to type all of that again.

Running Your Cukes

Even without an actual Cucumber feature, you should now be able to run Cuke4AS3. Go ahead and hit the Run button on the developer console. The compiler output window should show that it has built a file cuke4as3_steps.swf in your src directory. The Cucumber output window should show the familiar "0 scenarios, 0 steps" output.

If you're having trouble at this point, we suggest starting with the Cuke4AS3 wiki's troubleshooting page.[52]

It's time to add a scenario!

We're going to build a very simple game. Here's our scenario:

flash/src/features/epic_win.feature

```
Feature: Epic Win

  Scenario: Win the game
    Given the game is running
    When I play
    Then I should be the winner
```

Hit the Run button again in the developer console, and you should now see some ActionScript step definition snippets in the Cucumber output window.

52. https://github.com/flashquartermaster/Cuke4AS3/wiki/Troubleshooting

Paste those into the features/step_definitions/Steps.as file, adding an import statement at the top so that it looks like this:

```
package features.step_definitions
{
    import com.flashquartermaster.cuke4as3.utilities.*;

    public class Steps
    {
        [Given  (/^the game is running$/)]
        public function should_the_game_is_running():void
        {
          throw new Pending("Awaiting implementation");
        }

        [When  (/^I play$/)]
        public function should_i_play():void
        {
          throw new Pending("Awaiting implementation");
        }

        [Then  (/^I should be the winner$/)]
        public function should_i_should_be_the_winner():void
        {
          throw new Pending("Awaiting implementation");
        }
    }
}
```

The function names autogenerated by Cuke4AS3 are sometimes a bit odd, so feel free to change them to something more sensible. The name of the function doesn't affect whether the step matches; that's done by the previous annotation.

You should now be able to run the scenario from the developer console and see the first step fail with a pending exception.

Building the Game

Let's start building our game. We'll split the implementation into two layers: a user interface layer that displays our sophisticated game graphics, delegating to domain model layer that holds the actual game logic.

For the first iteration we'll concentrate on building the domain model. Here's the updated step definition file that calls an imaginary Game class:

```
package features.step_definitions
{
    import com.flashquartermaster.cuke4as3.utilities.*;
    import org.hamcrest.*;
```

```
    import org.hamcrest.object.*;
    import Game;

    public class Steps
    {
        private var _game:Game;
        [Given  (/^the game is running$/)]
        public function should_the_game_is_running():void
        {
          _game = new Game();
        }
        [When  (/^I play$/)]
        public function should_i_play():void
        {
          _game.play();
        }
        [Then  (/^I should be the winner$/)]
        public function should_i_should_be_the_winner():void
        {
          assertThat( _game.isWinner() );
        }
    }
}
```

Notice we've used the Hamcrest[53] assertion library for our Then step. We prefer these to the stock FlexUnit ones, because they make for more readable assertions. Cuke4AS3 bundles in these libraries automatically (though you can turn this off from the config tab), so you don't need to add them to the load path yourself.

We're importing and then calling a Game class, which we need to define. Create a file src/Game.as with the following code:

flash/src/Game.as

```
package
{
    public class Game
    {
        public function play():void
        {
        }

        public function isWinner():Boolean
        {
            return true;
        }
    }
}
```

53. https://github.com/drewbourne/hamcrest-as3

Run the scenario now from the developer console, and you should see the code compile and then pass the test. We're green!

It's time to enjoy that cup of tea for a moment; then we'll get to work on the user interface.

Adding the User Interface

It's delightfully easy to test ActionScript applications right up to the surface of the user interface, thanks to a very scriptable event API. We can even watch the game play out through the Cuke4AS3 developer console!

To achieve this, we'll use FlexUnit's UI Impersonation[54] library. The first thing you need to do is modify your Given step to hook up this library to the GameUI class we're going to build next.

flash/src/features/step_definitions/Steps.as

```
[Given  (/^the game is running$/, "async")]
public function should_the_game_is_running():void
{
    _game = new GameUI();
    Async.proceedOnEvent( this, _game, Event.ADDED_TO_STAGE );
    UIImpersonator.addChild( _game );
}
```

You'll notice that we're passing a string "async" to the Given annotation on the step definition method. This tells FlexUnit that this step contains asynchronous code. We want to make sure we wait until the UIImpersonator has fired the ADDED_TO_STAGE event before we proceed to the next step of the scenario.

To get this code to compile, you also need to add a few import statements at the top of the file and change the type declaration for the _game instance variable from Game to GameUI. We'll show you the full listing further down once we've finished working through the changes to this file.

The game will have a play button on the UI and a textbox that tells the player whether they've won. Now you need to change the last two step definitions to talk to these GUI widgets instead of the domain model.

flash/src/features/step_definitions/Steps.as

```
[When  (/^I play$/)]
public function should_i_play():void
{
    _game.playButton.dispatchEvent( new MouseEvent( MouseEvent.CLICK ) );
}
[Then  (/^I should be the winner$/)]
```

54. http://docs.flexunit.org/index.php?title=UIImpersonator

```
public function should_i_should_be_the_winner():void
{
    assertThat( _game.message.text, equalTo("You win!") );
}
```

The When step sends a mouse-click event to the play button, just as though the user had clicked it. The Then examines the text in the message to see whether it indicates that the user has won.

To get the scenario to pass, create src/GameUI.as and implement it as follows:

flash/src/GameUI.as

```
package
{
    import Game;
    import flash.display.Sprite;
    import flash.events.MouseEvent;
    import flash.text.TextField;

    public class GameUI extends Sprite
    {
        public var playButton:Sprite;
        public var message:TextField;
        private var _game:Game;
        public function GameUI()
        {
            _game = new Game();
            addPlayButton();
            addMessage();
        }

        private function handlePlayButtonClick( event:MouseEvent ):void
        {
            _game.play();
            if ( _game.isWinner() ) message.text = "You win!"
        }

        private function addPlayButton():void
        {
            var playButtonLabel:TextField = new TextField();
            playButtonLabel.text = "Play"
            playButton = new Sprite();
            playButton.graphics.beginFill( 0x00ff00 );
            playButton.graphics.drawRect( 0, 0, 100, 20 );
            playButton.graphics.endFill();
            playButton.addChild(playButtonLabel);
            playButton.addEventListener( MouseEvent.CLICK, handlePlayButtonClick );
            playButton.buttonMode = true;
            addChild( playButton )
        }
```

```
        private function addMessage():void
        {
            message = new TextField();
            message.height = 20;
            message.y = playButton.y + playButton.height + 5;
            addChild( message );
        }
    }
}
```

This is quite long but should be familiar to you if you're used to putting together ActionScript user interfaces from code.

The final listing for the step definitions should look like this:

flash/src/features/step_definitions/Steps.as

```
package features.step_definitions
{
    import com.flashquartermaster.cuke4as3.utilities.*;
    import org.hamcrest.*;
    import org.hamcrest.object.*;
    import flash.events.*;
    import org.flexunit.async.Async;
    import org.fluint.uiImpersonation.UIImpersonator;
    import GameUI;
    public class Steps
    {
        private var _game:GameUI;
        [Given  (/^the game is running$/, "async")]
        public function should_the_game_is_running():void
        {
            _game = new GameUI();
            Async.proceedOnEvent( this, _game, Event.ADDED_TO_STAGE );
            UIImpersonator.addChild( _game );
        }

        [When  (/^I play$/)]
        public function should_i_play():void
        {
            _game.playButton.dispatchEvent( new MouseEvent( MouseEvent.CLICK ) );
        }
        [Then  (/^I should be the winner$/)]
        public function should_i_should_be_the_winner():void
        {
            assertThat( _game.message.text, equalTo("You win!") );
        }
    }
}
```

With this in place, you should be able to run the scenario from the developer console and see it pass again. Try ticking the *visual mode* box to see the UI in all its glory.

Manual Testing

You can build your game into a full-fledged Flash application simply by calling mxmlc from the console.

```
$ mxmlc src/GameUI.as -output Game.swf
```

Open the resulting Game.swf in a browser and amuse yourself for hours.

Further Exploration

This game is pretty boring so far. Try changing the feature so that you win or lose the game on alternate plays.

```
Feature: Epic Win

  Scenario: Win on first play
    Given the game is running
    When I play
    Then I should be the winner

  Scenario: Lose on second play
    Given the game is running
    And I have played once
    When I play again
    Then I should lose
```

Can you implement the step definitions for the second scenario and then change the logic in Game.as to make it pass?

Recipe 36

Monitor a Web Service Using Nagios and Cucumber

Problem

You're monitoring the uptime of your web service with Nagios. The HTTP monitoring built into Nagios gives a quick up/down status. You want to add more advanced information to this report. Specifically, you want to run some acceptance tests to see whether your servers are showing the right content.

Ingredients

- A monitoring server running Nagios[55]
- The cucumber-nagios gem[56] for producing reports in a format easily understood by Nagios
- Webrat[57] for testing web pages
- Nokogiri[58] for parsing HTML results
- Bundler[59] for installing Ruby libraries onto the monitoring server

Solution

Nagios is an open source tool that gauges the health of your network. It does so by regularly running individual shell scripts—*plug-ins*, in Nagios parlance—and then collecting and presenting the results. A plug-in performs a single monitoring task, such as verifying that a web server is responding at a particular URL or connecting to a MySQL server to retrieve statistics.

The Nagios documentation describes a few simple output conventions for plug-ins to follow.[60] Plug-ins are not required to adhere to these, but doing so makes it easier for Nagios to display their reports.

---

55. http://www.nagios.org
56. http://auxesis.github.com/cucumber-nagios
57. https://github.com/brynary/webrat
58. http://nokogiri.org
59. http://gembundler.com
60. http://nagios.sourceforge.net/docs/3_0/pluginapi.html

cucumber-nagios is a Ruby gem that implements a Cucumber formatter for Nagios. With it, you can report pass/fail information in the style that Nagios expects to see. It also has a few helpers for generating new projects, which we don't need for this recipe.

In this recipe, we're going to write a Cucumber scenario that exercises a search feature on a public web server and then run that scenario regularly from a Nagios monitoring server.

Monitoring Server Setup

The installation instructions for Nagios vary quite a bit from platform to platform.[61] The good news is that once you have it installed, the procedure for administering it is the same. We used the Ubuntu installation instructions for this recipe;[62] if you're on a different operating system, you may need to tweak the paths a bit.

First, install Nagios and its plug-ins.

```
$ sudo apt-get install nagios3
```

Next, install Ruby and the libraries you'll need for web scraping.

```
$ sudo apt-get install rubygems ruby-dev libxml2-dev libxslt1-dev
```

Finally, install Bundler.

```
$ sudo gem install bundler
```

Your remote server now has all the software it needs to run a few basic Cucumber acceptance tests.

Development Machine Setup

Before we add the extra complication of monitoring, let's get a basic web scenario working locally in a development environment.

This recipe will use Bundler[63] for dependency management so that we can easily replicate our Ruby libraries later. If you haven't already installed Bundler, do so now.

```
$ gem install bundler
```

Next, create a Gemfile with the following contents:

---

61. http://nagios.sourceforge.net/docs/3_0/quickstart.html
62. https://help.ubuntu.com/community/Nagios3
63. http://gembundler.com

nagios/Gemfile
```
source :rubygems

gem 'cucumber-nagios'
```

cucumber-nagios lists Cucumber and Webrat as dependencies, so you don't have to name them explicitly. When you run Bundler, you'll have everything you need.

```
$ bundle install
```

Now that both machines are set up, we can turn our attention to the tests.

Cucumber Scenario

Let's imagine for this recipe that you're monitoring a web forum. You want to do more than a simple HTTP status code check; you want to actually perform a search once in a while to make sure the front end and database are still talking to each other. Place the following code in features/forum.feature:

nagios/features/forum.feature
```
Feature: Discussion forums

  Scenario: Search
    When I search the forums for "Ruby"
    Then I should see the most recent posts first
```

Here's the definition for the When step (this goes in features/step_definitions/forum_steps.rb):

nagios/features/step_definitions/forum_steps.rb
```
When /^I search the forums for "([^"]*)"$/ do |term|
  escaped = CGI::escape term
  visit "http://forums.pragprog.com/search?q=#{escaped}"
end
```

The visit() method comes with Webrat; we'll see how to make it available to Cucumber in a moment. First, let's finish out the second step definition.

nagios/features/step_definitions/forum_steps.rb
```
Then /^I should see the most recent posts first$/ do
  doc = Nokogiri::HTML response_body
  dates = doc.css('div.date').map { |e| Time.parse e.text }
  dates.should have_at_least(1).item
  dates.should == dates.sort.reverse
end
```

We grab the response_body() from Webrat, look for all the <div class="date"> elements on the page, and verify that they're in reverse sorted order.

These step definitions have used several dependencies: CGI for making the search term URL-friendly, Webrat for visiting the web page, Nokogiri for parsing the response, and so on. We need to make sure these are all visible from the step definitions. Create the file features/support/env.rb with the following contents:

nagios/features/support/env.rb

```
require 'time'
require 'cgi'
require 'webrat'
require 'nokogiri'

Webrat.configure do |config|
  config.mode = :mechanize
end
World Webrat::Methods
```

The scenario is now ready to run locally. Make sure to run it with the Nagios formatter, the same way you'll be running it on the server.

```
$ bundle exec cucumber -fCucumber::Formatter::Nagios
CUCUMBER OK - Critical: 0, Warning: 0, 2 okay | passed=2; failed=0; ...
```

Now that the scenario is passing on the local machine, it's time to hook it up to Nagios.

Reporting the Results

Transfer your project directory to the monitoring server, taking care to put them someplace visible to the nagios user, such as /var/lib/nagios/cucumber. Then, install and run Bundler to make sure you're using the same set of libraries as on your development machine.

```
$ gem install bundler
$ bundle install
```

Note that several of these gems have components written in C. If you get any errors during installation, make sure your server has a C compiler and Nokogiri's library dependencies installed.[64]

Nagios follows a chain of configuration files to monitor a server:

- The *host groups* file to describe logical collections of servers
- Each individual host's *config file* to specify what checks to run
- A *command definition* to map command names to scripts
- A *shell script* to implement each command

64. http://nokogiri.org/tutorials/installing_nokogiri.html

Let's start with the host groups file. On Ubuntu, this information lives in /etc/nagios3/conf.d/hostgroups_nagios2.cfg. Find the members line inside the http-servers group, and add pragprog, the name of the new host we'll be defining.

nagios/config/hostgroups_nagios2.cfg

```
define hostgroup {
        hostgroup_name  http-servers
                alias           HTTP servers

                members         localhost,pragprog
        }
```

Next, create pragprog_nagios2.cfg in the same directory with the following contents:

nagios/config/pragprog_nagios2.cfg

```
define host{
        host_name pragprog
        address forums.pragprog.com
        max_check_attempts 10
        check_command check_cucumber
        }
```

This will direct Nagios to run the check_cucumber command regularly against the forum server. You'll need to define this command as a Nagios plug-in in /etc/nagios-plugins/config/cucumber.cfg.

nagios/config/cucumber.cfg

```
define command{
        command_name    check_cucumber
        command_line    /usr/lib/nagios/plugins/check_cucumber
        }
```

The last piece of this Rube Goldberg contraption is to define the check_cucumber shell script that gets called by this command. By convention, this script goes in /usr/lib/nagios/plugins. All it needs to do is jump to the directory where you saved your scenario and then start Cucumber.

nagios/config/check_cucumber

```
#!/bin/sh
cd /var/lib/nagios/cucumber
bundle exec cucumber -fCucumber::Formatter::Nagios || exit 2
```

As one final test, you might try running check_cucumber manually from the shell. When you're satisfied that it's working, start the Nagios server and hit http://*server*/nagios3 in your browser. You should see something like Figure 30, *Viewing Cucumber results in Nagios*, on page 200.

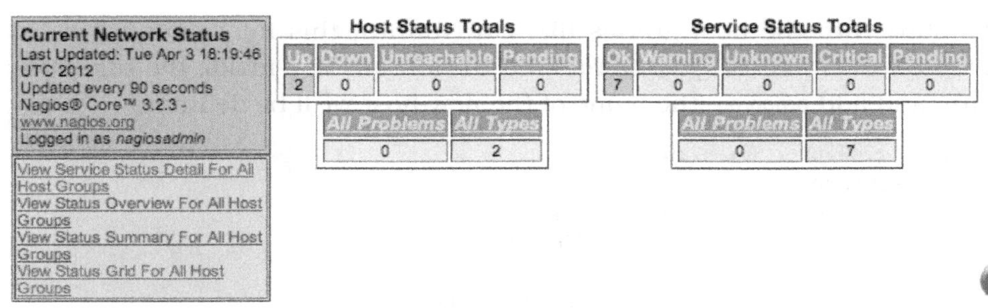

Host Status Details For All Host Groups

Host	Status	Last Check	Duration	Status Information
localhost	UP	2012-04-03 18:15:48	0d 2h 37m 43s	PING OK - Packet loss = 0%, RTA = 0.05 ms
pragprog	UP	2012-04-03 18:18:18	0d 0h 1m 7s	CUCUMBER OK - Critical: 0, Warning: 0, 2 okay

2 Matching Host Entries Displayed

Figure 30—Viewing Cucumber results in Nagios

CHAPTER 5

Other Languages and Platforms

This chapter is a roundup of Cucumber tips that don't fit neatly into the categories we've seen so far. We'll look at driving Python and Erlang code using Cucumber syntax. We'll also see a couple of recipes for specific operating systems, such as Linux and Mac OS X.

Recipe 37

Drive a Mac GUI Using AppleScript and System Events

Problem

You want to write Cucumber tests that exercise a Mac application through its user interface.

Ingredients

- System Events,[1] an Apple-provided API for simulating GUI events
- rb-appscript,[2] a bridge between Ruby and AppleScript
- Command-Line Tools for Xcode[3] to compile rb-appscript

Solution

Since the 1980s, Mac users have customized and automated their systems using the built-in AppleScript environment. Initially, this technology relied on software vendors to make their apps' features available in AppleScript. Now, users can perform basic GUI automation of just about any program through an AppleScript API known as System Events.

In this recipe, we're going to write a simple Cucumber feature to control a GUI. Our step definitions will use rb-appscript, a Ruby library that will give us access to AppleScript (and therefore System Events).

For our guinea pig, we'll choose Hex Fiend, an open source hex editor and binary file comparison tool. Figure 31, *Hex Fiend*, on page 203 shows a screenshot of Hex Fiend in action.

Setup

Hex Fiend is easy to install. Download the zip file from the official site,[4] double-click the file, and drag the Hex Fiend program to your Applications folder.

---

1. https://developer.apple.com/library/mac/#documentation/applescript/conceptual/applescriptx/concepts/as_related_apps.html
2. http://appscript.sourceforge.net/rb-appscript/index.html
3. https://developer.apple.com/xcode
4. http://ridiculousfish.com/hexfiend/files/HexFiend.zip

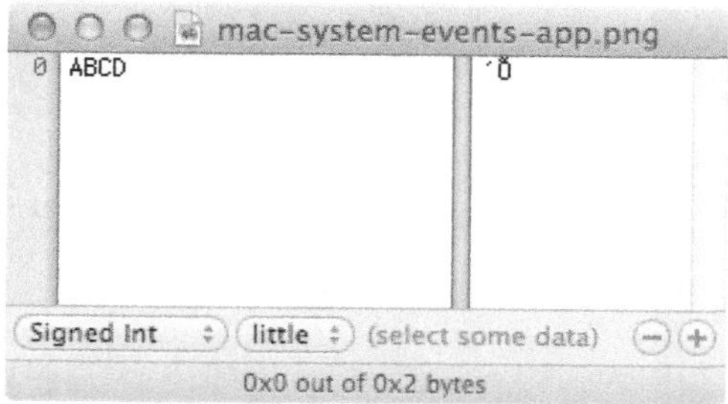

Figure 31—Hex Fiend

Before we can automate Hex Fiend's user interface, we need to enable the System Events API. Open your System Preferences, go to the Universal Access pane, and turn on the option marked "Enable access for assistive devices" (see Figure 32, *Enabling System Events*, on page 204). This will allow AppleScript to drive Hex Fiend's user interface.

Before you can install rb-appscript, you'll need a C compiler. Install the Xcode development environment from the Mac App Store.[5] Launch Xcode. Go to Preferences → Downloads and install the Command Line Tools package.

You have everything you need to install rb-appscript now.

```
$ gem install rb-appscript
```

Let's turn our attention to the app and its features.

Inspecting the GUI

Before we can write code to drive the GUI, we need to understand the structure: what are the main parts of the window and types of controls?

The easiest way to do this is to use the Accessibility Inspector, a tool provided by Apple that displays the type and placement of any control you hover the mouse over. To install it, you'll need an account on Apple's developer site;[6] the free level will work. Once you're signed in, visit the download page[7] and search for *Accessibility Tools for Xcode*. Download and open the .dmg file, and drag the two apps to your Applications folder.

Now, let's get a feel for how the tool works. Launch Hex Fiend, and then start Accessibility Inspector. Hover over the readout marked (select some data). You

5. http://itunes.apple.com/us/app/xcode/id497799835
6. http://developer.apple.com
7. https://developer.apple.com/downloads/index.action?name=for%20Xcode%20-#

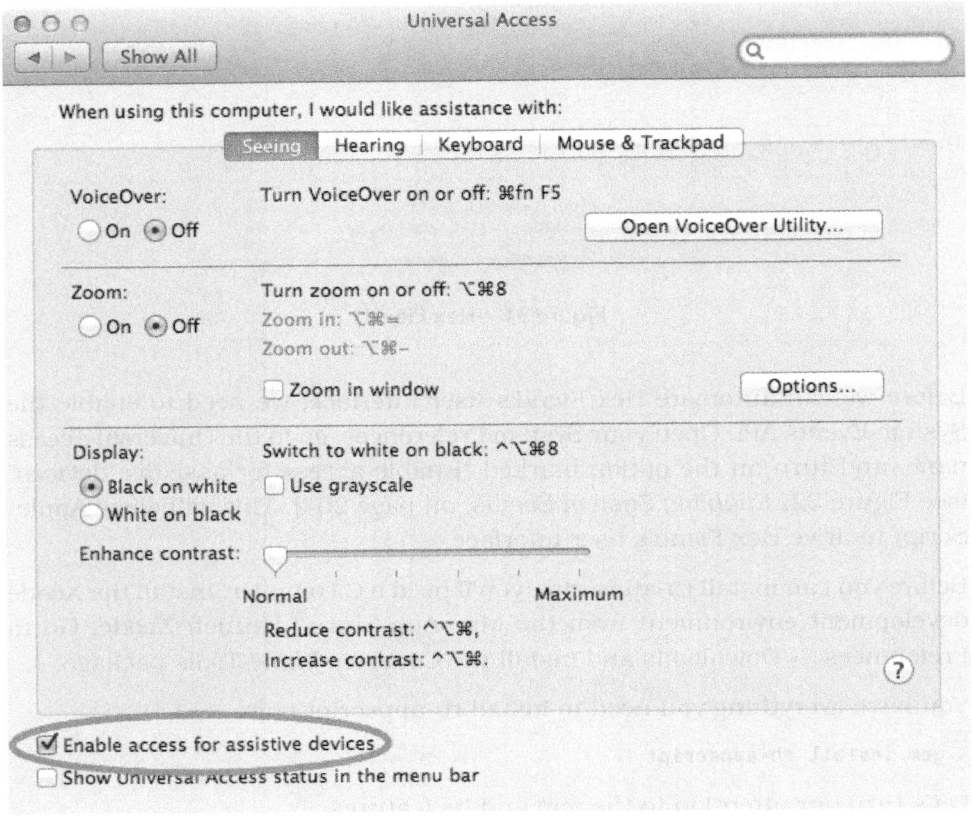

Figure 32—Enabling System Events

should see something like Figure 33, *Accessibility Inspector*. From this list, we can see that the control we're inspecting lives inside a table row, which in turn is embedded in a scroll area inside a splitter group. When we refer to these controls in Ruby, we'll need to know their exact place in the hierarchy.

While we're here, let's take a look at one more thing. Hover over the main editing area, and look at the Accessibility Inspector. You might expect to see a text field here, but instead we just see the main split group that takes up the whole window.

Like many OS X apps, Hex Fiend does a lot of custom rendering. In these situations, there's a limit to what Apple's built-in GUI scripting can do. For this recipe, we're not inspecting the contents of the text area—but we'd be out of luck if we needed to do that.

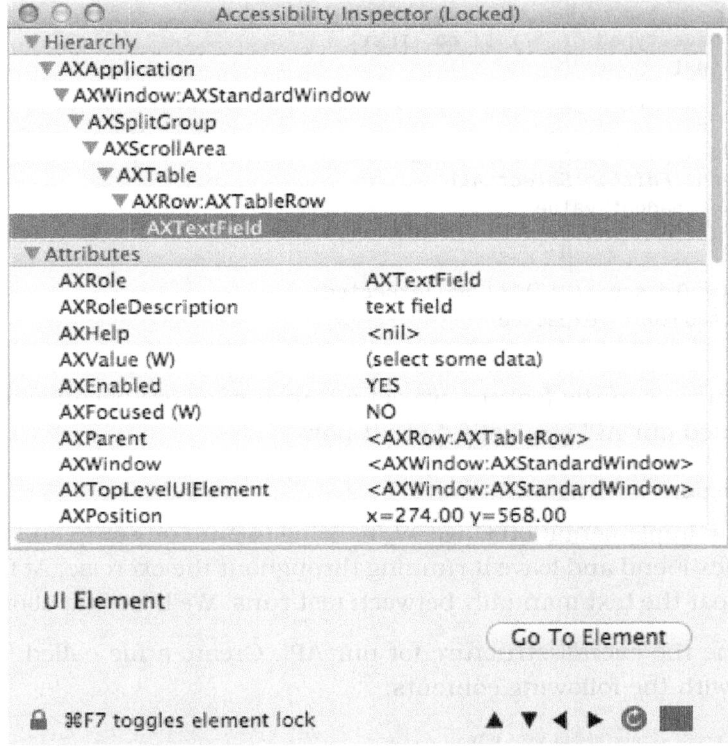

Figure 33—Accessibility Inspector

Feature

Let's write a simple Cucumber feature for one of Hex Fiend's basic operations: typing in a hexadecimal value and interpreting it as an integer. Put the following code into features/hex.feature:

mac_system_events/features/hex.feature

```
Feature: Hex editor

  Scenario: Convert to integer
    Given I have typed "ABCD"
    When I view the bytes as an integer
    Then I should see "-12885"
```

Go ahead and run the feature, and paste the step templates into features/step_definitions/hex_steps.rb. Now, let's fill in the definitions. AppleScript (and therefore rb-appscript) tends to be a bit chatty, so let's make these step definitions one-liners that call into support code. We'll code to an imaginary API for our app and then implement that API.

mac_system_events/features/step_definitions/hex_steps.rb

```
Given /^I have typed "(.*?)"$/ do |text|
  type_in text
end

When /^I view the bytes as an integer$/ do
  click_menu 'Edit', 'Select All'
  @actual = readout_value
end

Then /^I should see "(.*?)"$/ do |expected|
  @actual.should == expected
end
```

Now, when we run the feature, we get a bunch of errors because we haven't implemented our API yet. Let's do that now.

GUI Connection

For the first implementation stage, we're going to punt on setup and teardown. Launch Hex Fiend and leave it running throughout the exercise. At first, you'll need to clear the text manually between test runs. We'll fix that soon enough.

Let's define the overall structure for our API. Create a file called features/support/env.rb with the following contents:

mac_system_events/features/support/env.rb

```
require 'appscript'

include Appscript
module DrivesApp
  # helper methods go here...
end

World(DrivesApp)
```

We'll put all our GUI automation helper methods in the DrivesApp module so that they'll be accessible from the step definitions.

First, let's look at typing text. To type the letter *A* in AppleScript, we'd use the following code:

```
tell application "System Events" to keystroke "A"
```

The rb-appscript equivalent is as follows:

```
app('System Events').keystroke('A')
```

To type a whole string, you'd just call that code in a loop, like so:

mac_system_events/features/support/env.rb
```
def type_in(text)
  text.chars.each do |c|
    app('System Events').
      keystroke c
  end
end
```

Now, we need to be able to click menu items. To choose Edit → Select All in AppleScript, you'd use the following code:

```
tell application "System Events"
    tell process "Hex Fiend"
        click menu item ¬
                "Select All" of menu ¬
                "Edit" of menu bar item ¬
                "Edit" of menu bar 1
    end tell
end tell
```

Once again, rb-appscript maps that incantation to a more Ruby-like style. Add the following method to the DrivesApp module:

mac_system_events/features/support/env.rb
```
def click_menu(bar, item)
  app('System Events').
    processes['Hex Fiend'].
    menu_bars[1].
    menu_bar_items[bar].
    menus[bar].
    menu_items[item].
    click
end
```

The final piece of the puzzle is reading back the integer value. Rather than saying tell ... to click menu item ..., we need to say tell ... to get value of text field. Here's how we do that in rb-appscript:

mac_system_events/features/support/env.rb
```
def readout_value
  app('System Events').
    processes['Hex Fiend'].
    windows[0].
    splitter_groups[0].
    scroll_areas[0].
    tables[0].
    rows[0].
    text_fields[0].value.get
end
```

Now, rerun your step. All the steps should pass now. But we're not quite done. Our code doesn't launch the app before the first test or exit the app afterward. Let's fix that.

Starting and Stopping

How do we make sure our app is freshly launched and running from a known state before the first test? The most reliable way is to delete any preference files and launch the app before each test case. But this adds quite a bit of time to the process and makes our .feature files less useful for things like overnight stress testing.

The alternative is to launch the app once at the beginning of the test run and then find some way to put it in a known state before each test case. If your app supports some kind of factory preset action, you might choose this path.

Since this recipe has only one scenario, it doesn't matter too much. Let's just launch the app before the first step. We'll use the global hooks technique from Recipe 3, *Run Slow Setup/Teardown Code with Global Hooks*, on page 13. Place the following code in env.rb, just outside the definition of DrivesApp:

mac_system_events/features/support/env.rb

```
`open -a 'Hex Fiend'`
at_exit { app('Hex Fiend').quit :saving => :no }
```

Before the test starts, we use the Mac shell's built-in open command to ensure that Hex Fiend is launched and has a document open. After Cucumber finishes the last test, it will run our at_exit hook and quit the app without saving.

Further Exploration

In this recipe, we used a Cucumber technique called global hooks to launch the app once per test run. For more on how these work, see Recipe 3, *Run Slow Setup/Teardown Code with Global Hooks*, on page 13.

The AppleScript API is serviceable, but as you've noticed, it's a bit verbose. You have to specify the exact path from the root window of the user interface down to each control. In Recipe 38, *Drive a Mac GUI Using MacRuby and AXElements*, on page 209, we look at AXElements, a more Ruby-like way to drive Mac user interfaces.

Recipe 38

Drive a Mac GUI Using MacRuby and AXElements

Problem

You want to test a Mac GUI, but you don't want to use a bridge to AppleScript. Instead, you want to use an expressive Ruby-like API that will be easier to write and maintain.

Ingredients

- AXElements,[8] a Ruby wrapper around the Apple Accessibility APIs
- A nightly build of MacRuby,[9] an implementation of Ruby tied closely to the OS X runtime
- Spinach,[10] a Cucumber-like framework that's compatible with MacRuby
- Command-Line Tools for Xcode[11] to compile AXElements

Solution

AXElements is an easy-to-use library for Mac GUI automation. Rather than relying on AppleScript like traditional Mac scripting projects do, AXElements calls directly into Apple-provided APIs for interacting with on-screen controls. It is able to do so because it runs on MacRuby, a Ruby implementation that's able to call into the OS X system as easily as calling Ruby code.

The only catch is that MacRuby can't currently run Cucumber reliably. Instead, we'll use a test framework called Spinach. Spinach uses the same Given/When/Then syntax as Cucumber but is built around a simpler infrastructure that makes it easier to split up and reuse test steps. There are a few things that Spinach can't do—such as using parameterized steps like `When I type "(.*)"` —but we don't need those features for this recipe.

8. https://github.com/Marketcircle/AXElements
9. http://macruby.org
10. http://codegram.github.com/spinach
11. https://developer.apple.com/xcode

In this recipe, we're going to test Hex Fiend,[12] the same open source hex editor that we looked at in Recipe 37, *Drive a Mac GUI Using AppleScript and System Events*, on page 202. In the rest of this book, we've tried not to test the same app twice. Here, we choose to do so specifically because we want to compare two different Mac testing approaches side by side. Accordingly, we'll drive the app to do the same task as before: converting a hex number to decimal.

Setup

First, download the Hex Fiend zip file,[13] double-click to extract the contents, and drag the newly created Hex Fiend icon into your Applications folder. Launch the text editor and leave it running while we practice automating it. It should look something like this:

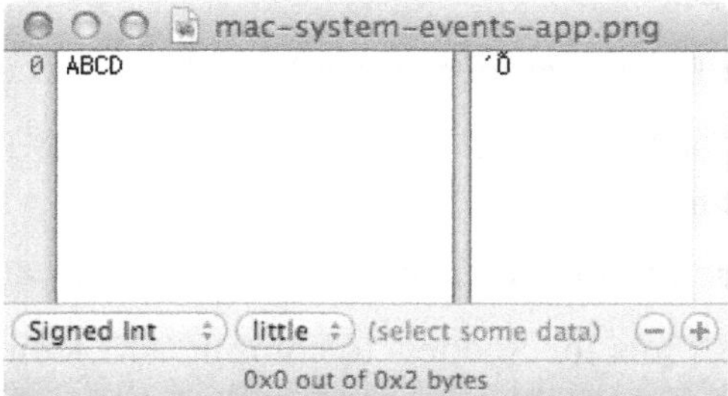

Next, we'll download MacRuby. AXElements requires features that were only recently introduced into MacRuby. Rather than running an official MacRuby release, you'll need to download and install the latest nightly build.[14]

You'll also need command-line C compilers to build AXElements. Install Xcode,[15] and then go into Xcode's Preferences menu and install the Command Line Tools add-on.

Now, you're ready to install AXelements. Because we're on MacRuby, we'll use the macgem command. Unlike other Ruby implementations, MacRuby installs to system folders—meaning that you're likely to need to preface the command with sudo.

```
$ sudo macgem install AXElements
```

The last step is to install Spinach. As part of the common setup we discuss in Section 3, *Getting the Tools You'll Need*, on page xiv, you'll also need the RSpec expectations library.

---

12. http://ridiculousfish.com/hexfiend
13. http://ridiculousfish.com/hexfiend/files/HexFiend.zip
14. http://macruby.macosforge.org/files/nightlies
15. http://itunes.apple.com/us/app/xcode/id497799835

```
$ sudo macgem install spinach rspec-expectations
```

Spinach is written for Ruby 1.9 specifically. MacRuby implements most of the 1.9 version of the language, so we're in pretty good shape here. There are just a couple of small compatibility tweaks we need to make, though. Create a file called helper.rb with the following contents:

mac_ruby/helper.rb

```
# A standard 1.9 feature that's not in MacRuby yet
#
def require_relative(path)
  require File.join(File.dirname(caller[0]), path.to_str)
end
# Spinach uses Ruby's standard StringIO class but doesn't load it
#
require 'stringio'
# Spinach's error reporting asks for the file and line number;
# MacRuby doesn't provide this
class Method
  def source_location
    ['', '']
  end
end
```

That's all we need to implement our recipe.

Feature

Spinach uses a pure-Ruby implementation of Cucumber's Gherkin language, so our feature will look just like a Cucumber one. Put the following text in features/hex.feature:

mac_ruby/features/hex.feature

```
Feature: Hex editor

  Scenario: Convert to integer
    Given a hex editor
    When I type some text
    Then I should be able to view the bytes as an integer
```

In Cucumber, we'd run the test here to generate step definitions on the console to paste into our Ruby code. Spinach can go one step further and actually generate the definition file for you; just pass the --generate flag.

```
$ macruby -rhelper -S spinach --generate
```

Spinach will create a file called features/steps/hex_editor.rb. Open it up and take a look:

```
class HexEditor < Spinach::FeatureSteps
  Given 'a hex editor' do
    pending 'step not implemented'
  end
  When 'I type some text' do
    pending 'step not implemented'
  end
  Then 'I should be able to view the bytes as an integer' do
    pending 'step not implemented'
  end
end
```

It looks quite a bit like a Cucumber step definition, except that the steps live inside a Ruby class. It's also worth noting that Spinach steps can't take parameters the way Cucumber steps can. In other words, we can't write a step that matches a regular expression like `When /^I type "([^"]+)"$/`.

Now that we have a place to put our step definitions, let's connect to our GUI.

Step Definitions

First, add the following lines to the top of `hex_editor.rb` to bring in the Ruby libraries we'll be using:

mac_ruby/features/steps/hex_editor.rb

```
require 'axelements'
require 'rspec-expectations'
```

Let's connect to our app. Replace the `Given` step definition with the following code:

mac_ruby/features/steps/hex_editor.rb

```
Given 'a hex editor' do
  @app = AX::Application.new 'Hex Fiend'
end
```

When we create a new `Application` object, AXElements will look for a running instance of the app. Once we have that object, we can type into the program's main window.

mac_ruby/features/steps/hex_editor.rb

```
When 'I type some text' do
  type 'ABCD', @app
end
```

Now we're ready to pull the results out of the user interface.

mac_ruby/features/steps/hex_editor.rb

```
Then 'I should be able to view the bytes as an integer' do
  edit_menu       = @app.menu_bar_item title:'Edit'
  select_all_item = edit_menu.menu_item title:'Select All'
```

```
  press select_all_item

  readout = @app.main_window.table.text_field
  readout.value.should == "-12885"
end
```

The first three lines locate and click the Select All item on the Edit menu. The final two lines locate the readout where the integer value will appear. This control is actually deeply nested inside a hierarchy: Window → SplitGroup → ScrollArea → Table → Row → TextField. But the beauty of AXElements is that we can cut through this hierarchy with a few simple search criteria: "Find me a text field buried somewhere within a table, no matter how deeply."

Now, when you rerun your Spinach feature, all the steps should pass. There's just one more thing we need to take care of.

Starting and Stopping

So far, we've just left the app running during the test. It would be nice to launch the app automatically before the run starts and exit afterward.

We can start the app by just shelling out to the command line at the top level of our step definition file.

mac_ruby/features/steps/hex_editor.rb

```
`open -a 'Hex Fiend'`
```

To exit the app, we can use a Spinach-provided hook called after_run().

mac_ruby/features/steps/hex_editor.rb

```
Spinach.hooks.after_run do
  hex_fiend = Accessibility.application_with_name 'Hex Fiend'
  terminate hex_fiend
  type '\CMD+d'
end
```

This will find and close the app and then press Cmd+D to dismiss the save dialog. Now, you should be able to rerun your Spinach tests and watch the app start and exit automatically.

Further Exploration

AXElements provides us with a very clean abstraction around GUI elements, but it's not without its trade-offs. Because it specifically requires the bleeding-edge version of MacRuby, you may encounter gems that aren't yet compatible. If you need to use a different Ruby version or you require specific Cucumber features, you may want to use AppleScript to drive your app instead; see Recipe 37, *Drive a Mac GUI Using AppleScript and System Events*, on page 202.

Recipe 39

Test Python Code Using Lettuce

Problem

You want to test a Python app from Cucumber; for consistency's sake, you want as much of your test code as possible to be in Python.

Ingredients

- Lettuce for testing Python using a Cucumber-like syntax[16]
- virtualenv for installing a Python sandbox to play in[17]
- colorama for viewing pass/fail results in color on Windows[18]

Solution

There are a few different ways to drive Python code in plain English, each with its own set of trade-offs. Lettuce is a test framework that strikes a careful balance: it's written in pure Python (so you won't have to install extra dependencies to use it) but understands basic Gherkin syntax (so you can write similar tests to the ones you'd use in Cucumber).

For this recipe, we'll use virtualenv to create a clean Python sandbox to play in. You'll need to have an installation of Python on your system to bootstrap virtualenv, but from there, everything we're doing will happen inside a separate environment.

First, download virtualenv.py to your system[19] and run it using your installed Python interpreter. On Mac or Linux, you'd type the following:

```
$ python virtualenv.py $HOME/sandbox
$ source $HOME/sandbox/activate
```

Here's the Windows equivalent:

```
C:\MyProject> python virtualenv.py C:\sandbox
C:\MyProject> C:\sandbox\Scripts\activate
```

16. http://lettuce.it
17. http://www.virtualenv.org
18. http://pypi.python.org/pypi/colorama
19. https://raw.github.com/pypa/virtualenv/master/virtualenv.py

Now, if you run python -v, Python will list where it's loading its various system libraries; these should be in the sandbox directory you passed to virtualenv.

Next, install Lettuce using the copy of pip that virtualenv provides.

```
$ pip install lettuce
```

If you're on Windows, you may also want to follow Erlis Vidal's procedure for enabling output colors.[20] Here's what Erlis recommends. First, install the colorama library.

```
C:\MyProject> pip install colorama
```

Then, add the following two lines to C:\sandbox\Lib\site-packages\lettuce__init__.py just after the last from ... import ... line:

```
from colorama import init()
init()
```

Now, you're ready to write tests. First, save the following code in python.feature:

python/python.feature

```
Feature: Python integration

  Scenario: Cucumber tests
    Given I am familiar with Cucumber tests
    When I write scenarios for Python code
    Then I can run them using Lettuce
```

When you run this using the lettuce command, you'll see the familiar missing-step messages, with Python boilerplate for you to paste into your step definitions.

```
$ lettuce python.feature

Feature: Python integration                    # python.feature:1

  Scenario: Cucumber tests                     # python.feature:3
    Given I am familiar with Cucumber tests # python.feature:4
    When I write scenarios for Python code  # python.feature:5
    Then I can run them using Lettuce       # python.feature:6

1 feature (0 passed)
1 scenario (0 passed)
3 steps (3 undefined, 0 passed)

You can implement step definitions for undefined steps with these snippets:

# -*- coding: utf-8 -*-
```

20. http://www.erlisvidal.com/blog/2010/10/how-install-lettuce-windows

```
from lettuce import step

@step(u'Given I am familiar with Cucumber tests')
def given_i_am_familiar_with_cucumber_tests(step):
    assert False, 'This step must be implemented'
@step(u'When I write scenarios for Python code')
def when_i_write_scenarios_for_python_code(step):
    assert False, 'This step must be implemented'
@step(u'Then I can run them using Lettuce')
def then_i_can_run_them_using_lettuce(step):
    assert False, 'This step must be implemented'
```

Paste those step definitions into python_steps.py, and rerun Lettuce to verify that you now have failing tests instead of undefined ones. Finally, change the body of each step definition to an empty function, like this:

python/python_steps.py

```
@step(u'Given I am familiar with Cucumber tests')
def given_i_am_familiar_with_cucumber_tests(step):
    pass
```

When you rerun the tests, they should all pass.

For this recipe, we've been using vanilla Cucumber format—nothing too exotic. Lettuce supports several of Cucumber's syntactical features, including scenario outlines and multiline strings. However, there are a few Cucumber techniques you can't yet apply in Lettuce at the time of this writing, such as tags and data tables.

Further Exploration

As we discussed at the beginning of this recipe, there are other ways to write plain-English tests for Python code. Cucumber actually ships with experimental Python support, which works by running a Python interpreter inside Ruby.[21] This approach has the advantage of supporting the full Gherkin syntax, but it isn't officially supported by the Cucumber team.

Another pure-Python project is Pyccuracy.[22] It shares Lettuce's advantage of not needing any runtimes other than Python installed. I chose to feature Lettuce here because its syntax is closer to Cucumber's.

21. https://github.com/cucumber/cucumber/tree/master/examples/python
22. https://github.com/heynemann/pyccuracy/wiki

Recipe 40

Test Erlang Code

Problem

You want to test your Erlang code using Cucumber-like syntax.

Ingredients

- cucumberl,[23] a pure Erlang implementation of basic Cucumber syntax
- rebar[24] for building cucumberl

Solution

cucumberl is an Erlang test framework that uses a subset of Cucumber's Gherkin syntax for describing test features. For this recipe, we're going to write a simple feature and connect it to Erlang step definitions. We'll start by installing cucumberl and its dependencies using your current Erlang installation. Then, we'll write a simple feature and see how to connect it to step definitions written in Erlang. Finally, we'll see how Erlang's pattern matching makes it easy to write multiple step definitions.

Setup

I've tested this recipe with Erlang R15B,[25] though it may work for you with other versions. The first thing you'll need is the rebar build tool.

```
$ git clone https://github.com/basho/rebar.git
$ cd rebar
$ make
```

This will build a rebar executable, which cucumberl's Makefile will call to build its source. Copy the rebar executable to a location on your $PATH.

Next, install cucumberl from Farruco Sanjurjo's fork (which has some updates for the latest Erlang builds).

```
$ git clone https://github.com/madtrick/cucumberl
$ cd cucumberl
$ make && make test
```

23. https://github.com/madtrick/cucumberl
24. https://github.com/basho/rebar
25. http://www.erlang.org/download.html

That will build cucumberl and then run a bunch of .feature files. The output should look something like a regular Cucumber run: a series of Given/When/Then steps scrolling by.

Features

In keeping with Erlang's origin in the telecommunications industry, let's write a test for a cellular base station. Put the following text in features/base_station.feature:

erlang/features/base_station.feature

```
Feature: Base station

  Scenario: Handoff
    Given a call on channel 140
    When the signal quality is better on channel 151
    Then the call should hand off to channel 151
```

As of this writing, cucumberl doesn't print sample test snippets for you to paste into your code. But it's pretty easy to implement step definitions on our own.

cucumberl looks for step definitions in a module named after your .feature file. For base_station.feature, we need to create a base_station module in src/base_station.erl.

erlang/src/base_station.erl

```
-module(base_station).
```

Each Given, When, or Then step in the .feature file needs a corresponding given(), when(), or then() function in Erlang. We'll need to export these three functions from our base_station module, plus a main() method to run the tests.

erlang/src/base_station.erl

```
-export([given/3, 'when'/3, then/3, main/0]).
main() ->
  cucumberl:run("./features/base_station.feature").
```

Now, let's turn to the step definitions.

Step Definitions

Here's the skeleton of a given() method for this scenario:

```
given([a, call, on, channel, Number], World, DebugInfo) ->
  todo.
```

The first parameter is simply the text from your scenario, broken into a list of atoms and parameters. Every literal word from your scenario (a, call, on, and channel) becomes an Erlang atom in the list, beginning with a lowercase letter.

To mark one of the words from your scenario as a placeholder for a quantity (e.g., Number in place of 140), you'd capitalize the entry in the list, making it a variable instead of an atom.

The DebugInfo parameter contains source file and line number information. We won't be using that for this recipe, so we'll use _ for that parameter name from now on. The World parameter is a bit like the World object from regular Cucumber; it carries context around from step to step. The difference here is that we explicitly return a new World at the end of each step, rather than modifying an existing one.

What should we put in that World variable? For this simple example, we'll just define a record so that we can stash current state like the channel with the best signal quality.

erlang/src/base_station.erl

```
-record(world,
        {bestChannel=none}).
```

Our given() method should return a new world record...

erlang/src/base_station.erl

```
given([a, call, on, channel, _], _, _) ->
  {ok, #world{}}.
```

which our when method can then fill in with the latest channel information. Note that because when is an Erlang keyword, we must enclose the function name in quotes.

erlang/src/base_station.erl

```
'when'([the, signal, quality, is, better, on, channel, Channel], World, _) ->
  {ok, World#world{bestChannel=Channel}}.
```

Finally, we can add an assertion to our test. We don't need any special assertion frameworks to do this; we just return true if the test passes or false if it doesn't. Erlang's =:= comparison operator will take care of this for us.

erlang/src/base_station.erl

```
then([the, call, should, hand, off, to, channel, Channel], World, _) ->
   World#world.bestChannel =:= Channel.
```

Running cucumberl

Now that you have definitions for all your steps, you can compile and run your project. cucumberl expects compiled Erlang code to be in the ebin directory of your project.

```
$ mkdir ebin
$ erlc -o ebin src/*.erl
```

To run cucumberl, make sure it's on your PATH and then invoke it from the command line.

```
$ cucumberl
```

This was a pretty small setup: one each of given(), when(), and then(). How do we prevent conflicts if we have more than one of these?

Multiple Definitions

So far, we've seen a scenario with exactly one Given, When, and Then step. Each of these goes with one Erlang given(), when(), or then() function.

What do we do if our scenario has more than one step of a certain type? For instance, consider the following feature:

erlang/features/handset.feature
```
Feature: Handset

  Scenario: Call
    Given a call is in progress

  Scenario: No call
    Given no calls are in progress
```

In classic Cucumber, we'd write a separate block of code to implement each of those two Givens. But in Erlang, we can't define two separate given() functions with the same signature.

What we *can* do is use Erlang's pattern matching. Here's the skeleton of a set of step definitions for this scenario:

erlang/src/handset.erl
```
given([a, call, is, in, progress], World, _) ->
    {ok, World};
given([no, calls, are, in, progress], World, _) ->
    {ok, World}.
```

With cucumberl, you can quickly and easily test your Erlang program's interface in the outside world with the familiar Gherkin syntax you've been using in Cucumber.

Further Exploration

cucumberl doesn't support the entire range of Gherkin syntax. But it does have scenario outlines,[26] which let you build a table of test data and run a set of steps repeatedly for all the data in the table.

---

26. https://github.com/cucumber/cucumber/wiki/Scenario-outlines

Recipe 41

Test Lua Code Using cucumber-lua

Problem

You want to test your Lua project using Cucumber.

Ingredients

- The Lua programming language, version 5.1[27]
- cucumber-lua,[28] a Lua implementation of the Cucumber wire protocol
- The LuaRocks package management system[29] to install cucumber-lua

Solution

Lua is an enjoyable programming language that's small, fast, portable, and extensible. cucumber-lua is a testing library written in Lua that implements Cucumber's wire protocol. With it, you can write your tests in Cucumber syntax and your step definitions in Lua.

Setup

You'll need both the base Lua language and the LuaRocks package management system—which is a bit like RubyGems. On the Mac, you can install both of these with one command if you're using Homebrew.[30]

```
$ brew install lua luarocks
```

Here's the Ubuntu equivalent:

```
$ sudo apt-get install lua5.1 luarocks
```

On Windows, you'd first download and install the base Lua language;[31] then you'd download the latest LuaRocks zip file[32] and run install.bat from where you extracted the contents.

Now, install cucumber-lua using LuaRocks.

27. http://www.lua.org/download.html
28. https://github.com/cucumber/cucumber-lua
29. http://luarocks.org/
30. http://mxcl.github.com/homebrew
31. http://code.google.com/p/luaforwindows
32. http://luarocks.org/releases

```
$ luarocks build \
  https://raw.github.com/cucumber/cucumber-lua/master/cucumber-lua-0.0-1.rockspec
```

Finally, launch the cucumber-lua server so it can listen for incoming test steps using Cucumber's wire protocol.

```
$ cucumber-lua
```

Leave that running in its terminal, and open a new terminal for your work in the next section.

Feature

Lua excels at making an existing system scriptable. Let's say we're dealing with a laboratory full of equipment and using Lua to let the end user customize how and when the tests are run. Place the following code in features/lab.feature:

lua/features/lab.feature

```
Feature: Laboratory
  Scenario: Voltage
    Given an empty test plan
    When I add a test to measure voltage
    Then I should see the following tests:
      | Measurement |
      | voltage     |
```

Since we're using the wire protocol, you'll need to create a .wire file to tell Cucumber where to look for step definitions. Create a file called features/step_definitions/cucumber-lua.wire with the following contents:

lua/features/step_definitions/cucumber-lua.wire

```
host: 0.0.0.0
port: 9666
```

cucumber-lua looks for a file called features/step_definitions/steps.lua. There's no reason that you can't use that file to load step definitions from elsewhere, but you do at least need to have a file with that name. Create an empty one now, and then run Cucumber to generate Lua templates for your step definitions.

```
$ cucumber features
...
You can implement step definitions for undefined steps with these snippets:

Given("an empty test plan", function ()
end)

When("I add a step to measure voltage", function ()
end)

Then("I should see the following tests:", function ()
end)
```

Go ahead and paste those into your empty steps.lua file, and then change the Given step to look like this:

lua/features/step_definitions/steps.lua

```
Given("an empty test plan", function ()
  tests = {}
end)
```

We're creating a new tests variable to hold the list of laboratory measurements. If this were a real project, you'd be calling into the storage API for your lab automation system here.

Now, let's look at the When step.

lua/features/step_definitions/steps.lua

```
When("I add a test to measure (%a+)", function (measurement)
  table.insert(tests, measurement)
end)
```

Lua doesn't support the same kind of regular expressions that Ruby does. Instead, it uses its own string-matching syntax. Here, %a+ means "one or more letters."

Once we've filled our list of measurements, we can compare them with what we're expecting.

lua/features/step_definitions/steps.lua

```
Then("I should see the following tests:", function (t)
  expected = {}

  table.remove(t, 1)
  for i, row in ipairs(t) do
    table.insert(expected, row[1])
  end

  assert(unpack(expected) == unpack(tests))
end)
```

When your .feature file has a table in it, cucumber-lua wraps up the contents into a Lua table and passes it into your step definition. The structure is simple: each row in your Cucumber scenario becomes one subtable inside the Lua table.

So, to get at the measurement names, we just delete the header row and then loop through the rest of the rows looking at the first (and only) cell.

Now, when you rerun Cucumber, your tests should all pass.

Further Exploration

In this recipe, we used Lua to pull apart tabular test data. To learn how to do this in regular Cucumber, see Recipe 1, *Compare and Transform Tables of Data,* on page 2. For more on the wire protocol, see Recipe 14, *Drive Cucumber's Wire Protocol,* on page 72.

Recipe 42

Test a GUI on Linux, Mac, or Windows with Sikuli

Problem

You're testing a Linux program written with a custom toolkit that's difficult to automate. Or, you'd like to test a cross-platform application from a single test suite.

Ingredients

- Sikuli,[33] a Java-based visual GUI testing tool from MIT
- JRuby,[34] a Ruby implementation written in Java that can call Sikuli's API
- The sikuli gem[35] to provide a few convenience wrappers in Ruby

Solution

Sikuli is a GUI testing tool that takes a bit of a different tack than its peers. Rather than finding controls on the screen by metadata such as CSS selectors or automation IDs, Sikuli takes a snapshot of the screen and recognizes controls by their appearance.

This approach presents a few challenges. For instance, what do you do when the designer changes the appearance of a control or when an OK button appears in multiple places on the screen? Sikuli offers a few ways around these issues: fuzzy image comparison, matching based on screen regions, optical character recognition, and so forth.

The typical way to write Sikuli scripts is to use the built-in IDE, which lets you mix text and little screenshots like so:

```
click([🔍])
```

You can also treat Sikuli as just another Java library and drive it from Cucumber. By doing so, you combine Sikuli's powerful image matching with Cucumber's plain-spoken language. We won't be able to drag screenshot images directly into our Cucumber features here, of course. But we can use image filenames, as in `click('search-button.png')`.

33. http://sikuli.org
34. http://jruby.org
35. https://github.com/chaslemley/sikuli_ruby

Like any testing technology, Sikuli is good fit for some situations, but not all. Dean Cornish, a test automation lead, explains further.

When Should You Use Sikuki?

by: Dean Cornish

We were testing an old Delphi app that was in a bit of a mess. It contained Win32 controls, as well as custom ones from a vendor. Both were concealed behind layers of unnecessary abstraction so that driving the interface through COM or .NET tools wasn't working.

The team recognized that they needed to refactor the code to make it more testable. I built a small test suite using Sikuli to give them some test coverage while they refactored. Shortly thereafter, they made the project testable through COM, which was a more sustainable approach. Sikuli helped us get through that transition period.

These are contexts where I've found Sikuli to be helpful:

- Native windows invoked from a web browser; e.g., Print dialogs
- File contents opened in a third-party application; e.g., PDFs
- Flash
- Overly complex UIs with mixed technologies and many layers

These are the drawbacks:

- Can't easily read text from the app
- Interactions such as scrolling make the tests much more complex
- Small UI changes can require many images to be re-captured
- Difficult to debug

For this recipe, we're going to write a cross-platform test that launches the Google Chrome browser and visits the Pragmatic Programmers website.

Setup

The Sikuli IDE is a wrapper around a powerful Java library. As we've discussed elsewhere in this book, there are multiple ways to drive a Java library from Cucumber. Here, we'll use JRuby for its simplicity.

First, download and run the appropriate JRuby installer for your platform.[36] If JRuby isn't your primary Ruby, you'll need to rerun the Cucumber setup instructions discussed in Section 3, *Getting the Tools You'll Need*, on page xiv.

```
$ jruby -S gem install cucumber rspec-expectations
```

If you're on a Mac, make sure you're using the default Java implementation from Apple. Sikuli isn't yet compatible with OpenJDK.

36. http://jruby.org/download

Next, download and install the Sikuli IDE,[37] which comes with the .jar files you'll need.

The last piece to install is the sikuli gem, which provides a few Ruby wrappers around the base Sikuli functions.

```
$ jruby -S gem install sikuli
```

Now, we're ready to write our feature.

Feature

This Cucumber feature will launch the browser, navigate to a specific page, and verify that the site's navigation bar correctly indicates what the current page is. Save the following code in features/browser.feature:

sikuli/features/browser.feature

```
Feature: Browser

  Scenario: Navigate to a magazine
    Given I am on "pragprog.com"
    When I click the "Magazine" link
    Then I should see an underlined "Magazine" link
```

You'll also need some screenshots of various screen elements. Launch Google Chrome and close any open tabs (so that the icon for the location bar becomes a magnifying glass). Take a screenshot by pressing Cmd+Shift+4 on your Mac or PrtSc on your PC. Crop the screenshot down to the magnifying glass, and save it as location-bar.png—or use the version from this book's source code.

Navigate to the Pragmatic Programmers home page,[38] and take a screenshot of the Magazine link, as shown:

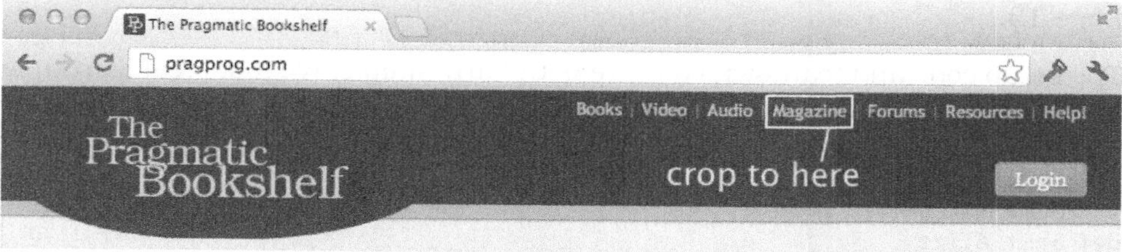

Now, click the link and take another screenshot of the same screen region, taking care to include the link's underline. Save these images as magazine.png and magazine-underlined.png, respectively.

You have everything you need to write the step definitions now.

37. http://sikuli.org/download.shtml
38. http://pragprog.com

Step Definitions

Let's fill in the step definitions. In a moment, we'll write a few helper methods with names like visit(), follow_link_to(), and so on. Create a file called features/step_definitions/browser_steps.rb with the following contents:

sikuli/features/step_definitions/browser_steps.rb

```
Given /^I am on "(.*?)"$/ do |url|
  visit url
end
When /^I click the "(.*?)" link$/ do |name|
  follow_link_to name
end
Then /^I should see an underlined "(.*?)" link$/ do |name|
  verify_underlined_link_to name
end
```

It's time to fill in those API method definitions. The standard place to put helper methods like these is a World object in features/support/env.rb.

sikuli/features/support/env.rb

```
require 'java'
require 'sikuli'
class BrowserWorld
  # API methods go here...
end
World { BrowserWorld.new }
After { close }
```

You'll notice we've also added an After hook to close the browser at the end of each scenario. This Cucumber suite has only one scenario—but if we had more and wanted to start and stop the browser only once, we'd use the techniques from Recipe 3, *Run Slow Setup/Teardown Code with Global Hooks*, on page 13.

The setup code and teardown code are both fairly simple. We just create a couple of Sikuli objects to represent the scripting context and screen and then start or stop the browser (adjust the path to where your browser is installed).

sikuli/features/support/env.rb

```
def initialize
  @screen = Sikuli::Screen.new                  # from the sikuli gem
  @script = org.sikuli.script.SikuliScript.new  # from the original Java lib
  @script.open_app '/Applications/Google Chrome.app'
  sleep 2
end
def close
  @screen.type 'W', KeyModifier::CMD
  @script.close_app '/Applications/Google Chrome.app'
end
```

To find or click a control, we call the Screen object's find() or click() method, either of which will throw an exception if the control doesn't exist.

sikuli/features/support/env.rb

```
  def follow_link_to(name)
    @screen.click "#{name}.png"
  end

  def verify_underlined_link_to(name)
    @screen.find "#{name.downcase}-underlined.png"
  end
end
World { BrowserWorld.new }
After { close }
```

The visit() method combines a mouse click with text entry, which is equally easy with Sikuli.

sikuli/features/support/env.rb

```
def visit(url)
  @screen.click "location-bar.png"
  @screen.type "#{url}\n"
end
```

And that's it! If you close all your Chrome tabs and exit and then run your Cucumber script, you should see the browser launch and go through its paces.

Recipe 43

Test an Arduino Project Using Serial

Problem

You want to use Cucumber to test an Arduino project or other embedded device with no network support.

Ingredients

- serialport,[39] a Ruby library for sending and receiving data over a serial port
- An Arduino-compatible board[40]
- The free Arduino IDE[41]
- A serial connection to your embedded device, either through a built-in port or with a USB to RS-232 converter
- (Optional) Pushbuttons, LEDs, and resistors if you want to hook up the controls for real

Solution

When we're testing an embedded device, we have to do without some of the luxuries of desktop or web apps, such as network connectivity or preexisting test libraries. But as long as we can create a serial connection to the device under test, we can still use Cucumber to test it.

In this recipe, we're going to program a simple Arduino game and test it from Cucumber.

Feature

The game consists of two buttons and two LEDs. The first player to click a button wins, and their LED lights up. We'll presume there's a referee making sure no one commits a false start.

39. https://github.com/hparra/ruby-serialport/
40. http://arduino.cc/en/Main/Hardware
41. http://arduino.cc/en/Main/Software

Here's a simple scenario that exercises the three possible outcomes. Put this in features/buzzer.feature:

serial/features/buzzer.feature
```
Feature: Buzzer

  Scenario Outline: Game
    Given a new game
    When the first buzz comes from <player>
    Then <led> should be lit

    Examples:
      | player       | led       |
      | player 1     | LED 1     |
      | player 2     | LED 2     |
      | both players | both LEDs |
```

Before we get to the step definitions, let's talk about hardware.

Setup

You can test the game logic from this recipe on just about any Arduino board, even without the physical buttons and LEDs to control the game. If you'd like to build the full device, you'll need two pushbuttons and two LEDs, plus wires and resistors for connecting them.

The intricacies of breadboards and pull-up resistors are a bit beyond the scope of this recipe, but the Arduino project has good tutorials for hooking up LEDs[42] and buttons.[43]

In addition to the Arduino IDE, you'll need the serialport gem for Ruby.

```
$ gem install serialport
```

The address of your serial port will vary widely based on your platform and serial adapter type. For Windows, it will typically be COM1, COM2, or similar. On Linux, it's often /dev/ttyS0. With a USB adapter on the Mac, it's typically a long code starting with /dev/tty-usbserial.

Once you've found the correct name for your serial port, create an environment variable so that we can keep this kind of configuration data out of our test script. On Windows, you'd type the following:

```
C:\> set SERIAL_PORT=COM1
```

Here's the Mac and Linux equivalent:

---

42. http://arduino.cc/en/Tutorial/Blink
43. http://arduino.cc/en/Tutorial/Button

```
$ export SERIAL_PORT=/dev/tty-usbserial-...
```

Now we're ready to implement our step definitions.

Step Definitions

First, let's look at the Given step. Since we're not including a reset function in this edition of the game, all we need to do is create a new SerialPort object and store it for use later. Put the following code in features/step_definitions/buzzer_steps.rb:

serial/features/step_definitions/buzzer_steps.rb

```
Given /^a new game$/ do
  @port = SerialPort.new ENV['SERIAL_PORT']
  @port.baud = 9600
end
```

Now, we need a way to simulate one (or both) of the players clicking a button. Let's invent a simple protocol: we'll send a 1, 2, or b to the device, depending on who pushed their button.

serial/features/step_definitions/buzzer_steps.rb

```
When /^the first buzz comes from (\d+)$/ do |first|
  character = case first
              when 'player 1' then '1'
              when 'player 2' then '2'
              when 'both players' then 'b'
              else raise 'unknown player'
              end

  @port.write character
end
```

We also need a protocol command to query which LED is lit. We'll send a single ? character, and the game will respond with the same 1, 2, or b as earlier.

serial/features/step_definitions/buzzer_steps.rb

```
Then /^LED (\d+) should be lit$/ do |led|
  expected = case led
             when 'LED 1' then '1'
             when 'LED 2' then '2'
             when 'both LEDs' then 'b'
             else raise 'unknown LED'
             end

  @port.write '?'
  @port.read.should == expected
end
```

One last bit of housekeeping: we need to require() the serialport library in features/support/env.rb.

serial/features/support/env.rb
```
require 'serialport'
```

Let's turn our attention to the game firmware.

Embedded Logic

In the Arduino development environment, create a new sketch called buzzer. At the top of your file, add a few definitions indicating which input and output pins you'll be using for the game.

serial/buzzer.ino
```
#include <Bounce.h>

const int BUTTON1 = 2;
const int BUTTON2 = 3;
const int LED1    = 9;
const int LED2    = 10;

Bounce button1(BUTTON1, 100);
Bounce button2(BUTTON2, 100);
```

Now, let's define the various characters in the serial protocol we designed in the previous section.

serial/buzzer.ino
```
#define QUERY   '?'
#define PLAYER1 '1'
#define PLAYER2 '2'
#define BOTH    'b'
#define NONE    -1

int winner = NONE;
```

As our game boots, we need to connect to the input and output pins and open a serial connection for listening. Start-up code like this goes into the special setup() function on Arduino boards.

serial/buzzer.ino
```
void setup() {
    pinMode(BUTTON1, INPUT);
    pinMode(BUTTON2, INPUT);
    pinMode(LED1,    OUTPUT);
    pinMode(LED2,    OUTPUT);

    Serial.begin(9600);
}
```

Now for the main loop() function, which the Arduino system will call repeatedly for us. All we need to do is read the physical buttons and the serial port, decide whether someone has pressed a button, and update the status.

serial/buzzer.ino

```
void loop() {
    int button = readButtons();
    int serial = (Serial.available() > 0 ? Serial.read() : NONE);
    int event  = (button != NONE ? button : serial);

    switch (event) {
    case PLAYER1:
    case PLAYER2:
    case BOTH:
        if (winner == NONE) setWinner(event);
        break;
    case QUERY:
        Serial.write(winner);
        break;
    default:
        break;
    }

    delay(50);
}
```

Reading the buttons is easy. Although cheap switches can actually fluctuate between on and off several times before settling one value, Arduino's built-in Bounce library can account for this automatically.

serial/buzzer.ino

```
int readButtons() {
    button1.update();
    button2.update();
    int b1Pressed = button1.risingEdge();
    int b2Pressed = button2.risingEdge();

    return b1Pressed ?
               (b2Pressed ? BOTH    : PLAYER1) :
               (b2Pressed ? PLAYER2 : NONE);
}
```

All that's left to do is turn on the appropriate LEDs for the winner.

serial/buzzer.ino

```
void setWinner(int value) {
    winner = value;
    digitalWrite(LED1, (winner == PLAYER1 || winner == BOTH));
    digitalWrite(LED2, (winner == PLAYER2 || winner == BOTH));
}
```

Compile and download your sketch to the Arduino device and run your Cucumber features. If you're feeling adventurous, connect real pushbuttons and LEDs to the circuit and try the game for real.

Further Exploration

The Arduino development system ships with a serial protocol called Firmata[44] for setting and querying analog and digital pins. We didn't use it for this recipe because Firmata can't override real data with simulated values like we needed to do here. But it can take a snapshot of your system state for remote debugging, which is really handy for more complicated embedded systems.

44. http://firmata.org

APPENDIX 1

RSpec Expectations

Many of the recipes in this book use test assertions written using the rspec-expectations library. This appendix provides a quick getting-started guide to writing this style of assertion.

A1.1 Basics

As the name implies, this library is part of the RSpec testing framework. However, you don't need the rest of RSpec to use it; you can install rspec-expectations as a stand-alone gem.

```
$ gem install rspec-expectations
```

The premise behind rspec-expectations is that test assertions should read like spoken sentences. The library adds a should() method to every Ruby object so that instead of writing assert(2 + 2 == 4), you can write readable code like this:

rspec/examples.rb
```
(2 + 2).should == 4
```

If the condition holds true, your Cucumber step will pass. If the condition is false, Cucumber will report a failure.

rspec-expectations comes with a number of *matchers*—these are different ways to use should() (and its counterpart, should_not(), which can be used anywhere in place of should()). Here are the most commonly used ones for comparing numbers, strings, and collections:

rspec/examples.rb
```
(2 + 2).should != 4
(2 + 2).should_not == 4

(2 + 2).should be > 3
(2 + 2).should be <= 5
```

```
Math.sqrt(2).should be_within(0.001).of(1.414)

'hello'.should start_with('hel')
'hello'.should =~ /ell/

[1, 2, 3].should include(2)
{:a => 1, :b => 2}.should have_key(:a)
```

RSpec also offers an easy way to test objects with Ruby-style method names like *xyz*? and has_*xyz*?.

rspec/examples.rb
```
# assuming some_object supports a has_flair?() method
some_object.should have_flair

# assuming some_object supports a festive?() method
some_object.should be_festive
```

If you need to verify that a piece of code throws a specific exception, you can use should raise_error().

rspec/examples.rb
```
lambda {
  SomeNonExistentClass.new
}.should raise_error(NameError)
```

These are the most common built-in matchers. RSpec ships with several more; see the official documentation for the full list.[1]

A1.2 Custom Matchers

As you work with rspec-expectations, you may find yourself wishing for a project-specific should() notation to make your assertions more legible. For example, let's say you wanted to write the following step to test a Book class:

rspec/examples.rb
```
    this_book.should please('developers')

class Book
  def pleases?(people)
    people == 'developers'
  end
end
```

rspec-expectations doesn't ship with a should please() matcher, but you can write a *custom matcher* and throw it in your env.rb.

1. http://rubydoc.info/gems/rspec-expectations

rspec/examples.rb
```
RSpec::Matchers.define :please do |people|
  match do |book|
    book.pleases?(people)
  end
end
```

When used in moderation, custom matchers can make your Cucumber step definitions easy to read and maintain.

A1.3 Alternatives

The should() method makes for nice, readable expectations. But it has a downside: it doesn't play well with unconventional Ruby objects like delegates.[2]

For these cases, RSpec supports a similar notation called expect() that isn't subject to these limitations.

rspec/expect.rb
```
expect(2 + 2).to == 4
```

Here are a few of the examples from earlier that have been adapted to use expect():

rspec/expect.rb
```
expect(2 + 2).not_to == 5
expect(2 + 2).to be > 3

expect('hello').to =~ /ell/
expect(some_object).to be_festive

expect {
  SomeNonExistentClass.new
}.to raise_error(NameError)

expect(this_book).to please('developers')
```

While Cucumber works well with rspec-expectations, you're certainly not required to use it. If you don't have rspec-expectations installed, Cucumber will fall back on the Test::Unit assertions that ship with Ruby. To use a different framework, all you have to do is require() it inside your env.rb.

2. http://myronmars.to/n/dev-blog/2012/06/rspecs-new-expectation-syntax

Bibliography

[Ada95] Douglas Adams. *The Hitchhiker's Guide to the Galaxy*. Ballantine Books, New York, NY, USA, 1995.

[Fow10] Martin Fowler. *Domain-Specific Languages*. Addison-Wesley Longman, Reading, MA, 2010.

[WH11] Matt Wynne and Aslak Hellesøy. *The Cucumber Book: Behaviour-Driven Development for Testers and Developers*. The Pragmatic Bookshelf, Raleigh, NC and Dallas, TX, 2011.

Index

SYMBOLS

$? variable, exit code, 31

=:= operator, 219

? character, protocol command for LEDs, 232

DIGITS

32-bit COM extension, Windows Phone emulator, 141

A

-a flag, testing across multiple machines, 38

accents, *see* international characters

Accessibility Inspector, 203–204

ActionScript, driving Flash apps with Cuke4AS3, 185–194

ActiveX and AutoIt, 135

Adobe Air, driving Flash apps with Cuke4AS3, 185–194

Adobe Flex SDK, driving Flash apps with Cuke4AS3, 185–194

After hook
- setup/teardown, 14, 64
- Sikuli testing, 228
- testing GUIs with Win32-Autogui, 138
- testing multiple interfaces, 64
- using global hooks instead, 13, 15

after_features(), custom formatting RTF reports, 9

after_run(), Spinach hook, 213

after_step_result(), custom formatting RTF reports, 11

AfterConfiguration hook, 17

Agile, vii–viii

aGlobals, Cuke4php, 177

all(), retrieving table elements, 163

Android, testing with Calabash, 153–159

ANSI escape codes, 118, 123

ANSICON, 118–123

antiques game, 71

APIWorld object, testing multiple interfaces, 61–66

AppleScript, driving Mac GUIs, 202–208

application driver DSL, refactoring to extract, 18–21

application styles, 181

Arduino testing, 230–235

Ashkenas, Jeremy, 164

assert, Clojure, 110

assertions
- C# syntax in .NET testing, 126
- Clojure, 110
- Erlang, 219
- Hamcrest, 190
- Node, 167
- PHP apps, 173–180
- rspec-expectations, xiv, 237–239
- Test::Unit, 239

Ast::Table, comparing and transforming tables, 2–6

asynchronous code, FlexUnit, 191

at_exit()
- driving Mac GUIs with AppleScript and System Events, 208
- global hooks for setup/teardown, 13–17, 46, 170, 208
- Guard, 46
- multiple browser testing with Watir, 170

audio watermarks, 71

authentication, remote machines, 37

AutoIt, GUI testing, 135–138

AutoitX3.Control, 138

automating
- with Guard and Growl, 41–46
- GUI testing with Win32-Autogui, 135–138
- Mac GUIs with AppleScript and System Events, 202–208
- Mac GUIs with MacRuby and AXElements, 209–213
- on continuous integration servers, 47–54

automation IDs
- locating controls in AutoIt, 136
- locating controls in White, 131, 133

AXElements, driving Mac GUIs, 209–213

B

balloon popping example of manipulating time, 67–71

bank balance example of global hooks for setup/teardown, 14–17

base station example of Erlang testing, 218–220

Before hook
- setup/teardown, 14
- using global hooks instead, 13, 15

Bernhardt, Gary, 184

BigDecimal, comparing and transforming tables, 2–6

BigInteger, using Cucumber directly with JRuby, 84–86

Bonjour, 39

book list examples
- collection example of Spring + Hibernate project, 92–97
- defining steps as regular Ruby methods, 22–26
- multiple browser testing with Watir, 170–172

bookmarking app example of Android testing, 153–159

Boost library, 82

Bounce, Arduino game, 234

browser(), global hooks, 16

$browser object, 15

@browser variable, 14

@@browser variable, 16

browsers
- cross-platform testing with Sikuli, 225–229
- global hooks for setup/teardown, 13–17
- refactoring to extract an application driver DSL, 18–21
- testing multiple with Watir, 168–172
- testing with cuke4php, 179–180

Bundler
- Guard and, 42
- monitoring web services with Nagios, 195
- testing across multiple machines, 38

button(), driving Swing with FEST, 114

buttons
- Arduino game, 230–235
- example of driving JavaScript/CoffeeScript, 165–167
- example of driving Swing with FEST, 112–115
- iOS app testing with Frank, 151
- locating in White, 131

buzzer, Arduino game, 233

C

C
- monitoring web services with Nagios, 198
- wire protocol listener, 75–82

C#
- driving Windows apps with White, 130–134
- testing .NET, 124–129
- Windows Phone app testing, 139–146

C# ATDD on a Shoestring, 129

C++, 82

Calabash, Android testing, 153–159

calabash-ios, 159

calculator examples
- driving Windows apps with White, 130–134
- iOS app testing with Frank, 148–152
- multiple interface testing, 62–66
- .NET testing, 125–129

callback parameter, CoffeeScript, 166

callbacks, parsing XML with, 7

campaign finance disclosures, 181

canned data, playing back with VCR, 181–184

Capybara
- JavaScript support, 70
- manipulating time in testing, 67–71
- parsing HTML tables, 160–163
- refactoring to extract an application driver DSL, 18–21

car dealer example of comparing tables, 2–6

cellular base station example of Erlang testing, 218–220

$centigrade parameter, 177

CGI, monitoring web services with Nagios, 198

CharacterStyle, custom formatting RTF reports, 10

chcp, pass/fail color output example, 118–123

check_cucumber, monitoring web services with Nagios, 199

check_element_exists(), calculator example with Frank, 152

Chrome, *see also* browsers
- cross-platform testing with Sikuli, 226–229
- multiple browser testing with Watir, 168–172

ChromeDriver, 168–172

chunky_png, comparing images, 27–32

CI (continuous integration) servers
- auto-testing, 47–54
- driving Windows apps with White, 130–134

circle example of comparing images, 28–32

classes, organizing step methods, 25

clbustos-rtf, custom formatting RTF reports, 7–12

click(), Sikuli testing, 229

click events
- Flash game, 192
- Sikuli testing, 229

Clojure
- using Cucumber directly with JRuby, 84
- using Cucumber with Leiningen, 109–110
- using Cucumber-JVM, 87

close(), testing multiple interfaces, 64

code page, Windows text output, 118, 121

CoffeeScript, driving with Cucumber-JS, 164–167

color
- comparing images, 27–32
- custom formatting RTF reports, 10

Ship To:

Ronald Hansen
248 PINE ARBOR CIR
ST AUGUSTINE, FL 32084-6541

Order ID: 112-6938597-3287412

Thank you for buying from MahlerBooks on Amazon Marketplace.

Shipping Address:	Order Date:	Thu, Jan 24, 2019
Ronald Hansen	Shipping Service:	Standard
248 PINE ARBOR CIR	Buyer Name:	Ronald A Hansen
ST AUGUSTINE, FL	Seller Name:	MahlerBooks
32084-6541		

Quantity	Product Details
1	**Cucumber Recipes: Automate Anything with BDD Tools and Techniques (Pragmatic Programmers) [Paperback] [2013] Dees, Ian; Wynne, Matt; Hellesoy, Aslak** **SKU:** 10GW18-634-014 **ASIN:** 1937785017 **Condition:** Used - Very Good **Listing ID:** 1122UG1N19M **Order Item ID:** 64150551790242 **Condition note:** This book is in very good condition; no remainder marks. It does have some cover shelfwear and corner wear. Inside pages are clean.

Python testing with Lettuce, 214–216
Windows text output, 118–123
colorama, Python testing with Lettuce, 214–216
columns, comparing and transforming, 3–6
COM extension, Windows Phone emulator, 141
COM object, testing GUIs with Win32-Autogui, 138
command definition, monitoring web services with Nagios, 198
Command-Line Tools
driving Mac GUIs with AppleScript and System Events, 202–208
driving Mac GUIs with MacRuby and AXElements, 209–213
need for, xiv
comparing
Erlang operator, 219
images, 27–32, 225
tables, 2–6, 159–163
cone of silence example of auto-testing on CI servers, 48–54
config file, monitoring web services with Nagios, 198
Consolas font, pass/fail color output example, 118–123
console output, Windows text, 118–123
continuous integration servers
auto-testing, 47–54
driving Windows apps with White, 130–134
@controlPanel, CoffeeScript, 166
controllers, Grails game, 102
controls
bookmarking Android app example, 157, 159
displaying with Symbiote, 149
identifying with Sikuli, 225, 229
locating in Ruby, 150
locating in White, 131, 133
locating with AutoIt, 136
convert_mi_to_km(), 136
converter examples
distance, 135–138
temperature, 173–180
copying tests to remote machines, 38
cores, testing across multiple, 33–35
Cornish, Dean, 226
cross-platform GUI testing with Sikuli, 225–229
CSS descriptors
in defining steps as regular Ruby methods, 23
locating HTML elements in Watir, 171
parsing with Nokogiri, 23
CSV stock price data, 183
The Cucumber Book, xiii, 17
cucumber-cpp, 77, 82
Cucumber-JS, driving JavaScript/CoffeeScript, 164–167
Cucumber-JVM
Grails, 99–103
Scala, 87, 104–108
Spring + Hibernate, 92–97
testing Java with, 87–91
Cucumber-JVM: Preparation, 91
cucumber-lua, 221–223
cucumber-nagios, 195–199
Cucumber-Scala, 104–108
Cucumber::Guard, 41–46
cucumberl, 217–220
Cuke4AS3, 185–194
cuke4php, 173–180
cURL
automating tests on CI servers, 47–53
calculator app example, 66
currencies, comparing and transforming tables, 2–6
custom formatting RTF reports, 7–12
custom matchers, rspec-expectations, 238

D

data
comparing and transforming tables, 2–6, 159–163
Erlang scenario outlines, 220
lack of support of data tables in Lettuce, 216
persistence in Spring + Hibernate project, 92–97
playing back canned with VCR, 181–184
databases
persistence in Spring + Hibernate project, 92–97
swapping drives, 19
debugging, remote, 235
DebugInfo parameter, 219
delays, removing, 67–71, 115
delegates and should(), 239
--delete flag, testing across multiple machines, 38
delta, comparing images, 27
dependencies
Clojure testing, 109
Cucumber + Spring project, 95
monitoring web services with Nagios, 196
desktop notifications, running tests automatically with, 41, 45–46
DevKit, xiv
diacritics, *see* international characters
diff!(), comparing and transforming tables, 5, 163
documents
custom formatting RTF reports, 7–12
publishing on Relish, 55–60
SpecRun reports, 128
domain module, swapping drives, 19
downsampling, comparing images, 27, 31
drawing program example of comparing images, 28–32
driver modules, swapping, 19
DSL
refactoring to extract an application driver, 18–21
swapping drives, 19

E

each(), testing across multiple cores, 34
Eclipse
  Android testing with Calabash, 153–159
  Cucumber-JVM, 91
embedded devices, testing with Serial, 230–235
EmuHost.exe, Windows Phone apps, 145
emulators
  Android testing, 154–159
  iOS app testing, 148–152
  UI Impersonation, 191
  Windows Phone app testing, 139–146
encoding, UTF-8, 120
environment variable
  choosing World with, 64
  iOS app testing with Frank, 151
  PHP apps, 175
  USE_GUI, 66
Erlang, 217–220
escape codes, ANSI, 118, 123
event handler, Windows Phone app, 145
event logging library autotesting example, 42–46
events, custom formatting RTF reports, 7–12
exceptions, verifying, 238
execute_script(), Capybara, 71
expect(), RSpec, 239
Expensify, 139
Express, 167
extracting
  application driver DSL with refactoring, 18–21
  HTML into Ruby module, 23

F

-f flag, 8
Fabók, Zsolt, 91
.feature files, publishing on Relish, 55–60
FEST, driving Swing with, 111–115
file scope, global hooks for setup/teardown, 15
find()
  parsing HTML tables, 163
  Sikuli testing, 229
finders, parsing HTML tables, 160–163
fingerprints, comparing images, 27, 31
Firefox, *see also* browsers
  global hooks for setup/teardown, 13–17
  refactoring to extract an application driver DSL, 18–21
  testing PHP apps with cuke4php, 179
Firmata, 235
firmware, Arduino game, 233
FIT (Framework for Integrated Test), ix
fixtures, FEST, 113
flags
  comparing images, 30
  formatting RTFs, 8
  Spinach --generate flag, 211
  testing across multiple machines, 38
Flash
  driving apps with Cuke4AS3, 185–194
  Sikuli, 226
  wire protocol, 72
FlexUnit, driving Flash apps with Cuke4AS3, 185–194
flight reservation example of testing across multiple machines, 36–40
floating-point numbers, 62, 136
follow_link_to(), cross-platform testing Sikuli, 228
fonts
  command prompt, 121
  pass/fail color output example, 118–123
format_args(), custom formatting RTF reports, 9
formatting
  documentation on Relish, 55–60
  HTML, 12
  Nagios, 198
  RTF reports, 7–12
  Windows text output, 118–123
forum search example of monitoring web services with Nagios, 197–199
Framework for Integrated Test (FIT), ix
Frank, iOS testing, 148–152
frankly_map(), 152
freeze(), TimeCop, 69
Furious Fowl game, 99–103
fuubar, 12
fuzzy image comparison, 225

G

games
  antiques, 71
  Arduino, 230–235
  driving Flash apps with Cuke4AS3, 185–194
  Furious Fowl example of Grails testing, 99–103
--generate flag, Spinach, 211
Get(), White, 133
Gherkin
  Erlang, 220
  .NET testing, 124–129
  Python, 214, 216
  Spinach, 211
Git, automating tests on CI servers, 47–54
given() method, Erlang testing, 218–220
global hooks
  driving Mac GUIs, 208
  driving Swing with FEST, 113
  Guard, 46
  setup/teardown, 13–17, 46, 170, 208, 228
  Sikuli testing, 228
  Watir, 170
GNTP (Growl Network Transport Protocol), 45
Google Chrome, *see* Chrome
Googlefight, 182
Grails, 99–103
grails-cucumber, 99–103
grocery bill example of .NET testing, 126–129
Groovy, Grails testing, 99–103
@group1 tag, testing across multiple machines, 37, 39
@group2 tag, testing across multiple machines, 37, 39

Growl, running tests automatically with, 41, 45–46

Growl Network Transport Protocol (GNTP), 45

Guard, running tests automatically with, 41–46

Guardfile, 42

GUIs
- driving Mac with AppleScript and System Events, 202–208
- driving Mac with MacRuby and AXElements, 209–213
- driving Swing with FEST, 111–115
- driving Windows apps with White, 130–134
- testing with Sikuli, 225–229
- testing with Win32-Autogui, 135–138

H

<h4> element, identifying, 171

Hamcrest, 190

hardware
- Arduino, 231
- testing, 63

hashes(), extracting table data, 5

headers, table
- comparing and transforming, 2–6
- Lua, 223

Hellesøy, Aslak, xiii

Hex Fiend
- driving Mac GUIs with AppleScript and System Events, 202–208
- driving Mac GUIs with MacRuby and AXElements, 210–213

hexadecimal interpretation examples
- driving Mac GUIs with AppleScript and System Events, 205–208
- driving Mac GUIs with MacRuby and AXElements, 210–213

hexagonal architecture and swapping drives, 19

Hibernate, 92–97

The Hitchhiker's Guide to the Galaxy, 165

hooks
- automating tests on CI servers, 47–54
- comparing images, 28
- driving Mac GUIs, 208, 213
- driving Swing with FEST, 113
- Furious Fowl game, 101
- Guard, 46
- iOS apps testing, 149
- in multiple browser testing with Watir, 170
- multiple interface testing, 64
- setup/teardown, 13–17, 46, 170, 208, 213, 228
- Sikuli testing, 228
- SpecFlow, 132
- Win32-Autogui, 138

host groups, monitoring web services with Nagios, 198

HSQLDB databases, Spring + Hibernate project, 96

HTML
- extracting into Ruby module, 23
- formatter, 12
- locating elements with Watir, 171
- parsing tables, 160–163
- parsing with Nokogiri, 23, 168, 171, 195
- SpecRun reports, 128

HTTP
- monitoring web services with Nagios, 195–199
- playing back canned data with VCR, 181–184
- simulating in Grails, 100
- testing multiple interfaces, 61–66

HTTParty, testing multiple interfaces, 61–66

Humpty Dumpty example of custom formatting RTF reports, 8–12

I

IDs
- bookmarking Android app example, 159
- locating controls in AutoIt, 136
- locating controls in White, 131, 133

images
- comparing, 27–32, 225
- matching with Sikuli, 225–229

import statements, Android apps, 158

in-memory option, Spring + Hibernate project, 96

Influence Explorer project, 181

input pins, Arduino game, 233

@integration tag, Grails apps, 100

Integration testing with Cucumber, 46

integration tests, *see also* continuous integration servers
- Clojure, 109–110
- Grails apps tag, 100
- PHP apps, 173–180

IntelliJ IDEA Community Edition, using Cucumber-JVM, 87–91

interfaces, testing multiple with World objects, 61–66, *see also* user interfaces

international characters, 118–123

invoke, wire protocol, 76, 79–80

IO object, formatting RTF documents, 9

iOS
- testing with Calabash, 159
- testing with Frank, 148–152

IP address, iOS app testing, 152

J

Java
- Clojure testing, 109–110
- driving Swing with FEST, 111–115
- Grails testing, 99–103
- GUI testing with Sikuli, 225–229
- Scala testing, 104–108
- Spring + Hibernate project, 92–97
- using Cucumber directly with JRuby, 84–86

using Cucumber-JVM, 87–91
wire protocol, 72

Java Persistence API (JPA), 95

JavaScript
antiques game, 71
Capybara support, 70
driving with Cucumber-JS, 164–167
manipulating time, 69–71

JavaScript Object Notation, *see* JSON

Jenkins
automating tests, 47–54
remote testing, 39

JFrameFixture, driving Swing with FEST, 114

JLabel, driving Swing with FEST, 114

JPA (Java Persistence API), 95

JRuby
driving Swing with FEST, 111–115
GUI testing with Sikuli, 225–229
start-up time and, 86
using Cucumber directly with, 84–86

jsmn, 79

JSON
bookmarking Android app example, 159
thermostat wire protocol listener example, 76, 79

JUnit
Scala testing, 104–108
using Cucumber-JVM, 87–91

JVM
Grails testing, 99–103
Scala, 104–108
Spring + Hibernate project, 92–97
using Cucumber directly with JRuby, 84–86
using Cucumber-JVM, 87–91

K

kelvinate(), 178

kelvinator app example, 173–180

keys
comparing tables, 5
remote machine key pairs, 37
Windows Phone emulator, 141

keyword, formatting RTF documents, 9

Kreeftmeijer, Jeff, 31

L

label(), driving Swing with FEST, 114

laboratory equipment example of Lua testing, 222–223

languages
comparing and transforming data tables, 2–6
Cucumber flexibility, xiii
international characters, 118–123

launch_app(), Frank, 152

launching
driving Mac GUIs with AppleScript and System Events, 208
iOS app testing with Frank, 152
in multiple browser testing with Watir, 170

Lavena, Luis, 123

lawn darts example of parsing HTML tables, 160–163

LEDs, Arduino testing, 230–235

lein-cucumber, Clojure testing, 109–110

Leiningen, Clojure testing, 109–110

Lettuce, Python testing, 214–216

libraries, testing, 46

libxml2, 169

libxslt, 169

Linux
GUI testing with Sikuli, 225–229
tools needed, xiv

listener, wire protocol, 75–82

living documentation, 59, *see also* documents

lobbyists, 181

locating
by name in Swing interface, 114
controls in AutoIt, 136
controls in Ruby, 150
controls in White, 131, 133
controls with Sikuli, 225, 229
elements in parsing HTML tables, 163
HTML elements with Watir, 171

@log variable, auto-testing with Guard and Growl, 44

logging library auto-testing example, 42–46

login, remote machines, 37

loop(), Arduino game, 233

Lua, 221–223

LuaRocks, 221–223

Lucida Console font, pass/fail color output example, 118–123

M

Mac GUIs, *see also* iOS
driving with AppleScript and System Events, 202–208
driving with MacRuby and AXElements, 209–213
testing with Sikuli, 225–229
tools needed, xiv

macgem, AXelements installation, 210

MacRuby, driving Mac GUIs, 209–213

main() method, Erlang testing, 218–220

manipulating time in testing, 67–71

map_column!(), converting tables, 4

map_headers!(), transforming tables, 3

Markdown, publishing documentation on Relish, 55–60

Marston, Myron, 181

match, formatting RTF documents, 9

matchers, rspec-expectations, 237–239

matching
C definitions, 79

digits in regular expressions, 136
images with Sikuli, 225–229
patterns in Erlang, 220
rspec-expectations matchers, 237–239
step definitions with Cuke4php, 176

Math.sqrt(), 66

Maven
- lack of artifacts in JRuby, 84
- Scala testing, 104–108
- Spring + Hibernate project, 92–97
- using Cucumber-JVM, 87–91

Mechanize, step definitions as regular Ruby methods, 22–26

Microsoft Visual Studio Professional, *see* Visual Studio Professional

missing columns, 5

mixins, refactoring to extract an application driver DSL, 18–21

models, Spring + Hibernate project, 94

monitoring web services with Nagios, 195–199

multiple browser testing with Watir, 168–172

multiple cores, testing across, 33–35

multiple interfaces, testing with World objects, 61–66

multiple machines, testing across, 36–40

multiple platform GUI testing with Sikuli, 225–229

mvn test, Spring + Hibernate project, 97

mxmlc, Cuke4AS3, 187, 194

N

Nagios, monitoring web services, 195–199

names
- columns, 3–6
- Cuke4AS3 functions, 189
- locating HTML elements in Watir, 171
- locating controls in White, 132
- property in Swing interface, 114
- publishing to Relish, 58
- serial port, 231

navigation, documentation on Relish, 57

.NET
- automation IDs, 132
- testing with Cucumber syntax, 124–129
- wire protocol, 72

Net::HTTP, VCR support, 182

Node Package Manager, driving JavaScript/CoffeeScript, 164–167

Node.js, driving JavaScript/CoffeeScript, 164–167

Nokogiri, HTML parsing, 23, 168, 171, 195

notifications, running tests automatically with, 41, 45–46

nth-of-type modifier, 163

NuGet
- .NET testing, 124–129
- Windows Phone app testing, 139–146

numbers, floating-point, 62, 136

numeric control IDs, 132

NUnit
- .NET testing, 124–129
- Windows Phone app testing, 139–146

O

object-oriented programming, vii, ix

Objective-C and Frank, 152

online resources, xv

open, driving Mac GUIs with AppleScript and System Events, 208

OpenCV, 32

OpenJDK and Sikuli, 226

optical character recognition, 225

option_pane(), driving Swing with FEST, 114

outlines, Erlang scenario, 220

output
- Arduino game, 233
- custom formatting RTF reports, 7–12
- Nagios conventions, 195
- pdiff flag, 30
- Python testing with Lettuce, 214–216
- Windows text, 118–123

outside-in development, xiii

P

page(), Capybara, 68

page object, defining steps as regular Ruby methods, 26

palindrome example of Windows Phone app testing, 140–146

parallel gem, testing across multiple cores, 33–35

parallel testing
- across multiple cores, 33–35
- across multiple machines, 36–40

Parallel.each(), testing across multiple cores, 34

parallel_tests gem, testing across multiple cores, 33–35

parameterized steps and Spinach, 209

parsing
- CSV stock price data, 183
- HTML tables, 160–163
- HTML with Nokogiri, 23, 168, 171, 195
- XML with callbacks, 7

pass/fail
- assertions in C# syntax in .NET testing, 126
- color output in Python testing with Lettuce, 214–216
- color output on Windows example, 118–123
- Nagios conventions, 195

passwords
- Jenkins, 49
- remote machines, 37
- VCR masking, 184

patterns
- in Agile development, viii
- matching in Erlang, 220
- parsing HTML tables, 160–163

pdiff, comparing images, 27–32
PEAR, 174
perceptual diff, comparing images, 27–32
performAction, Android testing with Calabash, 159
Perham, Mike, 31
permissions, Android testing with Calabash, 157
persistence
  JPA (Java Persistence API), 95
  Spring + Hibernate project, 92–97
phashion library, 31
phone apps
  Android testing with Calabash, 153–159
  iOS testing with Calabash, 159
  testing with Frank, 148–152
  Windows, 139–146
PHP
  testing with cuke4php, 173–180
  wire protocol, 72
PHPUnit test framework, 173–180
pie example of Clojure testing, 109–110
Pik, xiv
pixels, comparing images, 27–32
platforms
  cross-platform GUI testing with Sikuli, 225–229
  Cucumber flexibility, viii, xiii
plug-ins, Nagios, 195
PNG files, comparing images, 27–32
polling source code with Jenkins, 47, 50
pom.xml
  dependencies in Cucumber + Spring project, 95
  Scala testing stock broker example, 104
  using Cucumber-JVM, 88, 104
post-commit hooks, automating tests on CI servers, 47–54
Pragmatic Programmers website examples
  cross-platform testing with Sikuli, 226–229
  defining steps as regular Ruby methods, 22–26
  multiple browser testing with Watir, 170–172
PresentationClock example of driving Swing with FEST, 111–115
Presenter First, 180
protocol command for LEDs, 232
public key authentication, remote machines, 37
publishing documentation on Relish, 55–60
Pyccuracy, 216
Python, testing with Lettuce, 214–216

R

Rack
  manipulating time, 69–71
  parsing HTML tables, 161
Rake, automating tests on CI servers, 47–54
Rakefile, Jenkins, 48
raster font, 121
raw(), extracting table data, 5
rb-sppscript, driving Mac GUIs with AppleScript and System Events, 202–208
rbenv, xiv
rebar, Erlang testing, 217–220
Redcar text editor, 84
refactoring
  defined, 18
  extracting an application driver DSL, 18–21
  regular Ruby methods, 22, 25
regular expressions
  Cuke4php, 176
  floating-point numbers, 62
  Lua, 223
  matching digits, 136
  SpecFlow, 128
Relish, publishing to, 55–60
remote debugging, 235
remote testing across multiple machines, 36–40
renaming, columns, 3–6
reports
  custom formatting RTF, 7–12
  SpecRun, 128
require()
  Arduino game, 232
  PHP kelvinator app, 178
  stock price app, 183
reset button example of driving Swing with FEST, 112–115
Resharper, Windows Phone app testing, 143
respond_failure(), wire protocol listener, 81
respond_success(), wire protocol listener, 81
respond_with_match(), wire protocol listener, 80
response_body(), monitoring web services with Nagios, 197
result(), distance converter app, 136
Rich Text Format reports, custom formatting, 7–12
Robotium, Android testing with Calabash, 153–159
rotation, comparing images, 28, 32
rows(), extracting table data, 5
rows_hash(), extracting table data, 5
RSpec testing framework, 237
rspec-expectations, xiv, 237–239
rsync, testing across multiple machines, 36–40
RTF reports, custom formatting, 7–12
Ruby
  and should(), 239
  Arduino testing with Serial, 230–235
  auto-testing with Guard and Growl, 41, 45–46
  compared to Selenium, 168
  comparing and transforming tables, 2–6
  comparing images, 31

- custom formatting RTF reports, 7–12
- driving Flash apps with Cuke4AS3, 185–194
- driving Mac GUIs with MacRuby and AXElements, 209–213
- extracting HTML, 23
- global hooks for setup/teardown, 13–17
- GUI testing with Win32-Autogui, 135–138
- iOS app testing with Frank, 148–152
- locating controls, 150
- manipulating time, 69–71
- multiple browser testing with Watir, 168–172
- parsing HTML, 168, 171
- parsing HTML tables, 160–163
- PHP app testing with cuke4php, 180
- refactoring regular Ruby methods, 22, 25
- refactoring to extract an application driver DSL, 18–21
- step definitions as regular Ruby methods, 22–26
- VCR support, 182
- versions, xiv
- Windows text output, 118–123

ruby_gntp, auto-testing with Guard and Growl, 41, 45–46

RubyInstaller project, xiv

RunCukesTest, soda machine example, 89

RVM, xiv, 185

S

Safari, multiple browser testing with Watir, 168–172, *see also* browsers

SafariWatir, 168–172

Sanjurjo, Farruco, 217

Scala
- using Cucumber directly with JRuby, 84
- using Cucumber-JVM, 87, 104–108

ScalaCheck project, 108

scale, comparing images, 28, 32

scanf(), matching steps to implementations, 78

scenarios
- embedding Markdown to publish to Relish, 58
- Erlang outlines, 220
- skipping with tags, 54

Scott, Allister, 129

screenshots, matching with Sikuli, 225–229

search
- example of monitoring web services with Nagios, 197–199
- Shelley syntax, 150

SearchCriteria, White, 133

security, Jenkins, 49, 51

Selenium, compared to Ruby, 168

Selenium WebDriver
- global hooks for setup/teardown, 13–17
- testing PHP apps with cuke4php, 179–180
- testing multiple interfaces, 61–66

Serial, Arduino testing, 230–235

serialport, Arduino testing, 230–235

setup
- Arduino game, 233
- global hooks for, 13–17, 46, 170, 228
- Sikuli testing, 228
- Watir, 170

sharing
- in CoffeeScript/JavaScript, 166
- documentation on Relish, 55–60

shell script, monitoring web services with Nagios, 198

Shelley search syntax, 150

shipping example of testing across multiple cores, 33–35

should(), 237, 239

should raise_error(), 238

should_not(), 237

shutdown, *see also* teardown
- driving Mac GUIs with AppleScript and System Events, 208
- driving Mac GUIs with MacRuby and AXElements, 213
- iOS app testing with Frank, 152

Sikuli, 225–229

simulators, *see* emulators

Sinatra
- manipulating time in testing, 67–71
- parsing HTML tables, 160–163
- testing multiple interfaces, 61–66

skipping scenarios with tags, 54

sleep(), testing across multiple cores, 34–35

slingshot Grails game, 101

slow tests, *see* speed

Snarl, running tests automatically with, 41, 45–46

soda machine example of Cucumber-JVM, 88–91

SourceForge, 112

SpecFlow
- driving Windows apps with White, 130–134
- .NET testing, 124–129
- Windows Phone app testing, 139–146

special characters, 118–123

Specjour, 39

SpecRun
- driving Windows apps with White, 130–134
- HTML reports, 128
- .NET testing, 124–129
- Windows Phone app testing, 143

speed
- global hooks for setup/teardown, 13–17
- JRuby and start-up time, 86
- manipulating time in testing, 67–71
- testing PHP apps with cuke4php, 180
- testing across multiple cores, 33–35
- testing across multiple machines, 36–40

Spinach, driving Mac GUIs with MacRuby and AXElements, 209–213

Spring, 92–97
square root calculator example of testing multiple interfaces, 62–66
square_root_result(), 63
Squeaker example of refactoring to extract an application driver DSL, 18–21
src, Cuke4AS3, 187
SSH, testing across multiple machines, 36–40
start-up time, JRuby and, 86
status, formatting RTF documents, 9
step definitions
  Android testing with Calabash, 158
  Arduino game, 232–235
  C definitions, 78–82
  C# in .NET testing, 124, 126
  C# in Windows Phone app testing, 139–146
  Clojure, 110
  Cucumber-JVM, 89
  defining as regular Ruby methods, 22–26
  driving Flash apps with Cuke4AS3, 186–194
  driving Mac GUIs with AppleScript and System Events, 205–213
  driving Mac GUIs with MacRuby and AXElements, 211–213
  driving Swing with FEST, 112
  Erlang testing, 218–220
  Grails, 101
  Guard and Growl autotesting, 42–46
  GUI testing with Win32-Autogui, 135
  iOS app testing with Frank, 151
  JavaScript/CoffeeScript, 165–167
  Lua testing, 222–223
  manipulating time balloon popping example, 68–71
  monitoring web services with Nagios, 197–199
  multiple cores testing, 33–35
  multiple interfaces testing, 62–66
  parsing HTML tables, 162
  PHP apps, 175–180
  Python testing with Lettuce, 215–216
  refactoring to extract an application driver DSL, 18–21
  Scala, 107
  Sikuli cross-platform testing, 228
  Spring + Hibernate project, 93
  swapping driver modules, 19
  Swing, 114
  Watir multiple browser testing, 170
  White, 132–134
  Windows Phone app, 139–146
  Windows text output, 119
  wire protocol listener, 72–82
step methods, defining as regular Ruby methods, 22–26
step_matches, wire protocol listener, 76
steps_match, wire protocol listener, 79
stock examples
  playing back canned data with VCR, 182–184
  Scala testing, 104–108
strictEqual assertion, Node, 167
strings
  converting table cells, 3
  JSON, 79, 159
  Lua string-matching syntax, 223
  .NET apps, 132
success?(), comparing images, 31
sudo, AXelements installation, 210
Sunlight Labs, 181
SURF, comparing images, 28, 32
surplus columns, 5
swapping driver modules, 19
Swing, driving with FEST, 111–115
Symbiote, 149
synchronization
  antiques game, 71
  testing across multiple machines, 36–40
System Events, driving Mac GUIs, 202–208

T

-t flag, testing across multiple machines, 39
tables
  comparing and transforming, 2–6, 159–163
  Erlang scenario outlines, 220
  lack of support in Lettuce, 216
  Lua, 223
tags
  inside database transaction, 93
  integration testing environment, 100
  lack of support in Lettuce, 216
  skipping scenarios, 54
  testing across multiple machines, 36–40
  VCR, 182–183
take_square_root(), 63
TCP
  Android testing with Calabash, 153–159
  wire protocol, 72–82
<td> elements, comparing HTML tables, 163
teardown
  driving Mac GUIs with AppleScript and System Events, 208
  driving Mac GUIs with MacRuby and AXElements, 213
  global hooks for, 13–17, 46, 170, 208, 228
  Guard, 46
  Sikuli testing, 228
  Watir, 170
temperature converter example of testing PHP apps, 173–180
templates, Lua, 222
Test::Unit assertions, 239
tests variable, 223

text, *see also* documents
  custom formatting RTF reports, 7–12
  Windows output, 118–123
<th> elements, comparing HTML tables, 163
then() method, Erlang testing, 218–220
thermostat wire protocol listener example, 75–82
thin user interface, 180
this object, sharing in Cucumber-JS with, 166
time, manipulating in testing, 67–71
Time.now(), Ruby, 69
Timecop, manipulating time in testing, 67–71
-tolerance option, 31
touch(), calculator ecxample using Frank, 150–151
<tr> elements, comparing HTML tables, 163
transforming
  floating-point numbers, 62, 136
  tables, 2–6
transpose(), extracting table data, 5
@txn tag, Spring + Hibernate project, 93

U

UI elements, displaying with Symbiote, 149
UI Impersonation, FlexUnit, 191
UIA Verify, driving Windows apps with White, 130–134
UISpec, Shelley syntax, 150
Unicode, Windows text output, 118–123
Unit Converter, GUI testing, 135–138
USE_GUI environment variable, 66
used car example of comparing tables, 2–6
user interfaces
  driving Mac GUIs with AppleScript and System Events, 202–208
  driving Mac GUIs with MacRuby and AXElements, 209–213
  driving Swing with FEST, 111–115
  driving Windows apps with White, 130–134
  swapping drives, 19
  testing with Sikuli, 225–229
  testing with Win32-Autogui, 135–138
  thin, 180
UTF-8 encoding, 120
uuidgen utility, 51

V

-v flag, testing across multiple machines, 38
VCR, playing back canned data, 181–184
@vcr tag, 182–183
versions
  Erlang, 217
  Ruby, xiv
Vidal, Erlis, 215
virtualenv, Python testing with Lettuce, 214–216
visit()
  Capybara, 68
  cross-platform testing Sikuli, 228
  monitoring web services with Nagios, 197
  Sikuli testing, 229
Visual C# Express, .NET testing, 125, 129
Visual Studio Professional
  driving Windows apps with White, 130–134
  .NET testing, 124–129
  Windows Phone app testing, 139–146

W

Watchr, auto-testing with Guard, 43
watermarks, audio, 71
Watir, 168–172
Watir WebDriver, 168–172
web services, monitoring with Nagios, 195–199
WebDriver, multiple browser testing with Watir, 168–172
WebMock, playing back canned data with VCR, 181–184
Webrat, monitoring web services with Nagios, 195–199
weight in formatting RTF reports, 10
when() method, Erlang testing, 218–220
White, driving Windows app with, 130–134
Wilk, Joseph, 54
Williams, Nic, 46
Win32-Autogui, testing with, 135–138
win_gui, 138
@@window variable, FEST, 113
Windows
  driving apps with White, 130–134
  GUI testing with Sikuli, 225–229
  GUI testing with Win32-Autogui, 135–138
  .NET testing, 124–129
  phone app testing, 139–146
  RubyInstaller project, xiv
  text output, 118–123
Windows Phone Test Framework, 139–146
.wire file, 72–74
wire protocol
  driving Cucumber with, 72–82
  driving Flash apps with Cuke4AS3, 186
  listener, 75–82
  Lua testing, 221–223
  PHP app testing, 173–179
World()
  browser() and global hooks, 16
  choosing with environment variable, 64
  refactoring to extract an application driver DSL, 18–21
World object
  CoffeeScript/JavaScript, 166
  defining steps as regular Ruby methods, 24
  global hooks, 16
  testing multiple interfaces, 61–66

World parameter, Erlang testing, 219

Wynne, Matt, xiii, 56

X

xUnit.net, .NET testing, 124–129

Xcode
- driving Mac GUIs with AppleScript and System Events, 202–208
- driving Mac GUIs with MacRuby and AXElements, 209–213
- Mac tools, xiv

XML
- configuration for Sping + Hibernate project, 92
- parsing with callbacks, 7

XPath
- locating HTML elements in Watir, 171
- parsing HTML tables, 160–163

Y

YAML
- playing back canned data with VCR, 184
- publishing to Relish, 58

Explore Testing and Cucumber

Explore the uncharted waters of exploratory testing and delve deeper into Cucumber.

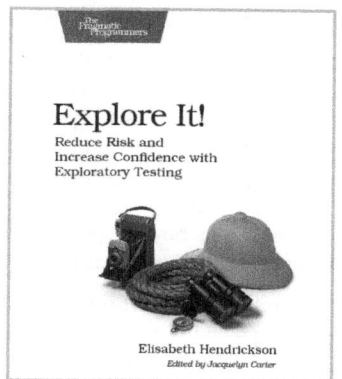

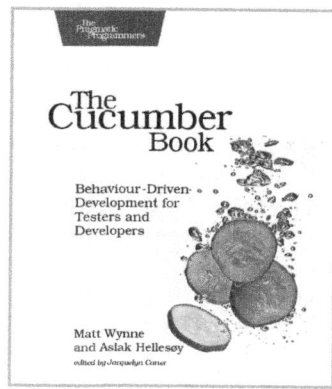

Seven Databases, Seven Languages

There's so much new to learn with the latest crop of NoSQL databases. And instead of learning a language a year, how about seven?

Data is getting bigger and more complex by the day, and so are your choices in handling it. From traditional RDBMS to newer NoSQL approaches, *Seven Databases in Seven Weeks* takes you on a tour of some of the hottest open source databases today. In the tradition of Bruce A. Tate's *Seven Languages in Seven Weeks*, this book goes beyond your basic tutorial to explore the essential concepts at the core of each technology.

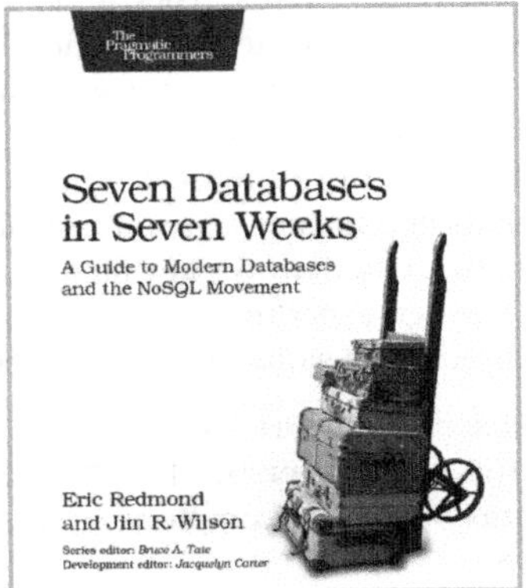

Eric Redmond and Jim R. Wilson
(354 pages) ISBN: 9781934356920. $35
http://pragprog.com/book/rwdata

You should learn a programming language every year, as recommended by *The Pragmatic Programmer*. But if one per year is good, how about *Seven Languages in Seven Weeks*? In this book you'll get a hands-on tour of Clojure, Haskell, Io, Prolog, Scala, Erlang, and Ruby. Whether or not your favorite language is on that list, you'll broaden your perspective of programming by examining these languages side-by-side. You'll learn something new from each, and best of all, you'll learn how to learn a language quickly.

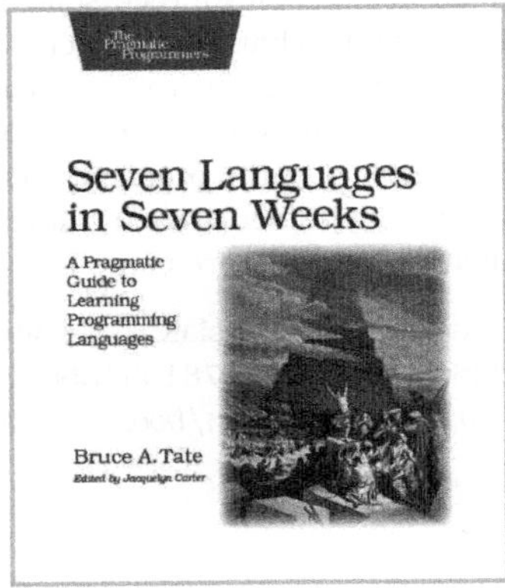

Bruce A. Tate
(330 pages) ISBN: 9781934356593. $34.95
http://pragprog.com/book/btlang

The Joy of Math and Healthy Programming

Rediscover the joy and fascinating weirdness of pure mathematics, and learn how to take a healthier approach to programming.

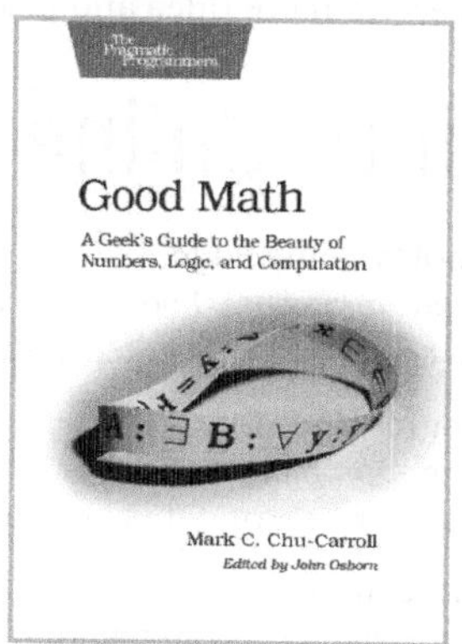

Mathematics is beautiful—and it can be fun and exciting as well as practical. *Good Math* is your guide to some of the most intriguing topics from two thousand years of mathematics: from Egyptian fractions to Turing machines; from the real meaning of numbers to proof trees, group symmetry, and mechanical computation. If you've ever wondered what lay beyond the proofs you struggled to complete in high school geometry, or what limits the capabilities of the computer on your desk, this is the book for you.

Mark C. Chu-Carroll
(282 pages) ISBN: 9781937785338. $34
http://pragprog.com/book/mcmath

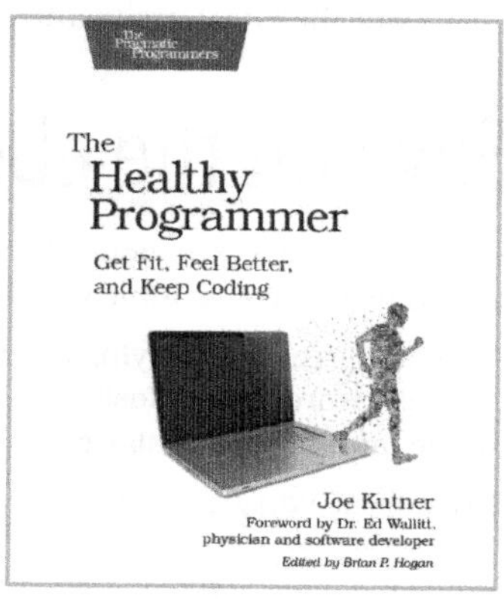

To keep doing what you love, you need to maintain your own systems, not just the ones you write code for. Regular exercise and proper nutrition help you learn, remember, concentrate, and be creative—skills critical to doing your job well. Learn how to change your work habits, master exercises that make working at a computer more comfortable, and develop a plan to keep fit, healthy, and sharp for years to come.

This book is intended only as an informative guide for those wishing to know more about health issues. In no way is this book intended to replace, countermand, or conflict with the advice given to you by your own healthcare provider including Physician, Nurse Practitioner, Physician Assistant, Registered Dietician, and other licensed professionals.

Joe Kutner
(254 pages) ISBN: 9781937785314. $36
http://pragprog.com/book/jkthp

The Pragmatic Bookshelf

The Pragmatic Bookshelf features books written by developers for developers. The titles continue the well-known Pragmatic Programmer style and continue to garner awards and rave reviews. As development gets more and more difficult, the Pragmatic Programmers will be there with more titles and products to help you stay on top of your game.

Visit Us Online

This Book's Home Page
http://pragprog.com/book/dhwcr
Source code from this book, errata, and other resources. Come give us feedback, too!

Register for Updates
http://pragprog.com/updates
Be notified when updates and new books become available.

Join the Community
http://pragprog.com/community
Read our weblogs, join our online discussions, participate in our mailing list, interact with our wiki, and benefit from the experience of other Pragmatic Programmers.

New and Noteworthy
http://pragprog.com/news
Check out the latest pragmatic developments, new titles and other offerings.

Save on the eBook

Save on the eBook versions of this title. Owning the paper version of this book entitles you to purchase the electronic versions at a terrific discount.

PDFs are great for carrying around on your laptop—they are hyperlinked, have color, and are fully searchable. Most titles are also available for the iPhone and iPod touch, Amazon Kindle, and other popular e-book readers.

Buy now at *http://pragprog.com/coupon*

Contact Us

Online Orders:	*http://pragprog.com/catalog*
Customer Service:	*support@pragprog.com*
International Rights:	*translations@pragprog.com*
Academic Use:	*academic@pragprog.com*
Write for Us:	*http://pragprog.com/write-for-us*
Or Call:	+1 800-699-7764

CPSIA information can be obtained at www.ICGtesting.com
Printed in the USA
LVOW02s1530231013

358273LV00047B/458/P

9 781937 785017